AF594859

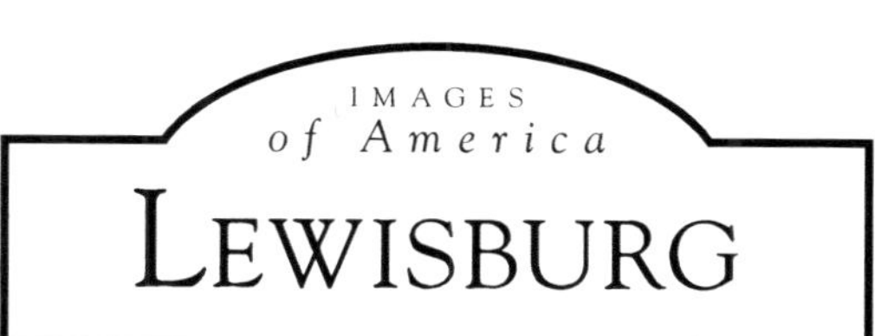
IMAGES
of America
LEWISBURG

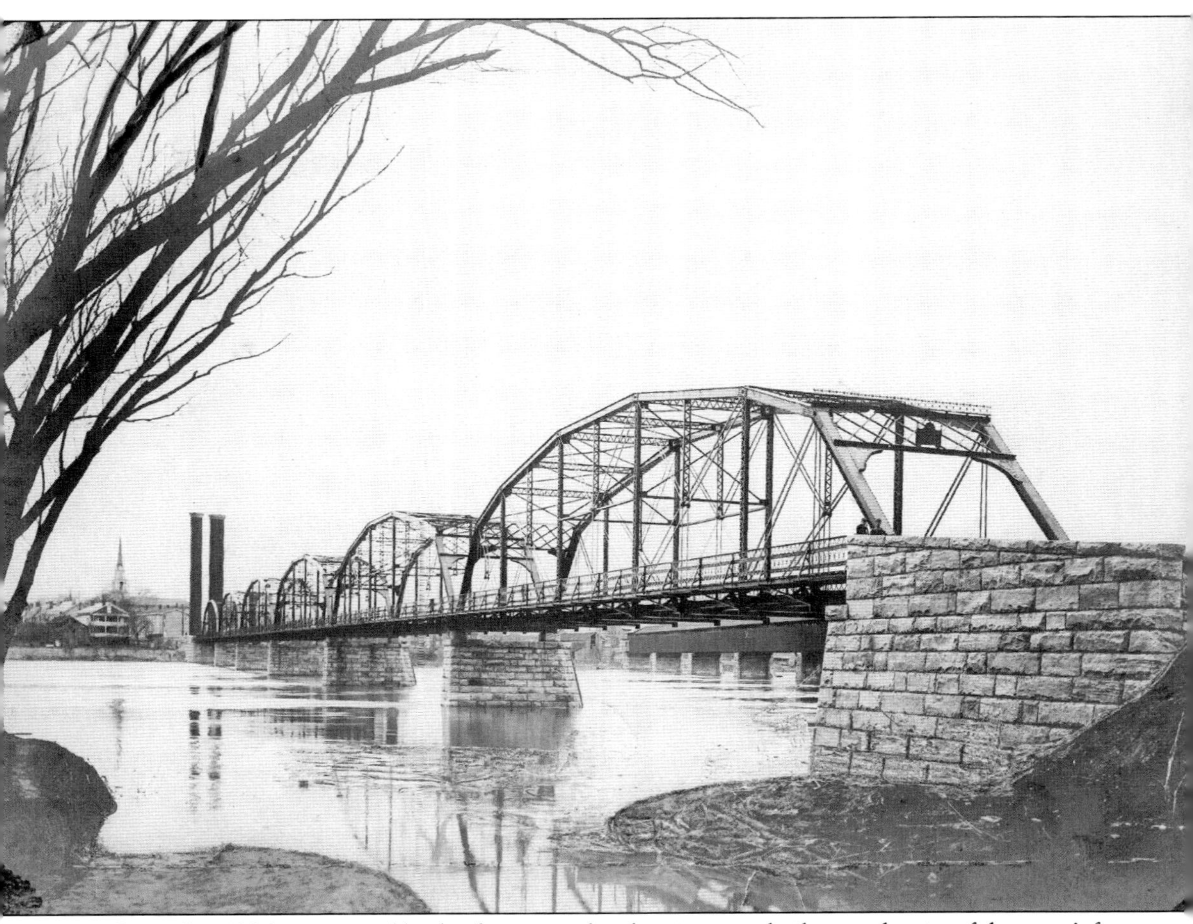

Started in 1906, a new steel bridge for cars and pedestrians was built near the site of the town's first wooden bridge at the east end of Market Street. Taken from the east bank of the Susquehanna River, the photograph shows the old crosscut canal entrance into the river in the foreground. For Lewisburg residents, easy access meant progress and prosperity. This bridge was replaced in 1988. (Union County Historical Society 80.7.20.)

On the Cover: Before the age of modern snow-clearing equipment, snow had to be removed the hard way. This winter scene captures the intersection of Market and Third Streets, with the early traffic signal visible on the right. Older residents of Lewisburg remember that the borough piled snow in the middle of the street; children walked on top of these piles, and when they slipped, they tried to avoid rolling under parked cars. (Union County Historical Society 90.13.9.)

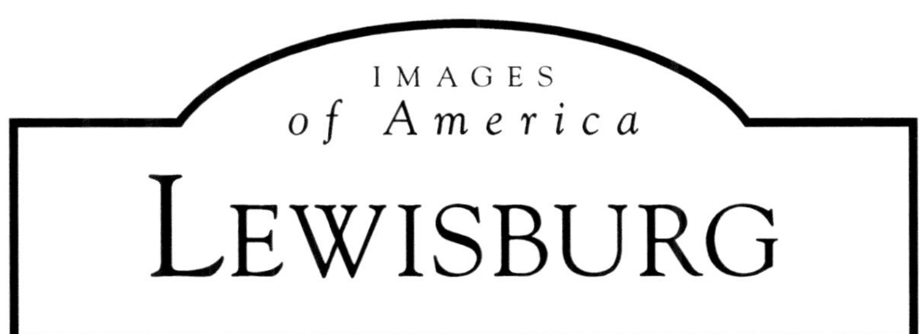

Marion Lois Huffines and
Richard A. Sauers

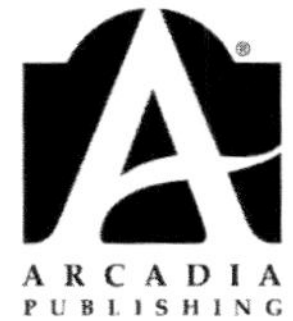

ISBN 978-0-7385-7335-9

Published by Arcadia Publishing
Charleston, South Carolina

Printed in the United States of America

Library of Congress Control Number: 2010921015

For all general information contact Arcadia Publishing at:
Telephone 843-853-2070
Fax 843-853-0044
E-mail sales@arcadiapublishing.com
For customer service and orders:
Toll-Free 1-888-313-2665

Visit us on the Internet at www.arcadiapublishing.com

Contents

Acknowledgments		6
Introduction		7
1.	Living	11
2.	Working	55
3.	Celebrating	89
4.	21st Century Lewisburg	125
Bibliography		127

ACKNOWLEDGMENTS

Jeannette Lasansky, vice president of the Union County Historical Society (UCHS), shared her extensive knowledge of both the historical society's photograph collection and the history of Union County. She also offered suggestions for revisions for the textual parts of the volume.

Alan Richard, of RichardHouse Photo Restoration, scanned the photographs selected from the collection of the Union County Historical Society, offered his help and advice in locating other images for the project, and used exceptional care to achieve the greatest clarity of each photograph.

Tiffini Scott, from Creative Images Plus, scanned the Packwood House Museum photographs and those donated by area residents.

Betsy Robertson, of Robertson Public Relations, edited all textual parts of the project, including all 220 captions.

Erin Vosgien from Arcadia Publishing was always graciously helpful by answering questions in a timely manner and encouraging us along the way to meet the deadlines.

The many people who offered their pictures, memories, and information include the following: Jeanne Bernt, Bucknell University, David Dunn, Russell Dennis, Gale Duque, Paul Ernst, Nada Gray, June Harmon, Dennis Hawley, Bruce Jackson, David Koch, Northeastern Federal Penitentiary, Owen Mahon, Carol Manbeck, Patsy Marra, James Mathias, Barry Maxwell, Ruth McCord, Michael McWilliams, David Mensch, Virginia Moore, National Archives, Ronald Nornhold, Isabella O'Neill, James Orbison, Ronn Palm, David Pearson, Playworld Systems, Dorothy Reish, Daniel Shannon, Graham Showalter, Donna Slear, Bradley Smith, Charlotte and Robert Smith, Robert Stackhouse, Harold Wagner, Harold Walters, Paul Yost, and John Zeller.

Unless otherwise noted, images in this volume appear from the collections of the Packwood House Museum (PHM, followed by an identification number) and the Union County Historical Society (UCHS, followed by an identification number).

INTRODUCTION

In 1770, Ludwig Derr, a Palatine German immigrant, built his house and gristmill where the Bull Run flows into the Susquehanna River. By 1785, he had laid out a town at first called Derr's Town and later Lewisburg—Lewis being the English counterpart of the German Ludwig. Derr may have laid it out, but it was the Susquehanna River that actually gave birth to the town and encouraged people to try their luck in this place. They worked to establish a way of life and to build a town that would ultimately prosper in good times and bad, through devastating floods and fires, and become a gateway that would lead into the Buffalo Valley.

Derr's Town officially became Lewisburg when it was incorporated in 1812. Union County, then twice its present size, was created from Northumberland County in 1813, at which time centrally located New Berlin was selected as the county seat. Absentee landowners, who showed little interest in their properties, hampered the early growth of Lewisburg. Yet by 1830, Lewisburg had grown to 979 people.

Crucial for the development and increasing importance of Lewisburg was the construction of the West Branch Division of the Pennsylvania Canal in 1830. In 1833, a crosscut canal linked Lewisburg to the Pennsylvania Canal. The crosscut canal, used primarily from 1834 to 1869, was about three-quarters of a mile in length, entering the Susquehanna River just below the covered bridge into Lewisburg. A dam across the river below the docks on South Water Street kept the river water deep enough for the boats. During the canal's heyday, Lewisburg enjoyed renewed vitality and growth.

The railroad came to Lewisburg on the morning of July 23, 1869, when the first train of the Lewisburg, Centre, and Spruce Creek Railroad chugged into town. This rail line eventually reached westward across Union County to Bellefonte and later was acquired by the Pennsylvania Railroad system (the Pennsy), which, after merging with New York Central to form the Penn Central Railroad, ended in bankruptcy in 1970.

The railroad era (1870–1920) brought still greater growth and prosperity to Lewisburg. By then, Lewisburg had far outgrown its phase as a pioneer town of struggle and sacrifice. Lewisburg now had an appetite for worldly things, nice worldly things. Prominent families built large elegant houses that still grace the streets of Lewisburg. The names of some of the families who owned those great homes are still found among the populace, on buildings and street signs.

A second railroad was constructed northward to Lewisburg in the 1880s. The Shamokin, Sunbury, and Lewisburg Railroad (1883), later called the Lewisburg-Tyrone Railroad, was later a part of the Reading Railroad. The railroad crossed the river at Sunbury and followed the west bank to Winfield and Lewisburg and then continued on to West Milton. The Reading depot stood just south of Market Street along Fifth Street. The Reading went into bankruptcy in 1971 and was acquired by Conrail five years later. What remains standing today is the freight station of the Reading Railroad on South Fifth Street.

When New Berlin wished to tax county residents to pay for a larger county courthouse, influential people from Lewisburg, among them George Miller, Eli Slifer, and William Cameron, began a campaign to divide the county and make Lewisburg the center of government for a new county. A popular vote created Snyder County in 1855, and Lewisburg was named the seat of a much smaller Union County. Lewisburg's victory in the competition with Mifflinburg to become the county seat was narrow. Only Lewisburg's rapid growth during the previous decade made it possible. Its leaders also offered a large sum of money for the costs involved, including money for the building of the courthouse.

By the time the new county courthouse opened in 1857, the borough had opened its first bank, the Lewisburg Dime Savings Institution, in 1851. The Frick and Slifer boatyard moved to town in 1850, and a steam-powered mill started operation in 1852. A gas works opened in 1859, and the Central Manufacturing Company, soon to be the Slifer, Walls, Shriner, and Company, began producing reapers, mowers, and other machinery in 1860. It was a thriving business that produced over 1,000 machines per year. Its competitor, Geddes, Marsh, and Company, manufactured harvesters and advertised as "a self-raking reaper and mower combined." For several decades, these two implement makers were the town's largest employers.

As Lewisburg's population passed 3,000 in the 1870s, the town included a modern music hall that opened in 1869, gas lights, several furniture makers, a modern fire engine company thanks to William Cameron, in addition to a number of other businesses. Three newspapers served the town. The *Lewisburg Chronicle* began publication in 1848 and the *Lewisburg Journal* in 1855. Both newspapers changed hands frequently, but the *Chronicle* and the *Journal* each had their political biases, with the *Chronicle* seen as a voice for the Republican Party and the *Journal* for the Democratic Party. The Lewisburg *Saturday News* first appeared in 1882.

In 1885, Lewisburg celebrated its 100th anniversary with fanfare. In his *Centennial History of Lewisburg*, I. H. Mauser printed a celebratory advertisement that described Lewisburg in 1885 as having, among other things, fine public schools, seven churches, flour mills with the celebrated White Gem flour at $1.25 per sack, two large sawmills, the nail works, woolen mills, a courthouse, an elegant opera house, finely built residences, a splendid fire department with its $10,000 engine, and two banks with over a half-million dollars "lying idle on Deposit." The University at Lewisburg was founded in 1846. It became Bucknell University after 1886, when William Bucknell rescued it from financial ruin. Destructive floods came in 1865 and again in 1889, as they would in 1936 and 1972. Each time, Lewisburg rebuilt and continued to grow.

By 1900, Lewisburg was beginning to take on the look of a modern town. Families with money were building Italianate Victorian homes that remain a trademark of the borough's reputation. A number of major employers continued to provide enough wealth for the town to continue to expand. Paving began on Market Street in 1915, as did the introduction of the now famous three-globe streetlights. A sewer system began in 1927, and the predecessor to the present Evangelical Community Hospital opened its doors in 1926. The completion of the Northeastern Federal Penitentiary in 1932 in Kelly Township also brought more residents and jobs to Lewisburg.

To serve the growing and demanding population of Lewisburg and its surrounding area and to provide an inviting environment for new businesses and industry, Lewisburg provided infrastructure, enhanced government, and medical facilities. It also offered opportunities for leisure activities, recreation, and support for the arts. Buffalo Valley Telephone Company formed in 1904. A free river bridge replaced the toll bridge at Market Street in 1906. Citizens' Electric Company formed in 1911. The Lewisburg Civic Club developed a park next to the river bridge where the old water towers once stood so prominently. The Federal Building at the corner of Market and Third Streets was erected in 1932. In 1941, the art deco Campus Theatre opened on Market Street.

Lewisburg's post–World War II growth continued with zest. The JPM Company started business in 1949. The Silver Moon drive-in theater opened in 1952. In 1953, the modern Evangelical Community Hospital opened it doors. The community pool was completed in 1960. More traffic led to the widening of Route 15 to four lanes in 1961, the same year that the Moore Business Forms plant opened, and the Lewisburg Chair Company became Pennsylvania House. Wolfe Field opened in 1967, and 1968 saw the first Festival of the Arts. In 1969, a municipal parking lot replaced the old Cameron Engine Company building and the site of the opera house. Also in 1969, Kentucky Fried Chicken opened its doors for business, the first of several fast-food restaurants in Union County.

In the later years of the century, sprawl along Route 15 also began to endanger the downtown shopping area, which had always been the borough's core. However, the 1960s demolition of older structures, such as the Christian Church and both railroad stations, spurred a grassroots effort to ensure that Lewisburg did not lose its distinctive Victorian buildings, streetscapes, and vibrant downtown. The downtown continued to be home to several longtime local businesses such as Purity Candy, the Edwin D. Mensch Agency, and Stein's Flowers. However, in the early 21st century, Lewisburg suffered the loss of some long-standing major businesses, such as Pennsylvania House, International Paper, and JPM, as well as smaller but important enterprises, such as the 130-year-old Donehower's Sporting Goods and the 60-year-old Wagner's Stationery.

Lewisburg, along with the rest of Union County, celebrates the bicentennial of Union County in 2013. The Lewisburg Borough population now stands at 5,454, with a total of 15,852 people living in the 17837 zip code. Market Street continues to attract new ventures and small businesses. Bucknell University endeavors to play a larger role in the town by moving its Barnes and Noble Bucknell University Bookstore into downtown (which was done on June 26, 2010) and by establishing its offices into other downtown buildings. The Lewisburg Downtown Partnership strives to continue the heritage of a strong downtown, encouraging new businesses and services to settle in the Lewisburg core area. The town and its abutting townships provide a strong and talented workforce in a region that has both the services and variety of much larger cities and the charm and care of a small community. In 1993, Lewisburg was named one of the 100 best small towns in America, and in 2004, the Lewisburg downtown historical district was placed on the National Register of Historic Places.

Through periodic floods, when mud filled streets and houses, destructive fires, business failures, and just plain bad luck, Lewisburg and its neighboring East Buffalo and Kelly Townships persevered. They participated in the progress that came from the hard work and hopeful vision that were the hallmarks of small-town American life. Lewisburg had an important presence on the west bank of the Susquehanna River and thrived as a river and canal town, a railroad town, and later as a stop on the busy highways at the intersection of Routes 15 and 45. Even more recently, Interstate 80, just 8 miles north, connects Lewisburg to cities to the east and to a faster west route. The interstate system as a whole was responsible in large part for the demise of the railroads and their freight-moving efficiency.

Lewisburg had business, industry, and culture, and it valued education and recreation. It rightfully celebrated itself with festivals and clubs and parades. In 1885, on the occasion of the Lewisburg centennial, J. W. Shriner stated, "With all these advantages, no one can doubt what the second Lewisburg centennial will be with its 100,000 inhabitants." It did not quite work out that way, and some would say, "thank heavens." But Lewisburg is proud of its history. This book honors the achievements of those who have gone before and looks forward to a proud future.

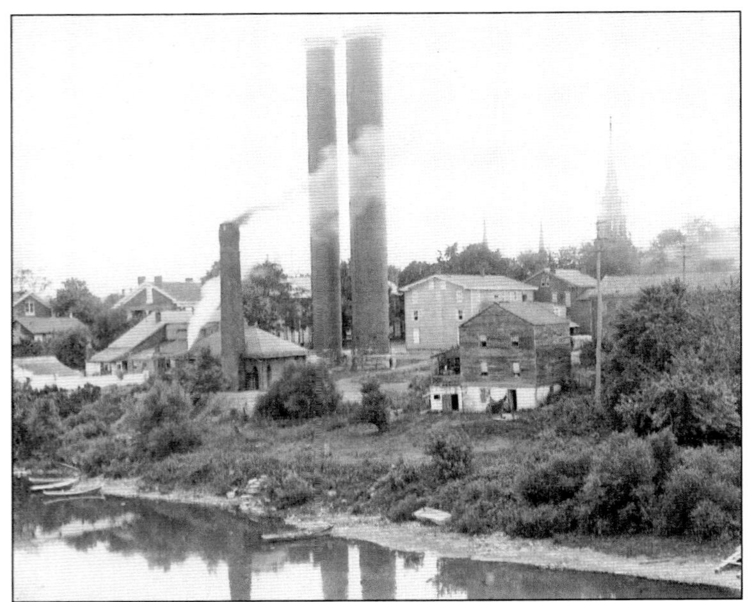

The Lewisburg Water Works was completed in December 1883 and consisted of a pump house, seen to the left of the towering pipes. Water taken from the river was pumped into the standing pipes for distribution. The pipes stood at 130 feet, with a diameter of 12 feet, and were a commanding feature of the Lewisburg landscape for four decades. (UCHS 89.5.20.3.)

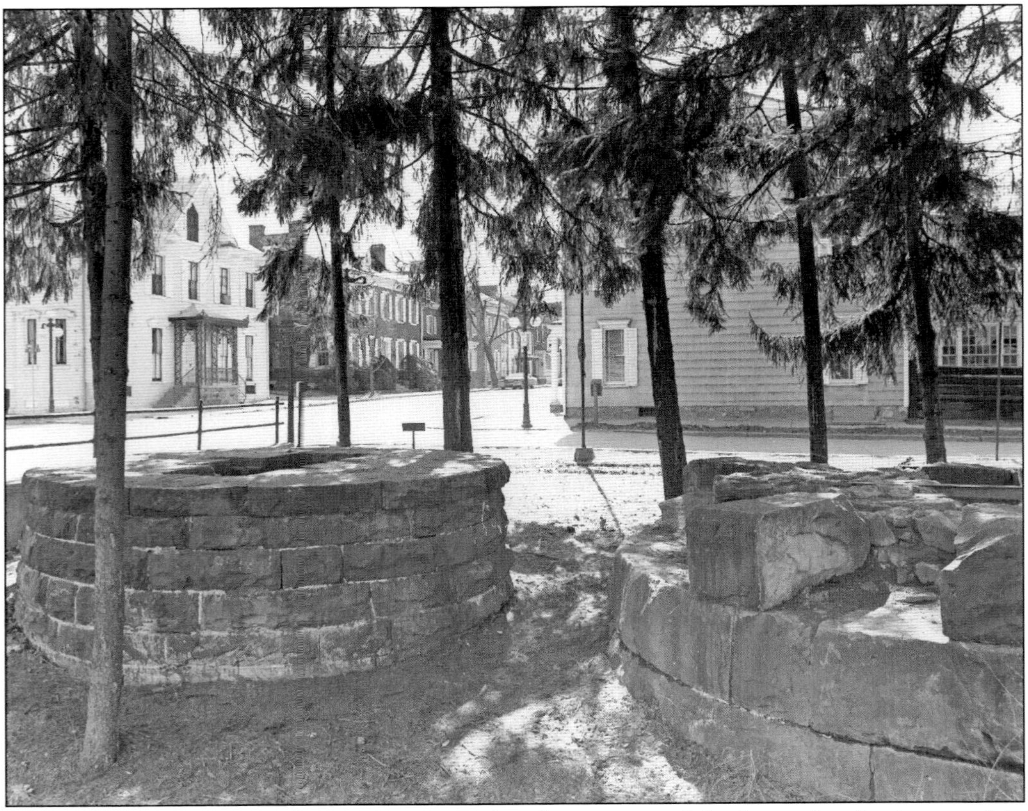

The standing pipes came down in 1923. Today the remains of the base of each pipe stand in Soldiers' Memorial Park at the corner of Market and Water Streets. The park is now owned by the Borough of Lewisburg. In the background to the right, one sees Packwood House Museum, former home of Edith and John Fetherston. Part of the building served as a tavern in earlier times. (UCHS 89.5.27.1A.)

One

Living

The people who live in Lewisburg understand the importance of community, beginning in 1785 when Ludwig Derr laid out the town in partnership with the Susquehanna River. Ever after, the Susquehanna played an important role in what Lewisburg became. Starting in the 1830s, the canal brought people and goods; bridges opened up a way for the railroads and people traveling from a distance. Floods marked periods of rebuilding, challenging the residents in a common effort to start again and improve the community.

Lewisburg gained wealth and status from its location on the river, and with this wealth, a town emerged with resources and public works that formed a sturdy foundation. An opera house and a university brought opportunity not readily available elsewhere. Churches served social causes as well as spiritual needs. An orphanage provided a home and a way to grow up safely. A community hospital grew and helped those in physical distress, while homes for the elderly developed into large complexes with multiple ways to live and be cared for.

Lewisburg was a town filled with opportunities to make a living in health care, education, transportation, manufacturing, and construction. Lewisburg depended on the produce from the fertile fields surrounding the town and the hard work of its farmers. When goods or services became scarce because of hard times, distant wars, floods, and fires, the citizens persevered, because they were a community.

Both elegant and plain homes line the streets; other buildings open their doors to business. Neighboring farm fields blend into the horizon of ridges and the Buffalo Valley. Even the Northeastern Federal Penitentiary up the road declares its presence with an Italian Renaissance–style smokestack. Now that the tall water towers beside the Susquehanna River are gone, church steeples, the courthouse cupola, the university on the hill, and the prison smokestack define the Lewisburg skyline. This skyline orients the citizenry, reminding them of community, where people greet friends on the street and join with each other in hard times and good.

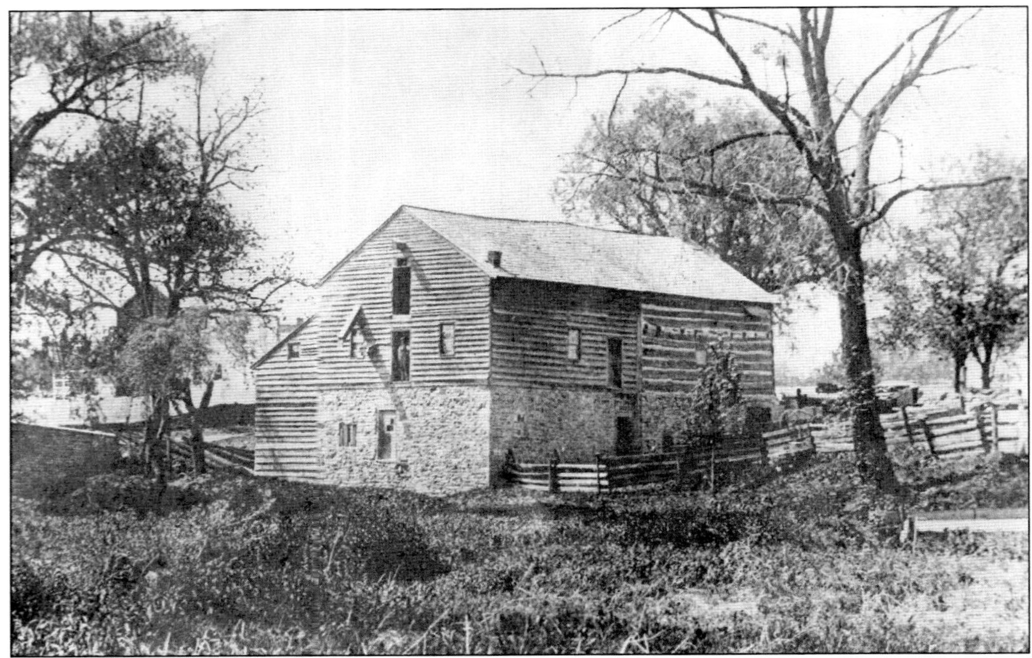

Ludwig Derr's original mill in Lewisburg was photographed in 1860, nearly a century after it was first built. The mill stood near the mouth of Spring Run, later called Limestone or Wilson Run, and more recently Bull Run. Ludwig Derr laid out a plan for the town in 1785 and sold plots, sometimes by auction. (UCHS 89.5.6.7.)

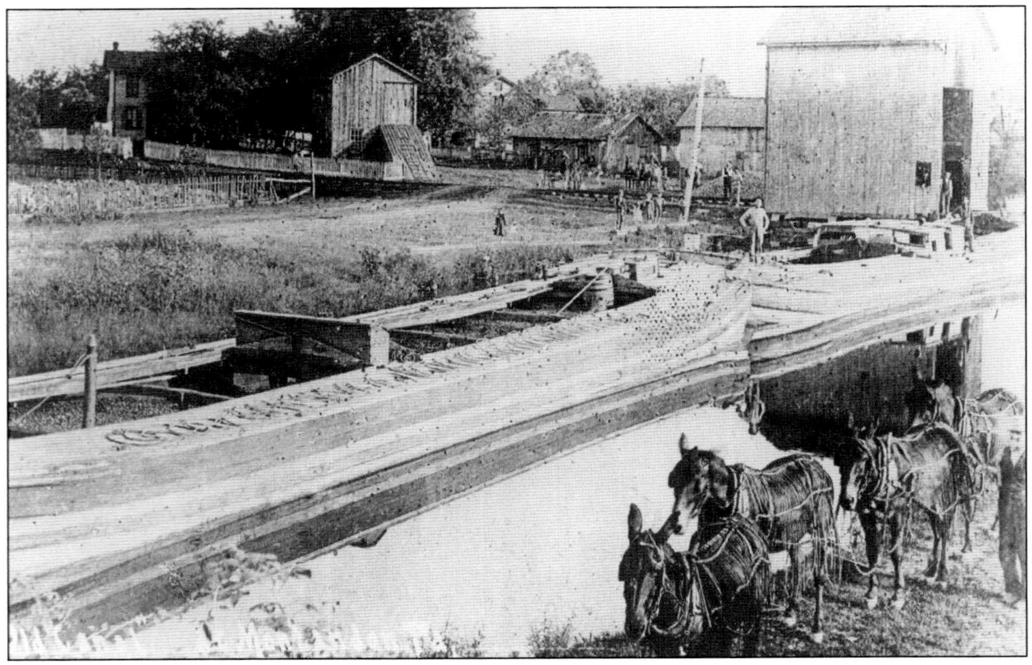

Barges were pulled by mules on a towpath along the Pennsylvania Canal. Lewisburg was on the wrong side of the river to enjoy the major benefits of the Pennsylvania West Branch Canal. In 1833, a crosscut canal was completed, linking Lewisburg to the Pennsylvania canal system. It was three-quarters of a mile in length. (UCHS 89.5.21.2.)

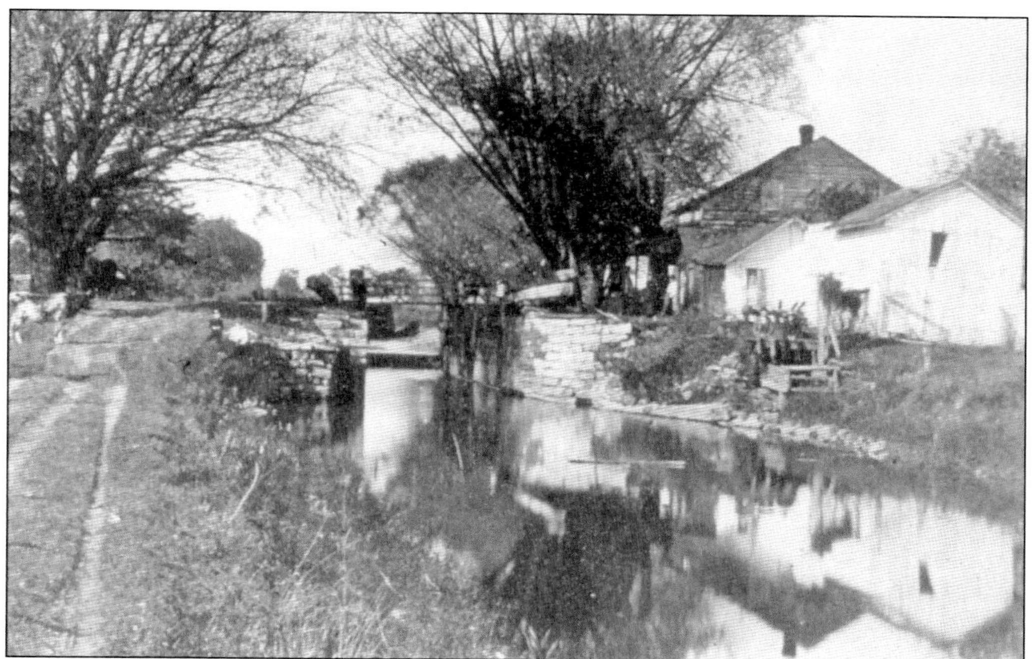

Locks on the canal raised the level of the water to accommodate boats regardless of the weather-driven level of the water. The Lewisburg crosscut canal consisted of a dam across the river and three locks. The canal entered the Susquehanna River below the covered bridge. Remains of the dam are still visible south of the Lewisburg Bridge when the water is low. (PHM.)

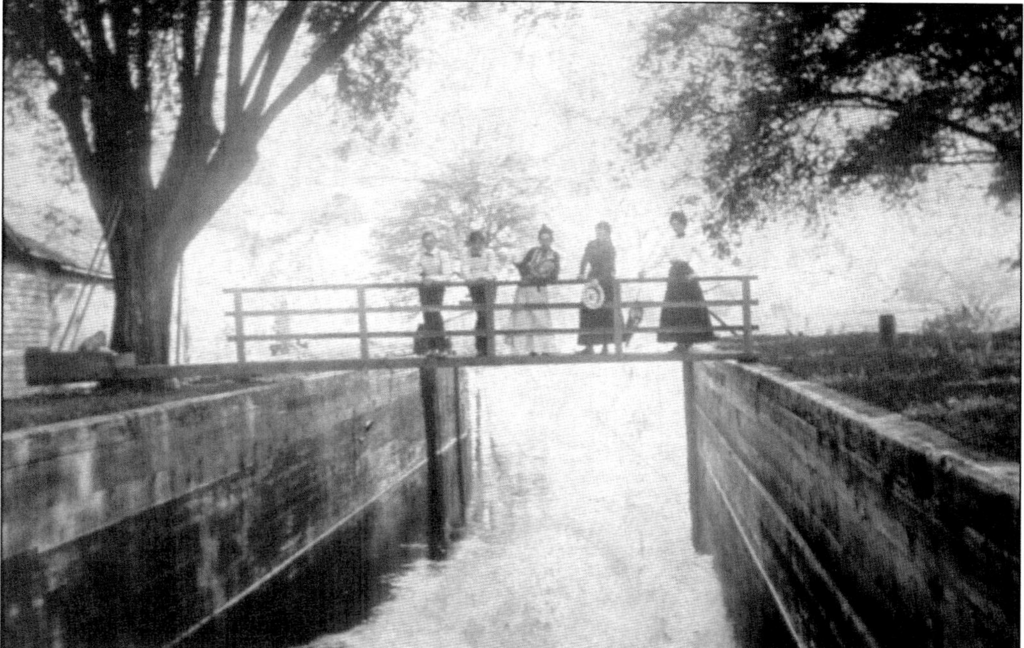

Three women and two men enjoy viewing a lock. Lewisburg's crosscut canal paid large dividends to the town. A period of intensive growth quickly occurred, as local farmers and businesses now had an easier way to get their goods to more distant markets. Potential residents could also reach the town more easily. (PHM.)

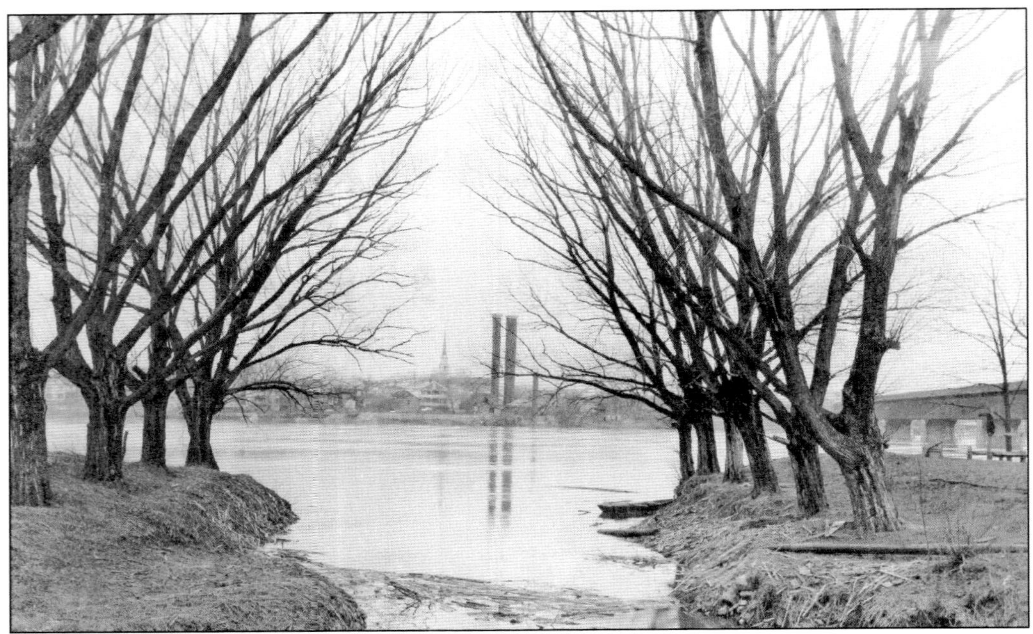

The view of Lewisburg from the east bank of the river shows the entrance into the Susquehanna River by the crosscut canal near present-day May's. The pump house and the standing pipes can be clearly seen along with the Presbyterian church steeple. The covered train bridge is visible to the far right. Railroads drastically lessened the need for the canal, moving goods and people more quickly and easily. (PHM.)

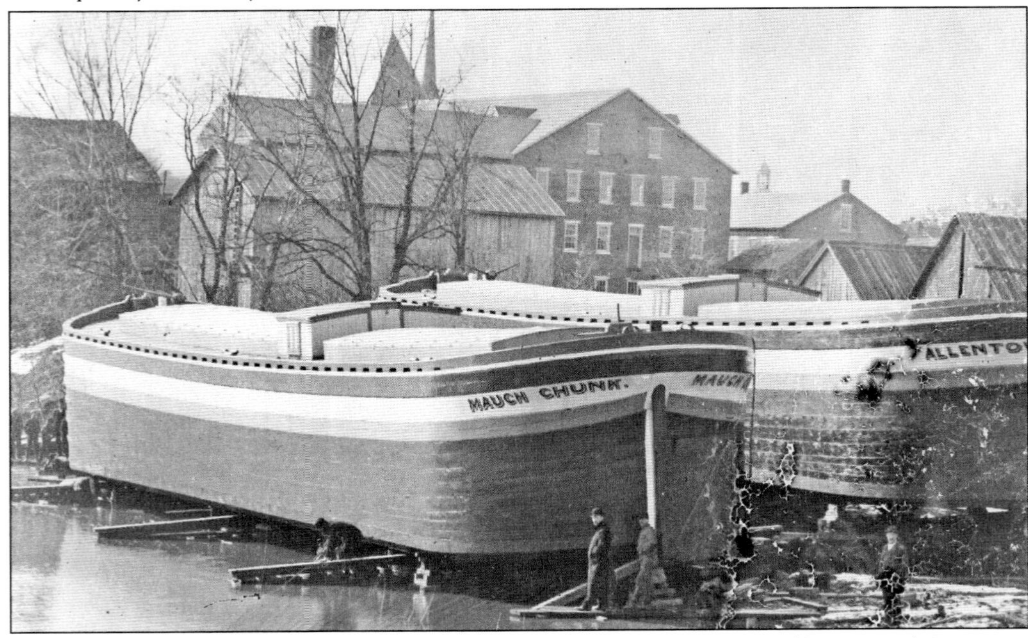

The canal boats *Mauch Chunk* and *Allentown* are docked at the Phillip Billmeyer and Company boatyards on North Water Street around 1865. These canal boats were larger than those used on the West Branch of the Pennsylvania Canal and were about 85 feet long and 13 to 14 feet wide. Built for service on the larger Lehigh and Delaware Canals, they would be transported downstream when the spring flood deepened the rivers. (UCHS 89.5.21.3.)

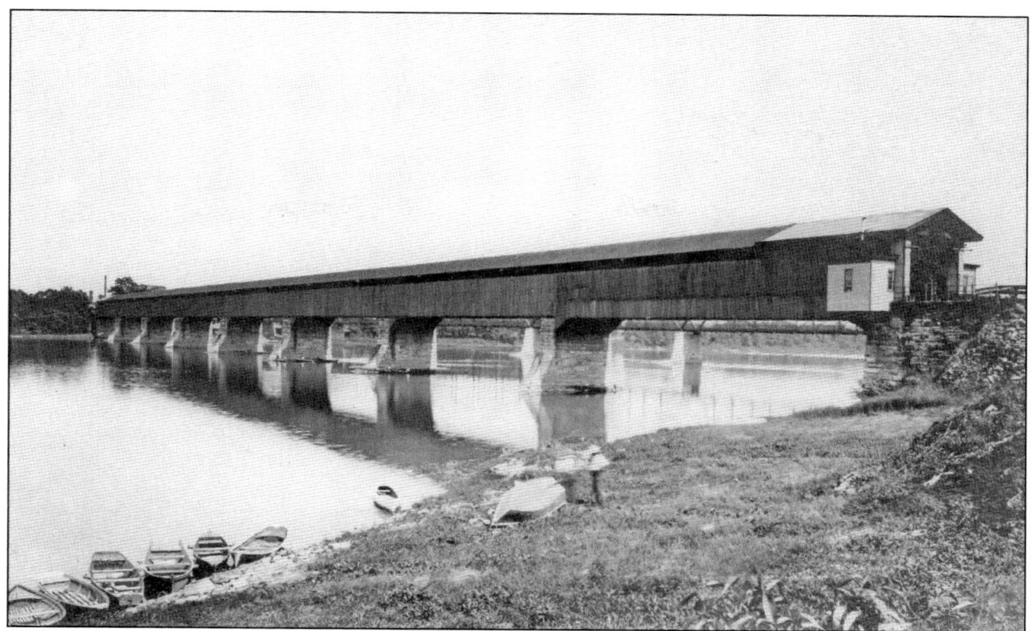

The covered toll bridge accommodated trains, trolleys, pedestrians, and horse-drawn vehicles. A major flood in 1865 heavily damaged much of Lewisburg's first wooden bridge, which had opened in 1818. Shortly after its loss, the Lewisburg Bridge Company, a private corporation, built a new wooden, covered toll bridge, about 400 feet to the north, near St. John Street. It was replaced in 1912 by a steel trestle bridge. (PHM.)

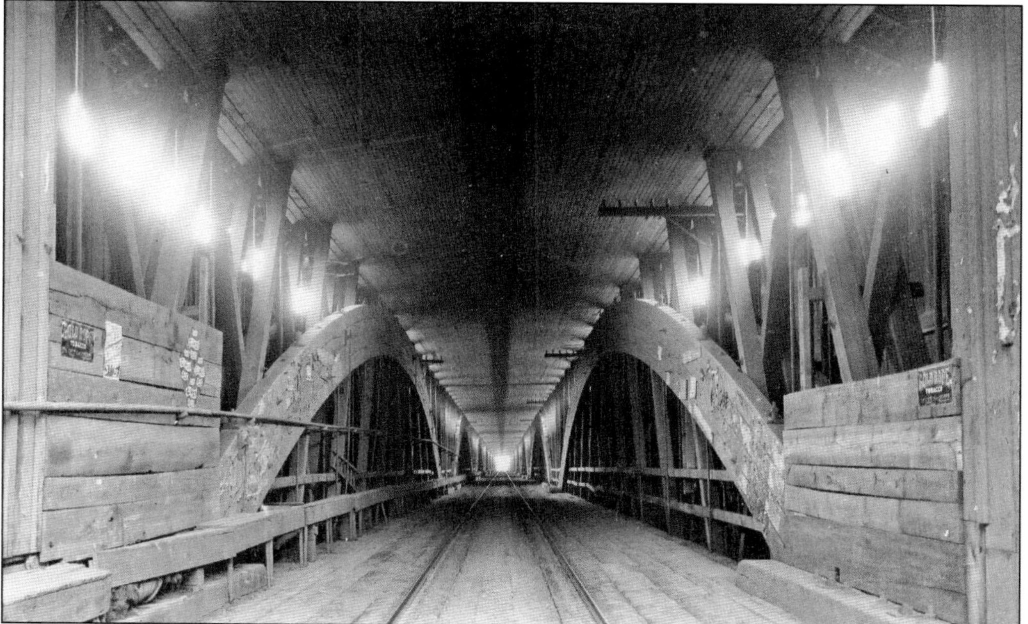

The interior of the covered wooden train bridge shows that the bridge structure was a Burr arch truss type, probably the most common structural system for covered bridges. The Burr arch, invented by Theodore Burr and first used in 1804, consists of a pair of segmented arches sandwiched between two multiple kingpost trusses. Wooden bridges were covered to keep the structure dry and to prevent or delay decay. (UCHS 92.9.91.132.)

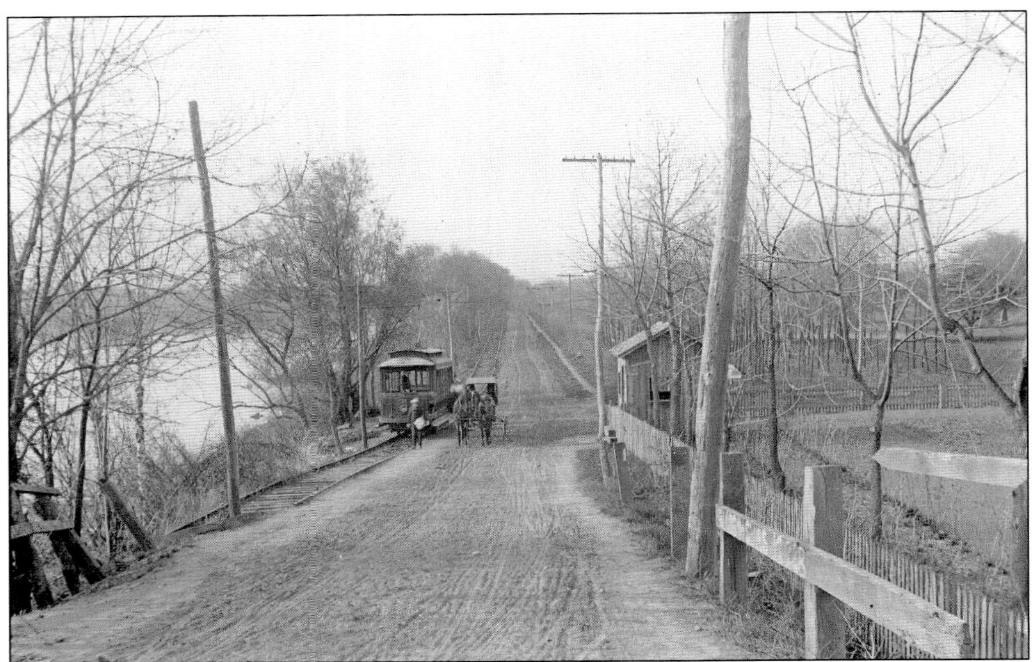

The Lewisburg/Milton/Watsontown trolley traveled on the east bank of the river. The electric-operated trolley car ran from 1898 to 1928. In the early years, the trolley went only as far as the Montandon side of Lewisburg's earlier wooden toll bridge until the covered toll train bridge was operative. In 1912, service was added to Mifflinburg. (UCHS 83.39.02.)

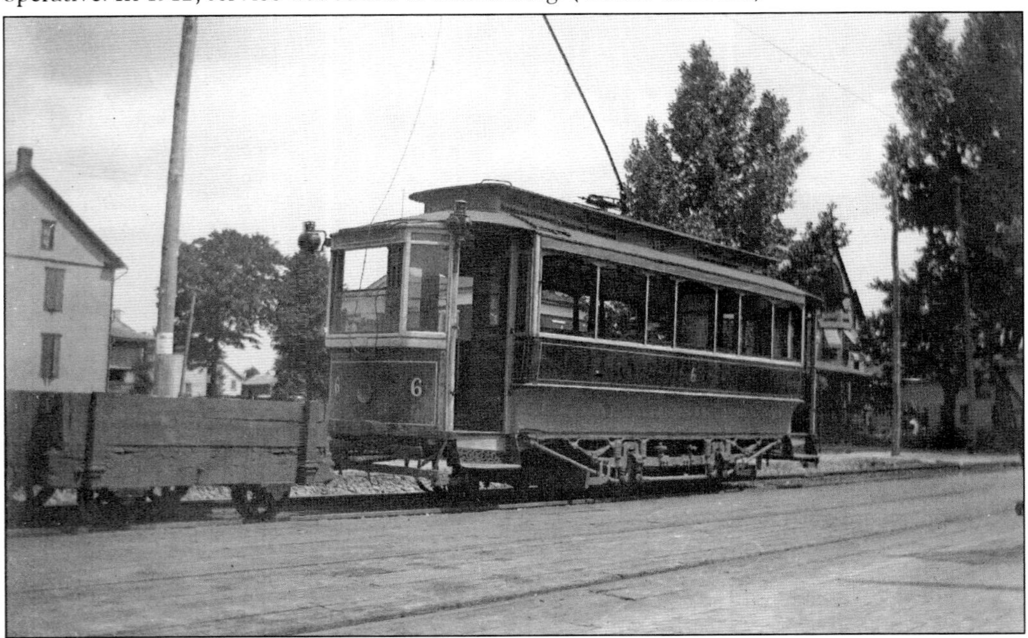

The trolley used the covered toll bridge. The grade from the riverbank to the railroad bridge at East Lewisburg was steep and difficult to negotiate. Before crossing the bridge, the conductor called the Pennsylvania Railroad station agent at Lewisburg on the telephone to request a clear track. He then opened the switch, crossed the bridge, and pulled onto a siding at the station at North Second and St. John Streets. (UCHS 83.55.1.)

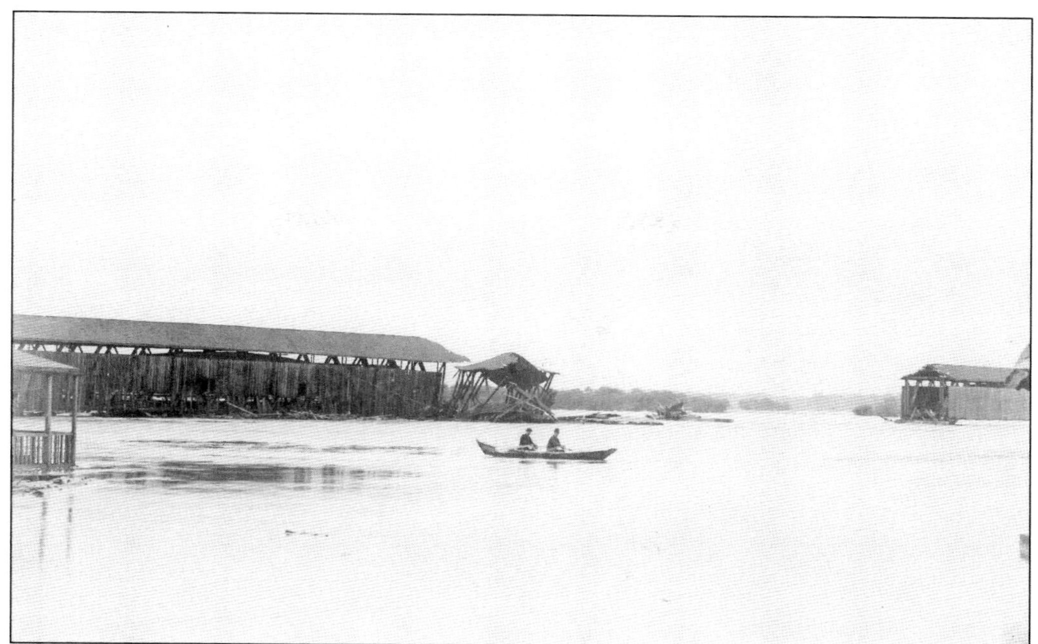

The floodwaters of 1889 (the Johnstown flood) severely damaged the covered toll train bridge. A large midsection was washed downriver. The damaged section was rebuilt as quickly as possible in order to avoid interrupting traffic and commerce for a lengthy period of time. Severe flooding damaged the bridge periodically. (David Koch and Alan Richard.)

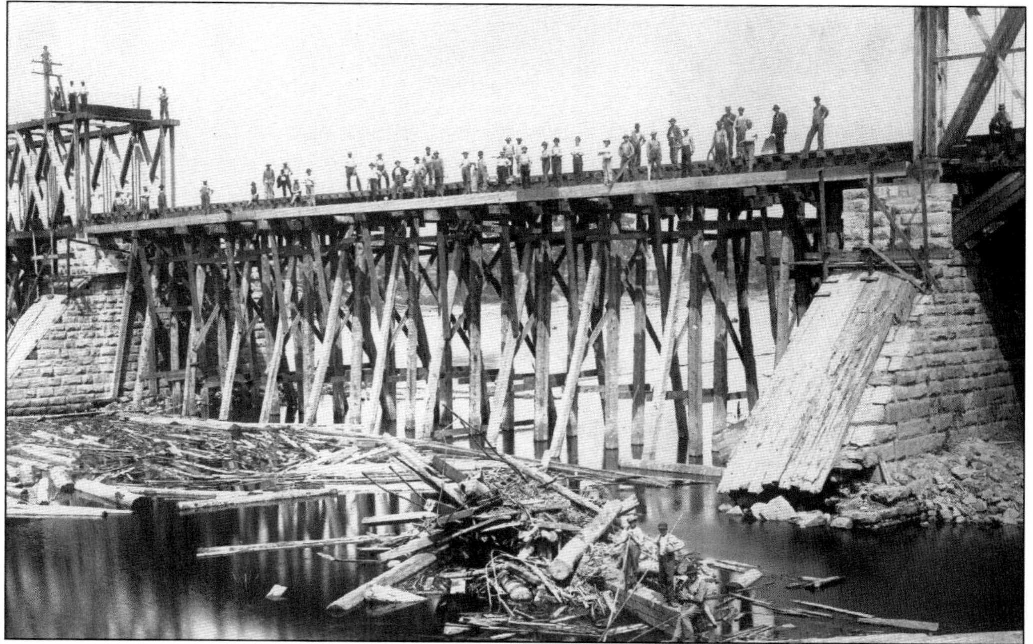

The Lewisburg covered toll bridge was rebuilt after the destruction from the 1889 (Johnstown) flood. The first bridge over the Susquehanna River at Lewisburg was the covered bridge constructed in 1818. It was damaged in the 1865 flood and then rebuilt, destroyed, and rebuilt after the 1889 flood. In 1912, a steel railroad and trolley bridge on the original piers replaced it. (David Koch and Alan Richard.)

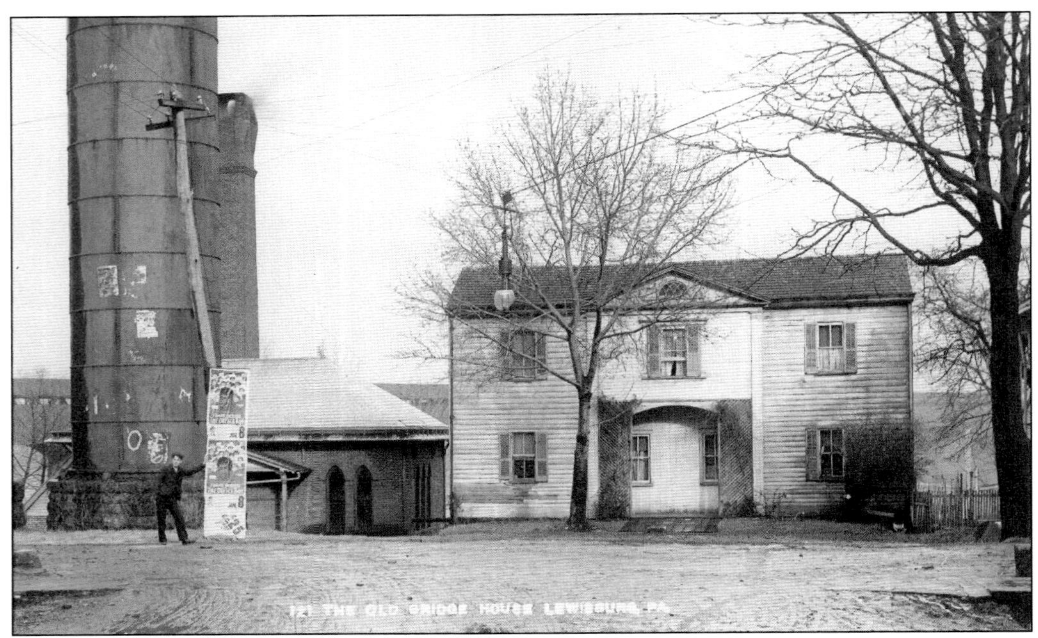

The tollhouse stood at the eastern end of Market Street. In 1905, long obsolete, it had been converted into a home but blocked access to the proposed new free bridge. The house was auctioned off for $56.50 and subsequently moved to the southwest corner of North Water and St. Anthony Streets. The house seen here is flanked by the Lewisburg Water Company and its water towers or standpipes. (UCHS 92.9.91.154.)

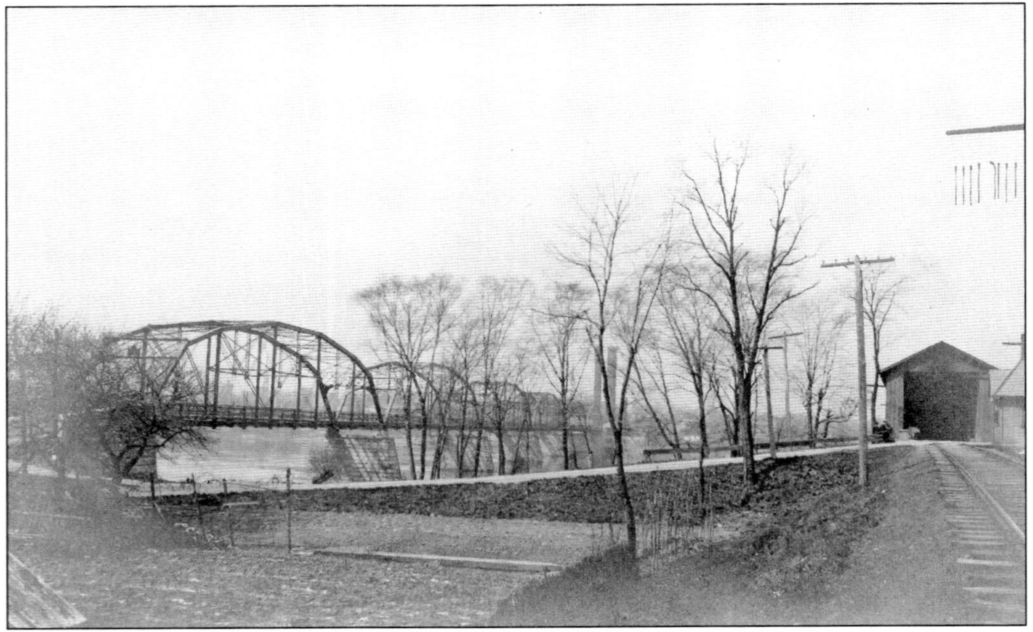

The steel bridge, constructed in 1906, required no toll. The covered toll train bridge, seen here to the right, also accommodated pedestrians and wagons. A steel railroad bridge replaced it in 1912. The photograph gives the unusual perspective of the steel bridge, which exited on Market Street, adjacent to the railroad bridge that exited on St. John Street and was still wooden. (UCHS 92.9.91.161.)

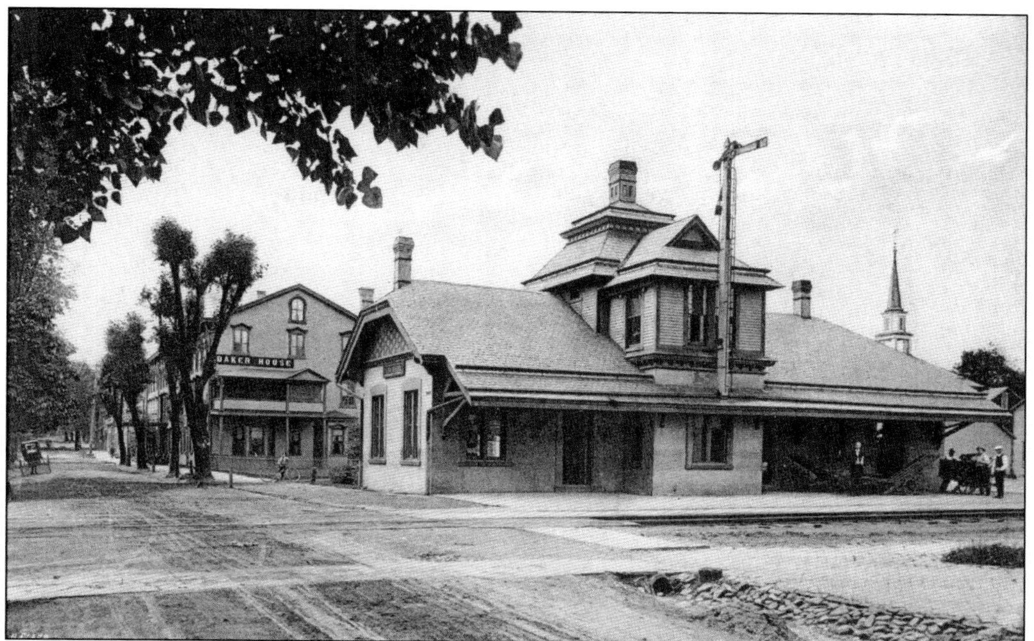

The Pennsylvania Railroad passenger and freight station, built in 1869, was located at the southwest corner of North Second and St. John Streets. This rail line—initially called the Lewisburg, Centre, and Spruce Railroad and later the Lewisburg and Tyrone Railroad—was later acquired by the Pennsylvania Railroad. The line ran west through Union County. It was the first railroad in the county. The structure was demolished in the 1960s. (UCHS 92.9.90.25.)

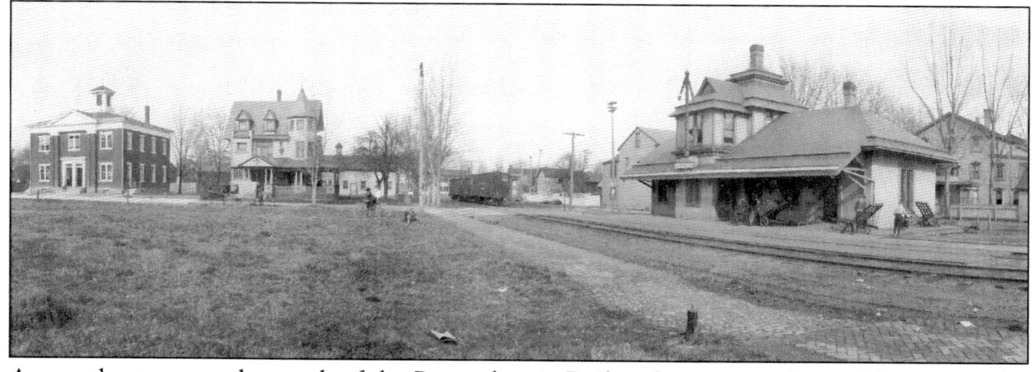

Across the street to the north of the Pennsylvania Railroad station on Second Street was the brick North Ward School, and next to it on the right was the Barnhart-Comstock House. The house was built in 1885 and is a romantic example of the Queen Anne style, having turrets, a round tower, and oriel windows. To the south of the railroad station was the Baker House Hotel. (UCHS 79.481.14.1.)

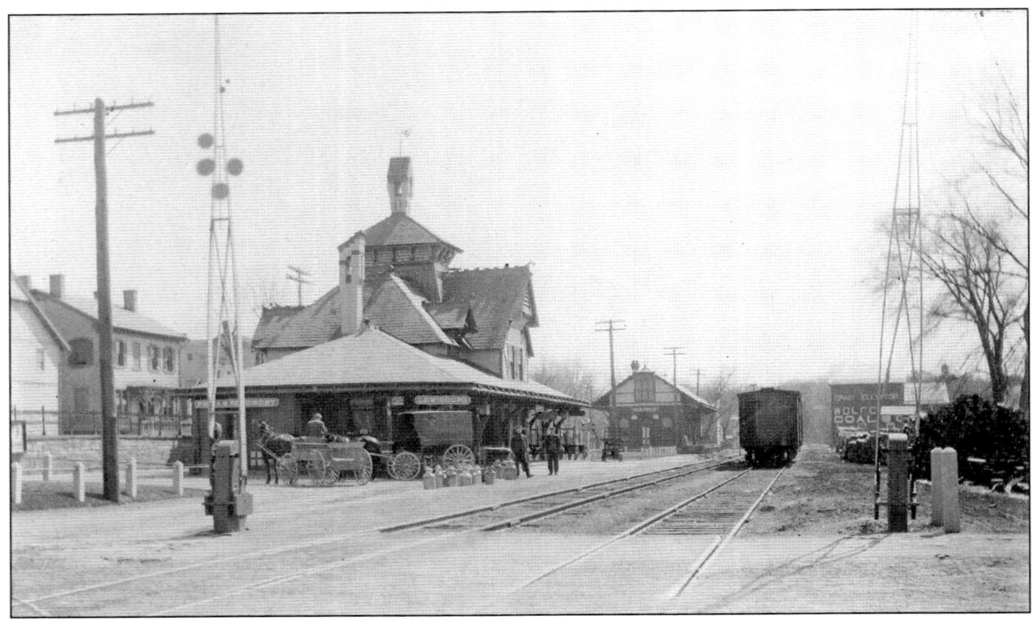

The Philadelphia and Reading Railroad station was located at the corner of Market and South Fifth Streets and built in 1882–1883. Originally the Shamokin, Sunbury, and Lewisburg Railroad, it was the second rail line to enter the county. It ran along the county's eastern edge from Winfield to Allenwood and north to Williamsport. (UCHS 80.7.20.)

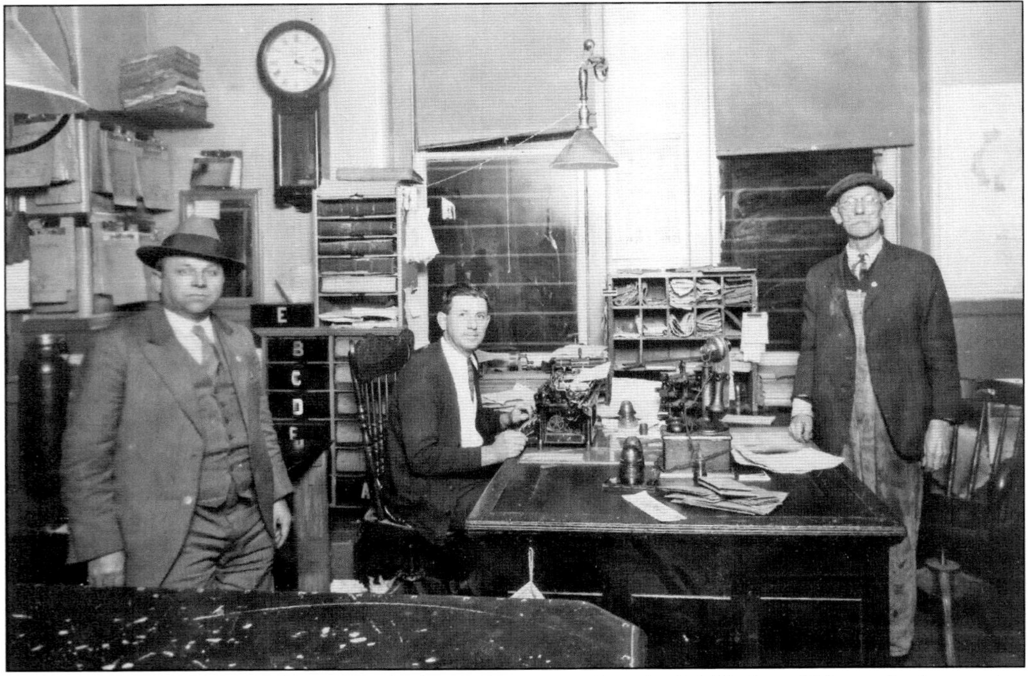

The Reading station was the envy of others. As reported in the *Mifflinburg Telegraph*, the station had a telegraph office on the second floor as well as a separate baggage room and two waiting rooms. Of the Reading station, only the freight station remains standing. It benefits from adaptive reuse as the Lewisburg Borough offices and police station. The passenger station was razed in the 1960s. (UCHS 95.10.2.)

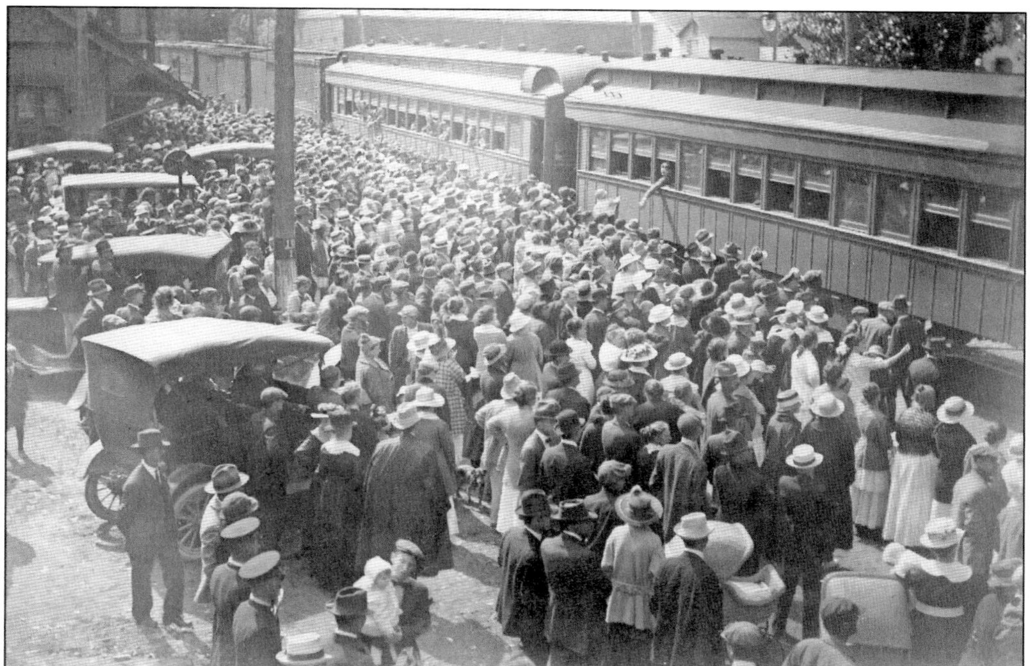

Scores of local residents send off Union County soldiers of the 103rd Motor Battalion at the Pennsylvania Railroad Station on North Second Street in February 1917. Even from the old photograph, the excitement and anxiety seem palpable. This scene repeated itself in small towns and cities throughout the United States. (UCHS 89.19.2a.)

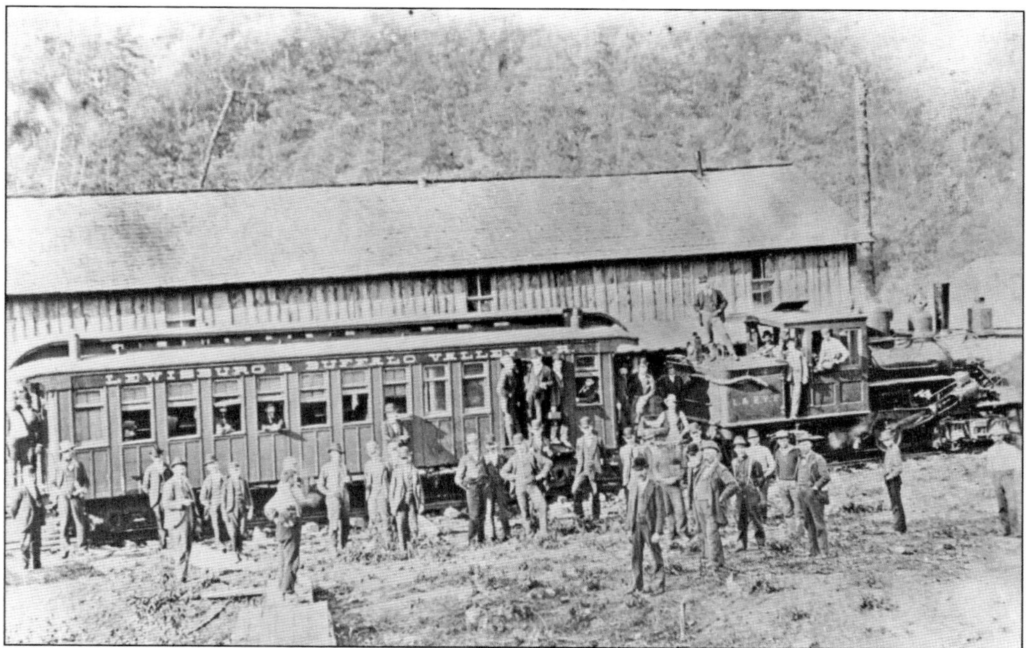

The Kulp narrow gauge railroad operated primarily for the timber interests of the Kulp timber operations, but it would also take passengers to the farthest northwesterly point in Union County, Tea Springs. The line ran from 1897 to 1906. The timbering industry used it to transport logs to distant mills or to the river. (UCHS 89.5.11.41.)

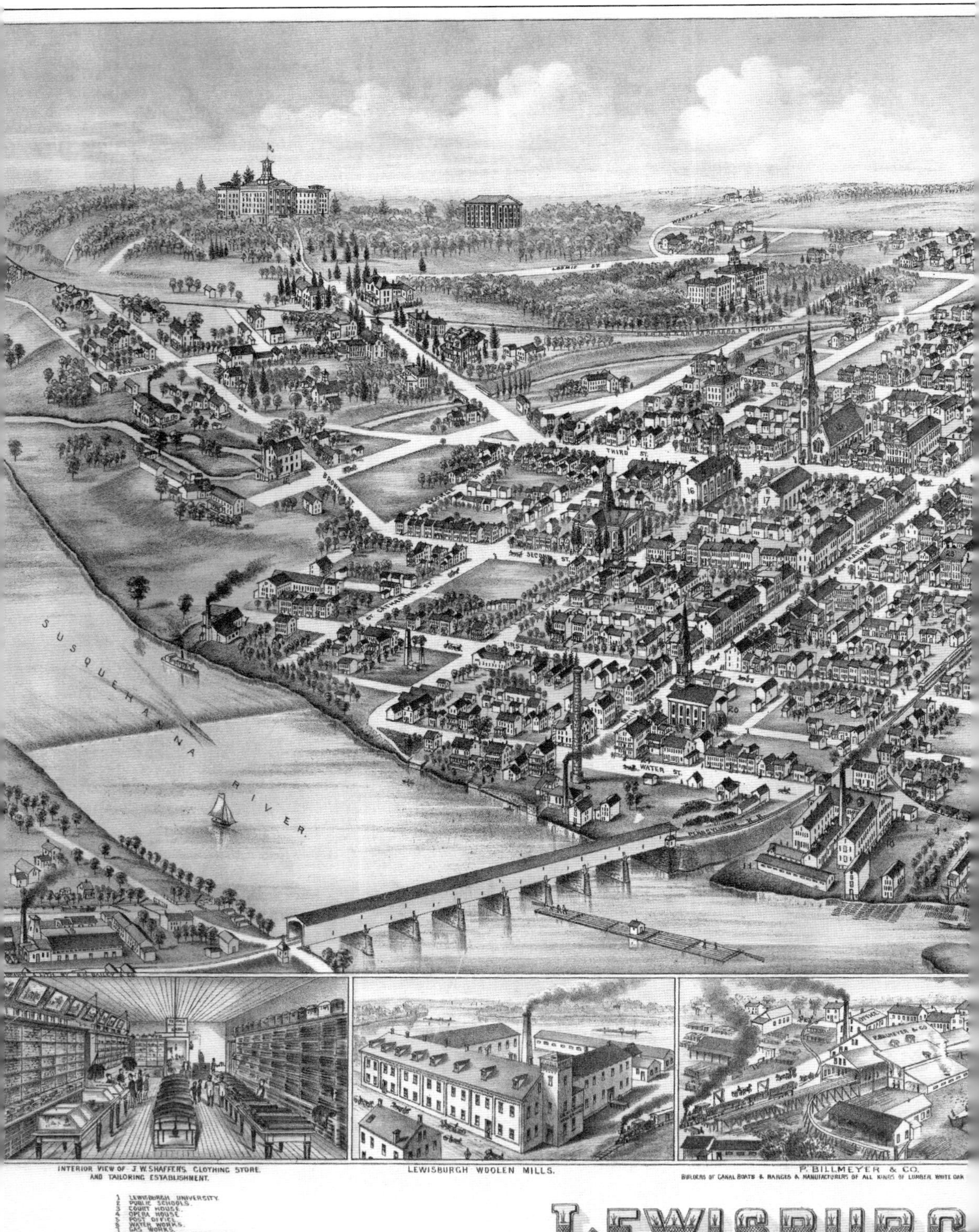

SUSQUEHANNA RIVER

INTERIOR VIEW OF J. W. SHAFFER'S CLOTHING STORE AND TAILORING ESTABLISHMENT.

LEWISBURGH WOOLEN MILLS.

P. BILLMEYER & CO.
BUILDERS OF CANAL BOATS & BARGES & MANUFACTURERS OF ALL KINDS OF LUMBER. WHITE OAK

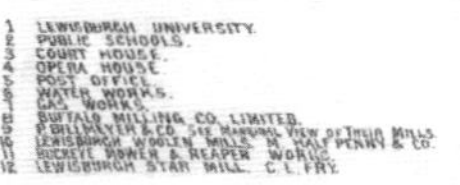

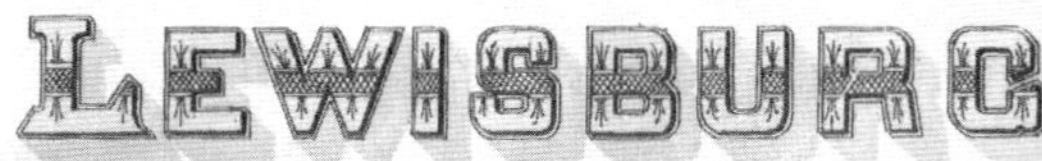

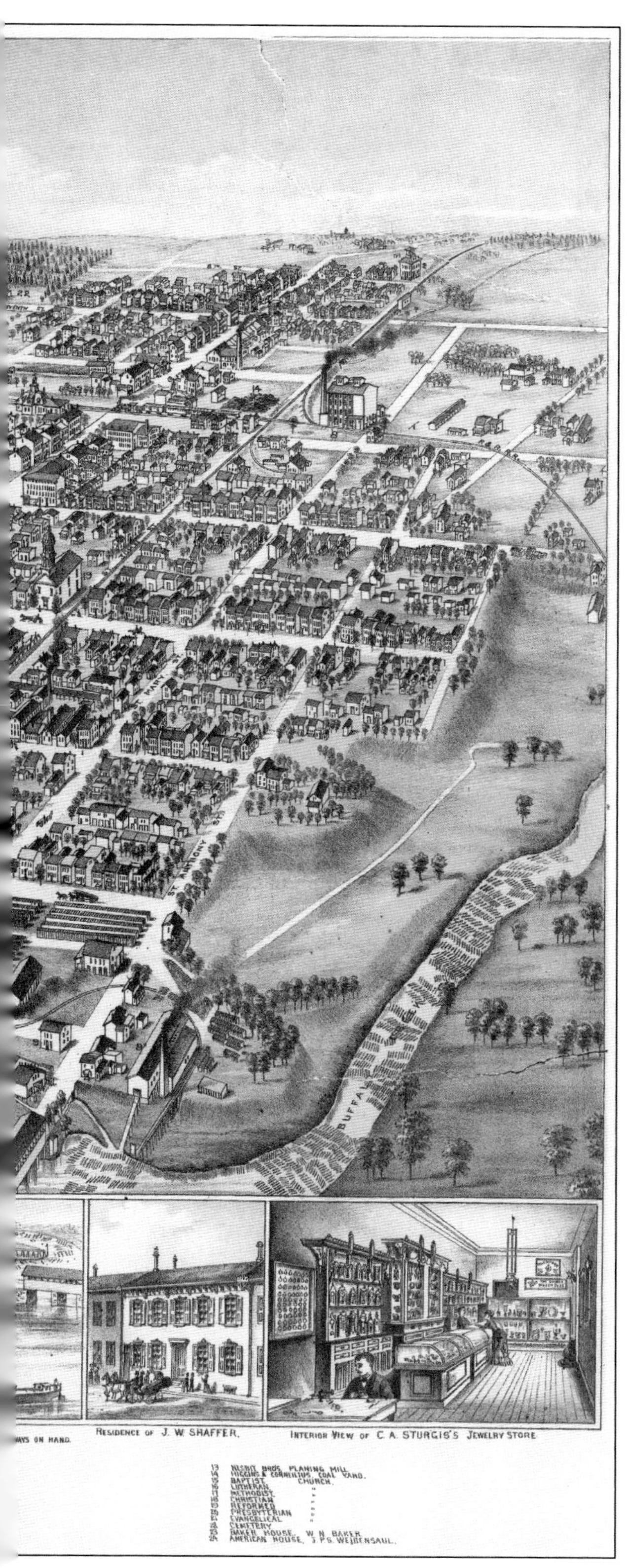

This 1884 map of Lewisburg illustrates the extent to which the town had developed by then. To the upper left, the University at Lewisburg, chartered in 1846 and renamed Bucknell University in 1886, sits on its hill with Old Main, begun in 1849 and completed in 1858, one of the earliest structures on the campus. Off to the right is the Academy Building, the oldest structure on campus (1849). The river shows the dam, which was part of the crosscut canal and the covered toll bridge. One standing pipe of the Lewisburg Water Company and the pump house is close to the river. In the town, the steeples of both the Presbyterian church and the Baptist church stand out significantly. (UCHS 89.5.4.)

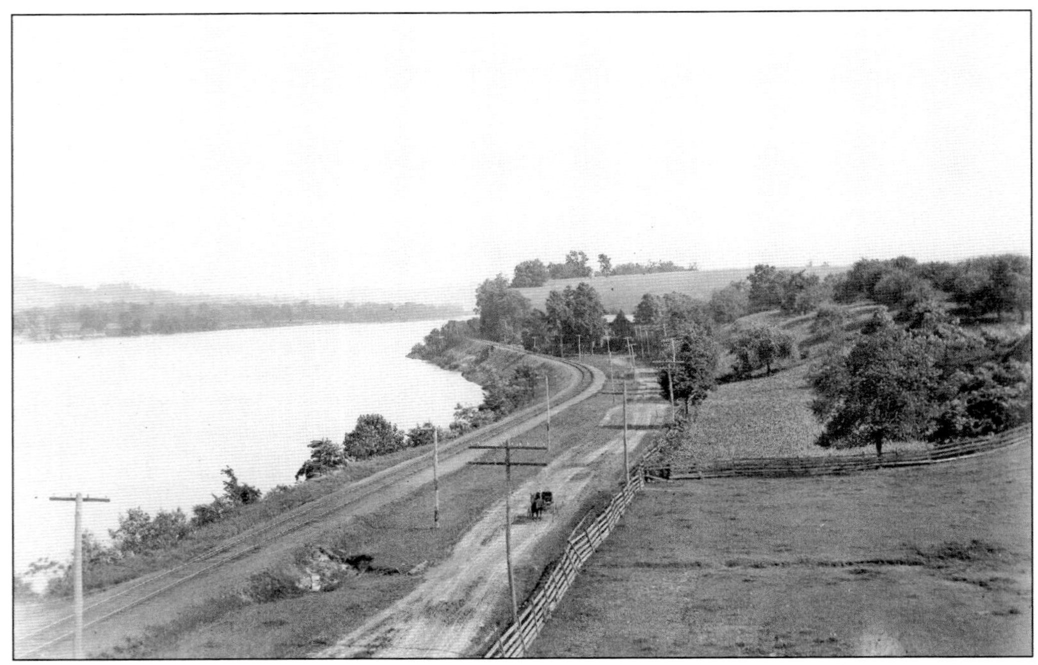

This horse-drawn carriage makes its way south on River Road toward the Gundy Farm. A section of the Reading Railroad line parallels River Road, having crossed the Susquehanna River at Sunbury. The river on the left and farm fields to the right suggest the rural nature of the landscape that still surrounds Lewisburg. (UCHS 82.4.3.23Ea.)

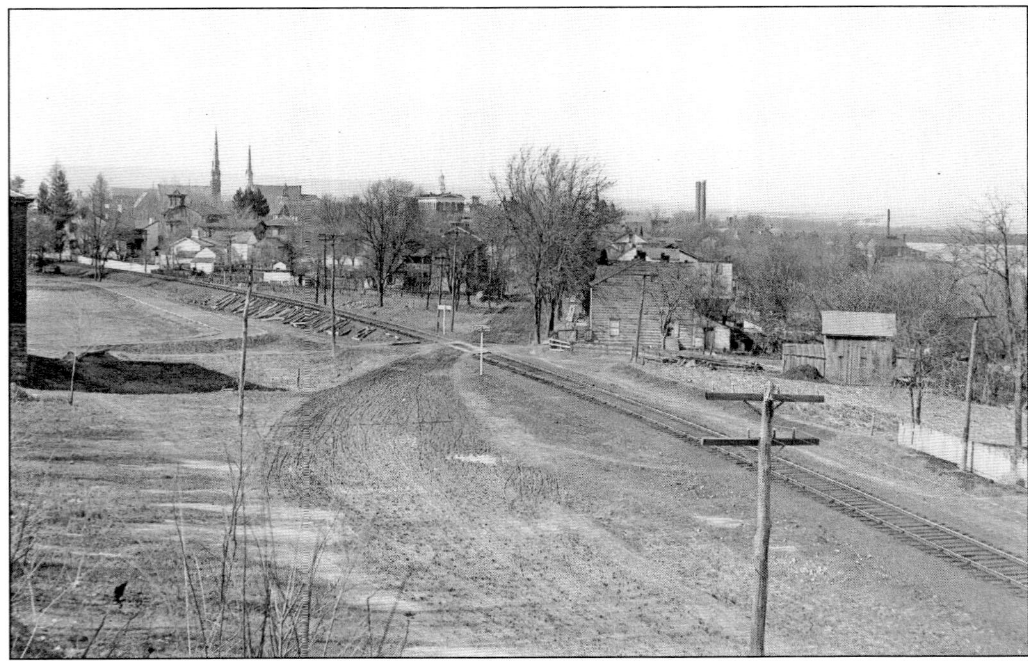

The Reading Railroad enters Lewisburg where River Road meets Brown Street. Though street paving did not begin until 1915, the skyline of Lewisburg is in no way that of a mere frontier town. One notes the standing water pipes right of center, the 1855 courthouse cupola, which was designed by nationally known architect Lewis Palmer, and the church steeples to the left. (UCHS 1991.25.2.)

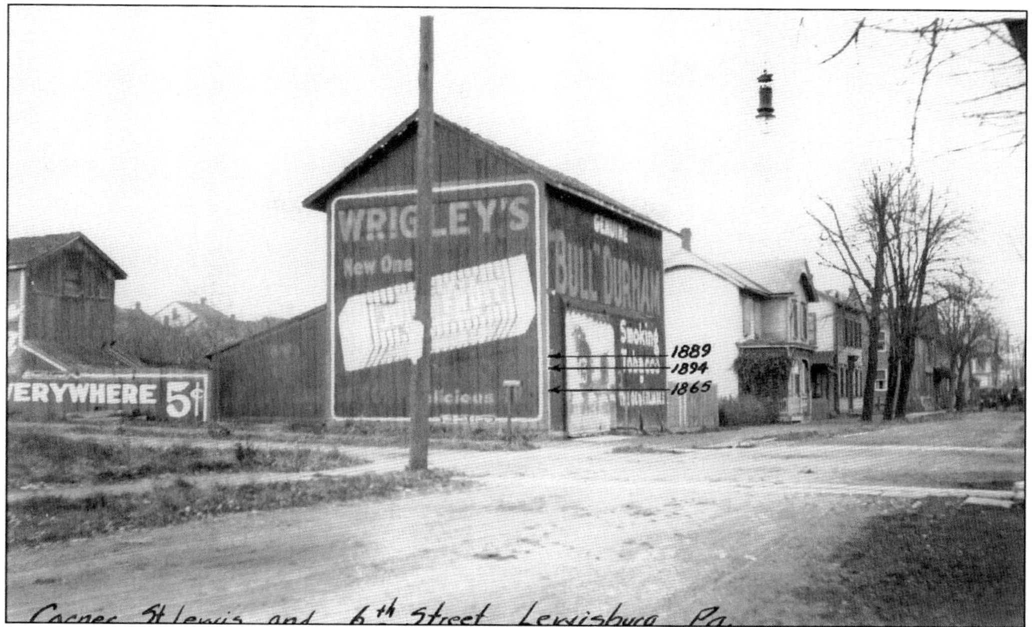

The owner of this picture of the corner of St. Louis and Sixth Streets marked it to indicate the levels of flooding in the years 1865, 1889, and 1894. The floods of 1936 and then 1972 exceeded these levels significantly. Flooding has frequently played a role in the history of Lewisburg, washing away bridges and filling the streets. The residential areas were not spared, nor was the downtown core. (UCHS 2008.18.5.)

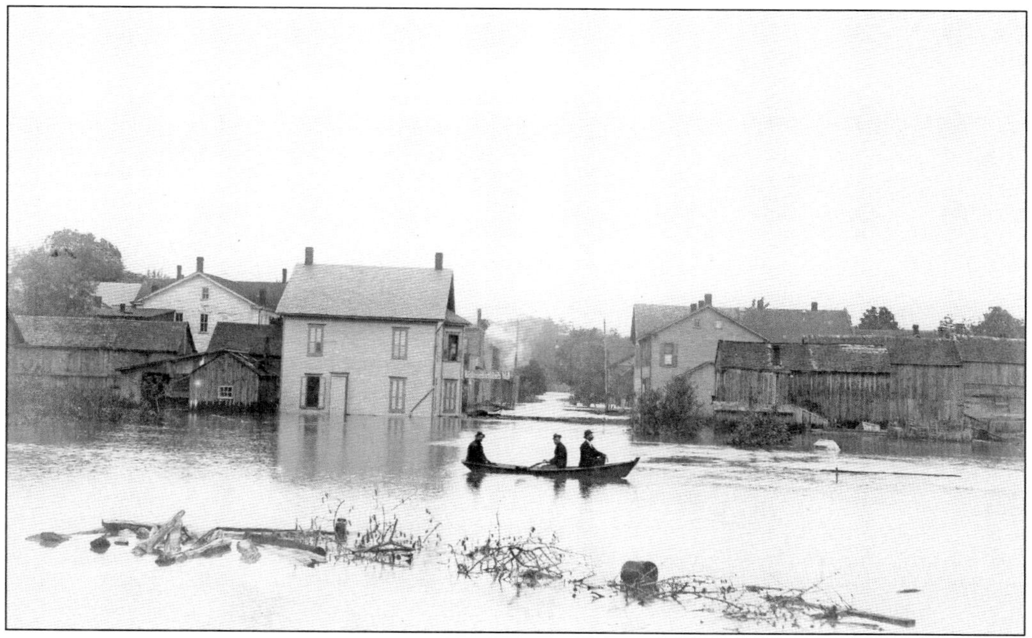

A boat rower conveys two gentlemen down a street flooded in 1889. House basements were fully filled with water, and the floodwaters clearly entered the first floors. Residents who did not anticipate the flood's depth in a timely manner and carry their belongings to higher levels would have had furniture, appliances, furnaces, and any goods stored at ground level or below destroyed. (UCHS 2006.15.1.)

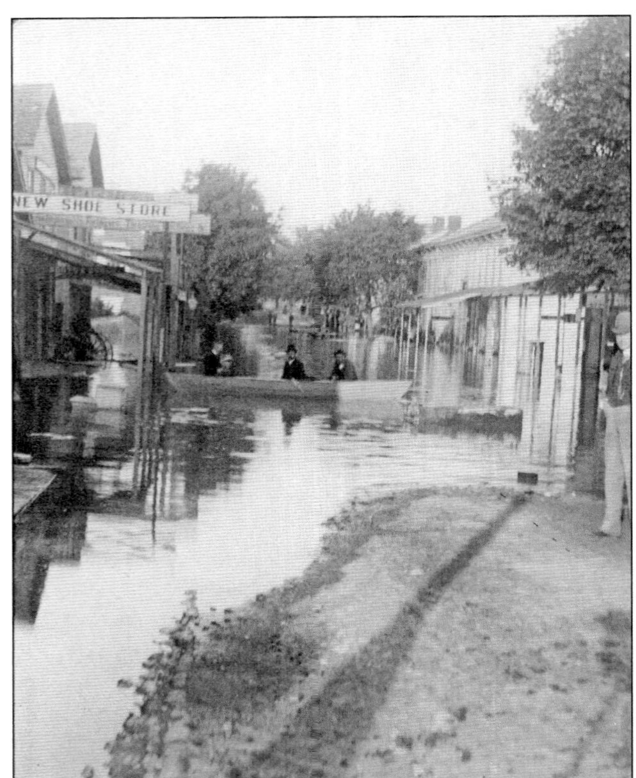

Because of the floodwaters at Market Street near Sixth Street, three men row in the town where businesses would have lost a major portion of their inventory. Another person to the right in the photograph studies the water level. This flood was called the "Johnstown Flood" because 2,200 people lost their lives when a dam above that town collapsed. (UCHS 92.9.33.)

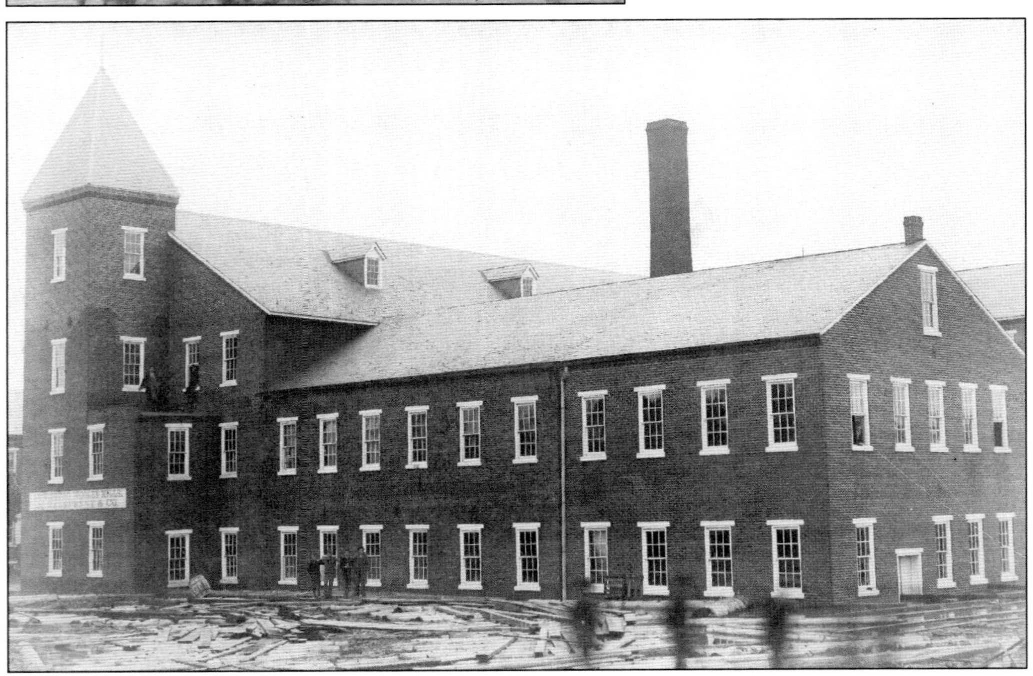

The Halfpenny/Lewisburg Woolen Mill, flooded in 1889, was surrounded by water and debris. The mill survived the flood, having already rebuilt from a devastating fire in 1878. It became the upholstery plant for Pennsylvania House in 1959, was acquired by La-Z-Boy in 2000, and finally closed in 2004. It currently houses the Street of Shops, an antiques and collectibles center. (UCHS 2005.15.3.)

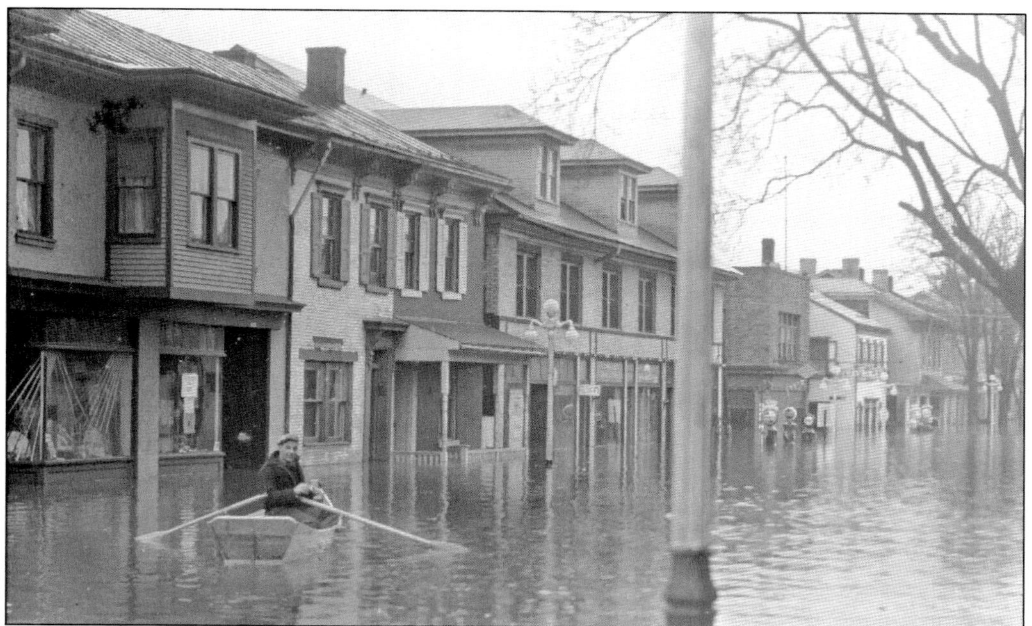

The March 1936 flood of the Susquehanna River resulted in the highest water yet seen in Lewisburg, surpassing even that of the severe 1889 flood. The man in the rowboat is seen just starting to head west down Market Street between Fifth and Sixth Streets. Most of the buildings seen in this image no longer exist; they were torn down after the 1972 flood to create Hufnagle Park. (Northeastern Federal Penitentiary.)

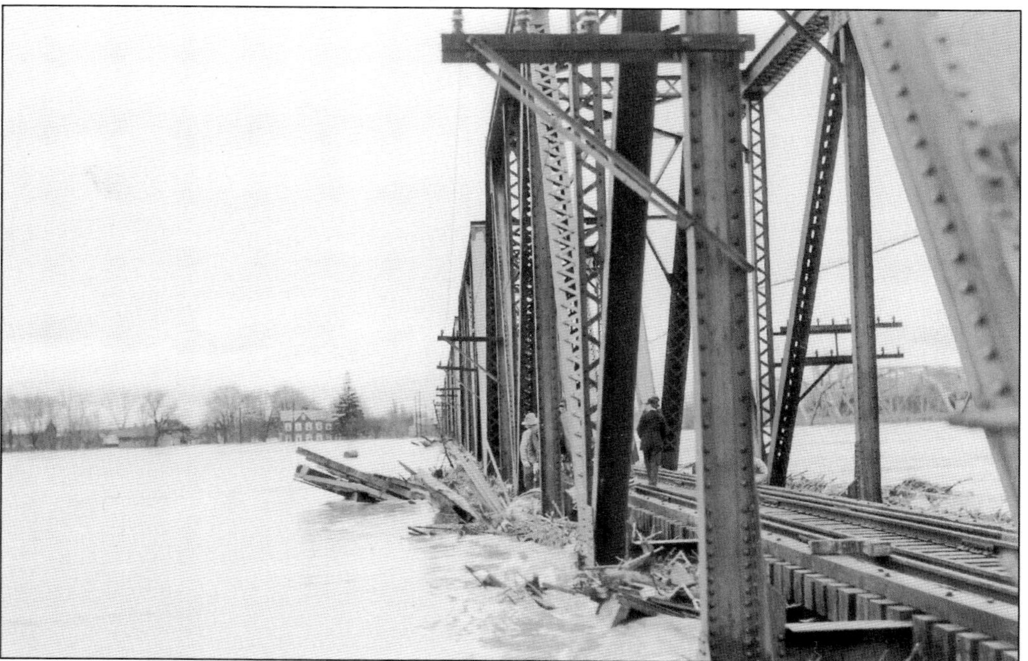

The debris washed into the Susquehanna River by the 1936 flooding crashes up against the north side of the Pennsylvania Railroad bridge. The river level rose onto the bridge, leaving the railroad tracks just above water. This view is taken from the Lewisburg side of the river looking east. In the background is the steel automobile bridge built in 1906. (UCHS 89.5.12.20.)

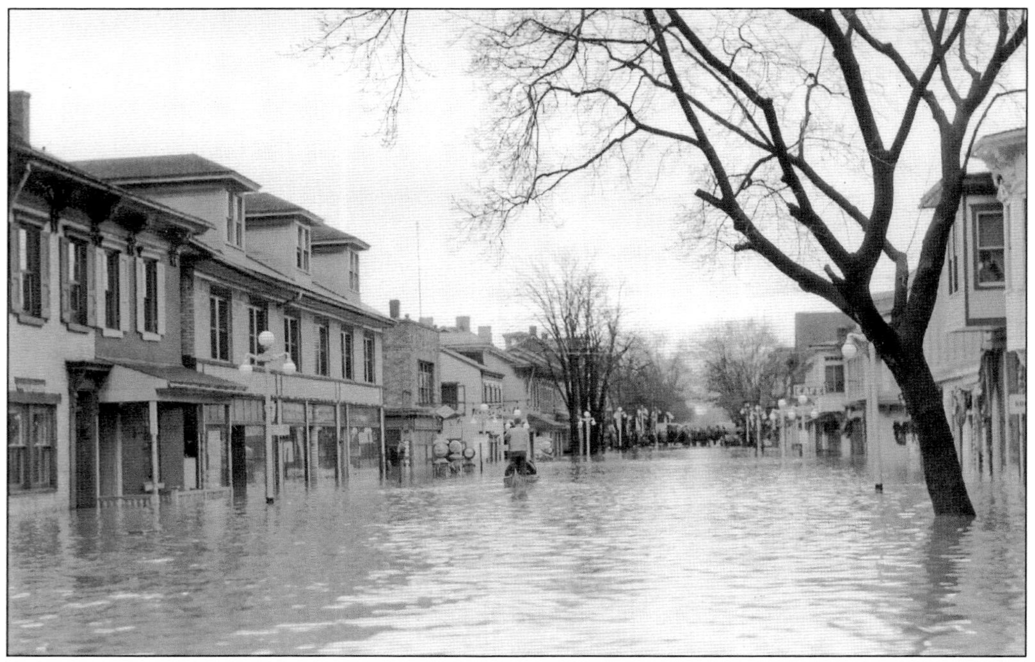

Taken on March 19, 1936, this image shows a man in a canoe rowing west on Market Street during the flood of that year. He is in the middle of the block between Fifth and Sixth Streets and near the spot where Bull Run flows under the street; this stream's flooding was made all the worse because of building over the creek. (UCHS 79.481.10.2.)

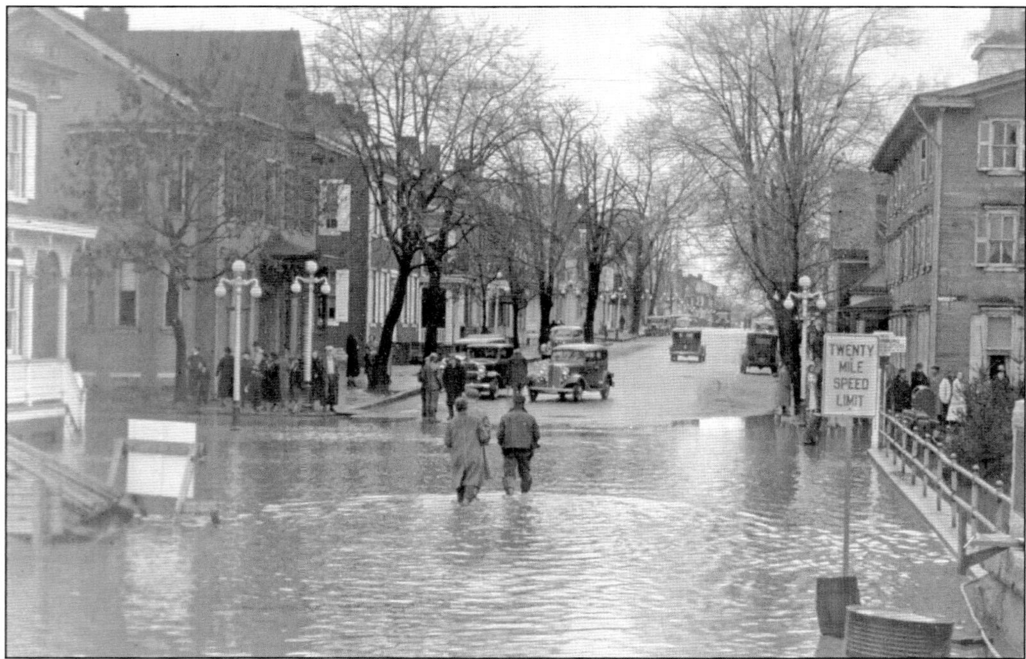

A brave photographer waded through the cold water of March 1936 to snap this image of the west end of the Susquehanna River bridge. The dilapidated frame house on the right would become the home of John and Edith Fetherston later that year; it is now the Packwood House Museum. (Northeastern Federal Penitentiary.)

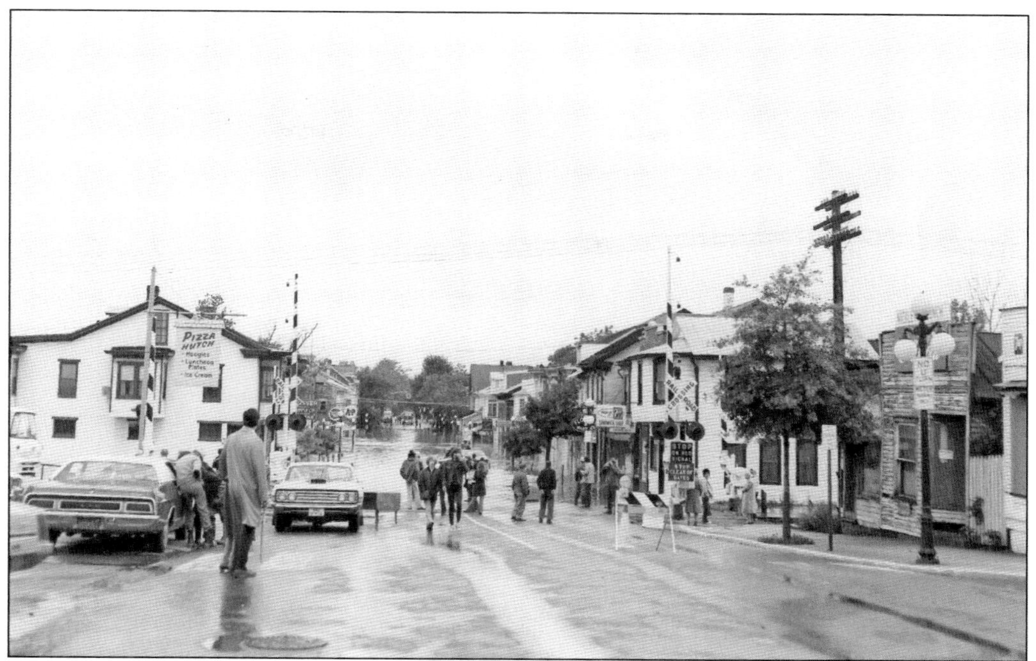

Hurricane Agnes struck Pennsylvania in June 1972. Lewisburg and other towns in the Susquehanna Valley were hit hard by the high water. This view, looking west on Market Street, shows the water just beginning to rise as Bull Run overflows its banks. This small stream had been built over earlier in the century, resulting in quick flooding whenever it rained hard. (UCHS 89.5.12.31.)

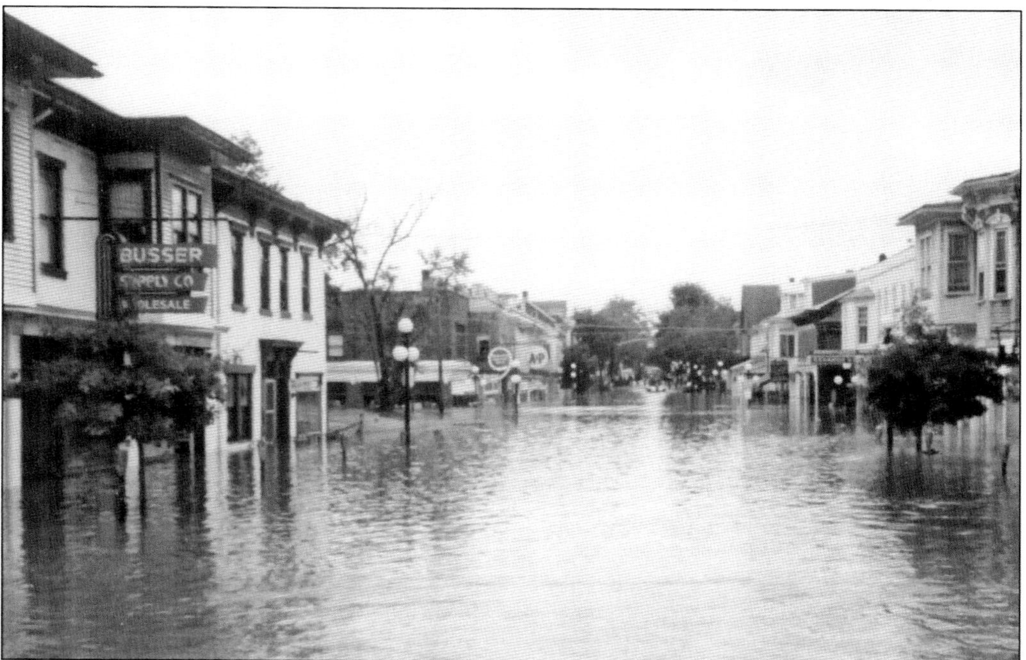

This view shows Bull Run at the height of the June 1972 flood. By this time, much of the town was under water. Damage was so severe that all the buildings on the left, from Busser Supply Company and the Western Auto store to the A&P grocery store, were torn down afterwards. (Daniel Shannon.)

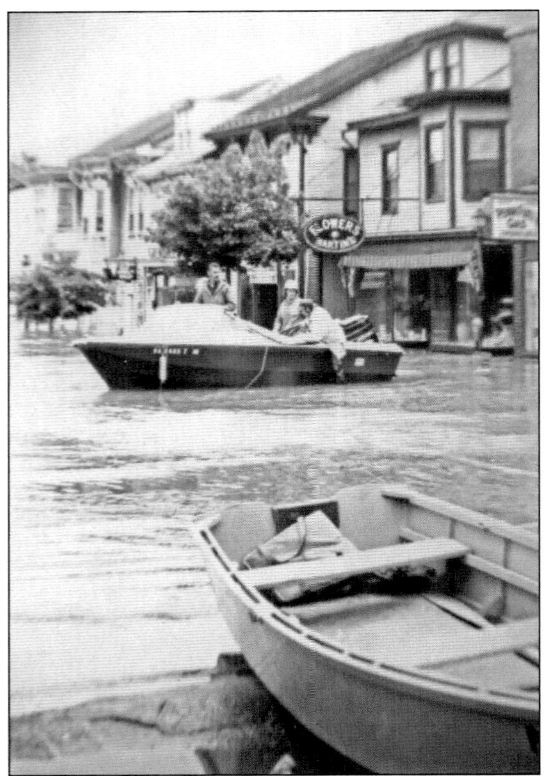

At the height of the 1972 flood, authorities used both motor and hand-powered boats to rescue stranded residents and maintain order in the chaos of evacuations. Former police chief Gordon Hufnagle drowned while trying to rescue an elderly couple who had been swept out of the boat by the raging currents; all three drowned. (PHM.)

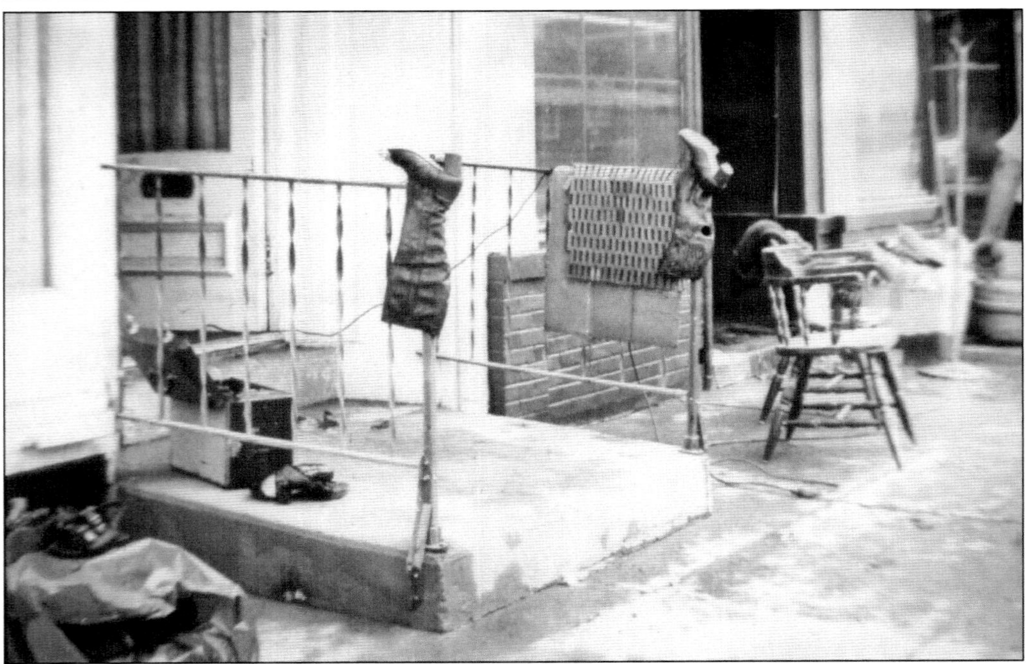

Hurricane Agnes left much of Lewisburg under water. Even those families whose houses saw only their basements flooded had plenty of cleaning up to do. Residents remember that the 1972 floodwater was dirty and muddy, resulting in weeks of cleanup afterward. Here one can see furniture, boots, and floor mats hung out to dry as beleaguered residents worked hard to clean. (PHM.)

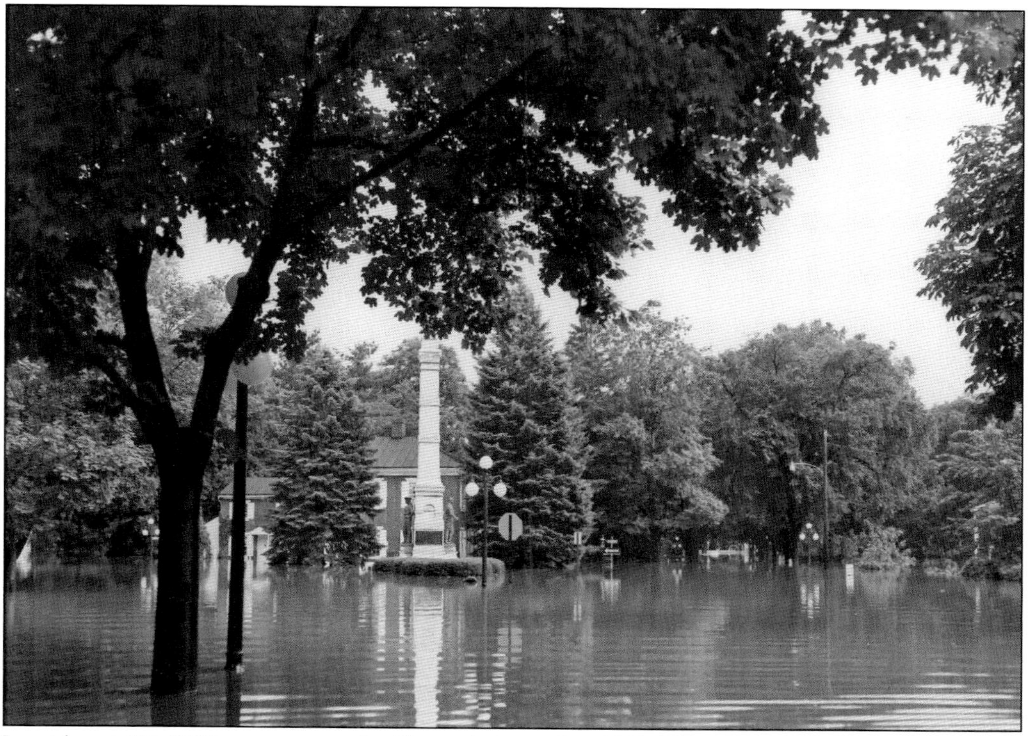

Lewisburg's Civil War monument had been dedicated in 1901. This is how it looked in June 1972, surrounded by high water from Hurricane Agnes. Located near the intersection of St. George and South Third Streets, the monument remembers the sacrifices of the town's soldiers during the four bloody years of the Civil War. (UCHS 89.5.12.30.)

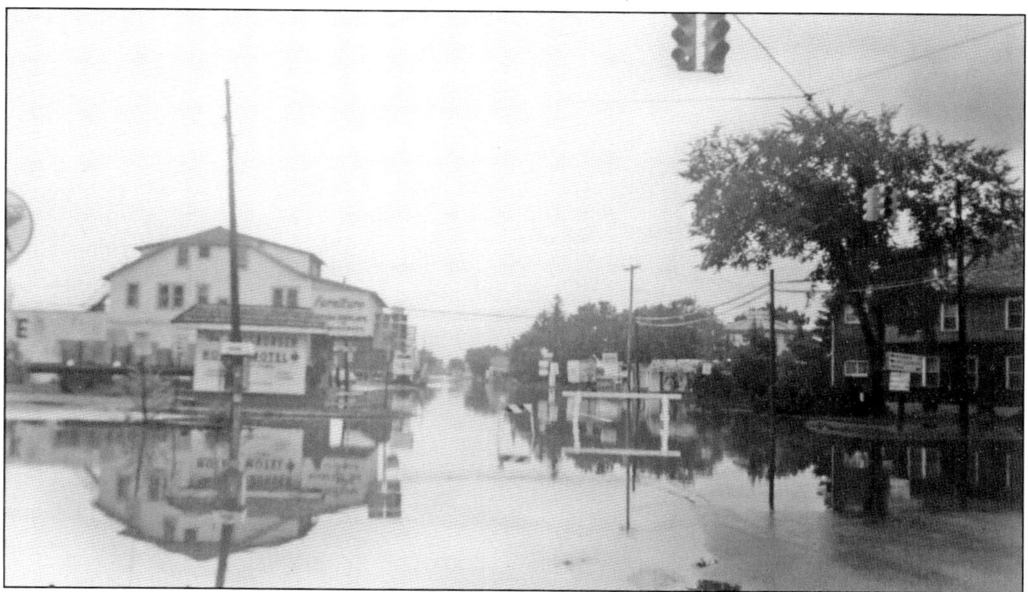

The flood of 1972 reached across Lewisburg to close Route 15, a mile from the river. This view looks north on Route 15 from its intersection with Market Street, also known as PA Route 45. Sherman Doebler's Texaco gas station is on the left, next to a large sign advertising the Lewisburger Hotel. Lewisburg High School is just to the right of this photograph. (UCHS 82.4.1.10Ee.)

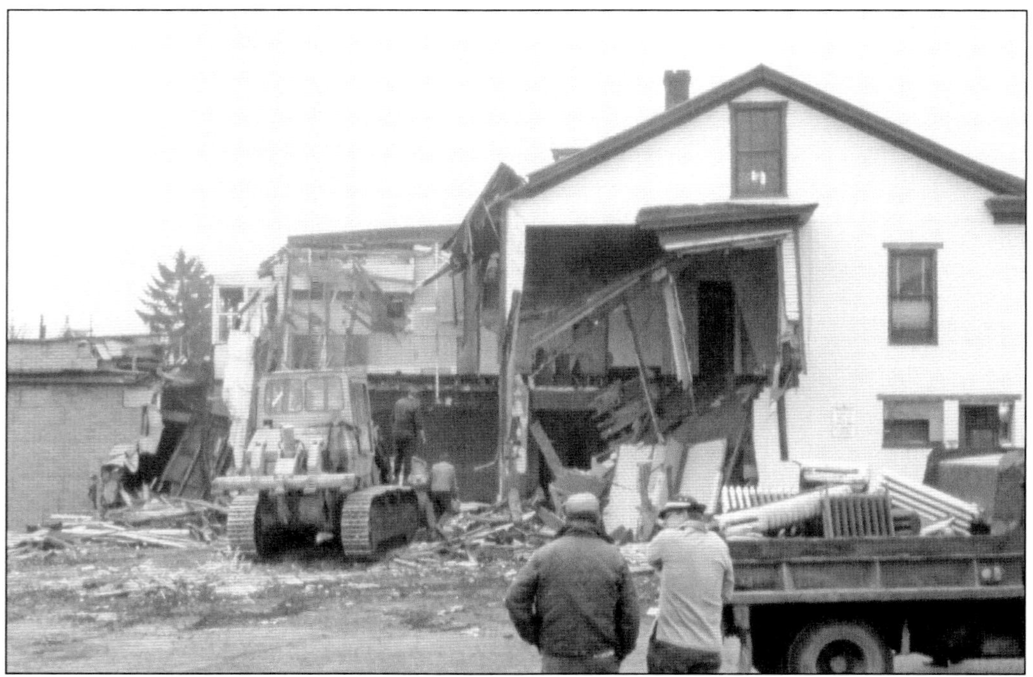

Hurricane Agnes severely damaged many sections of Lewisburg. As a result, several buildings were torn down. This scene shows a wrecking crew at work near Bull Run, just south of the intersection of Market and Fifth Streets. Bull Run ran through this area, and its powerful current was part of the reason that the high water fatally damaged so many structures. (Daniel Shannon.)

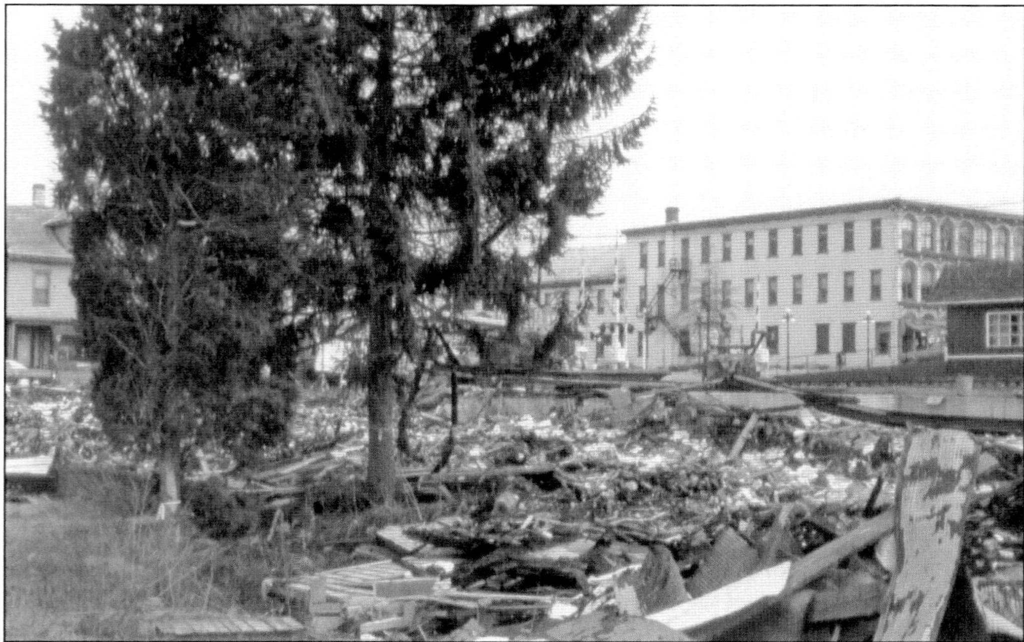

This is the scene after the wrecking crew, shown in the photograph above, finished demolishing the white building. The large pine tree shown here can also be seen in the background of the previous image; the tree still stands in Hufnagle Park. The Chamberlin building stands in the right background. (Daniel Shannon.)

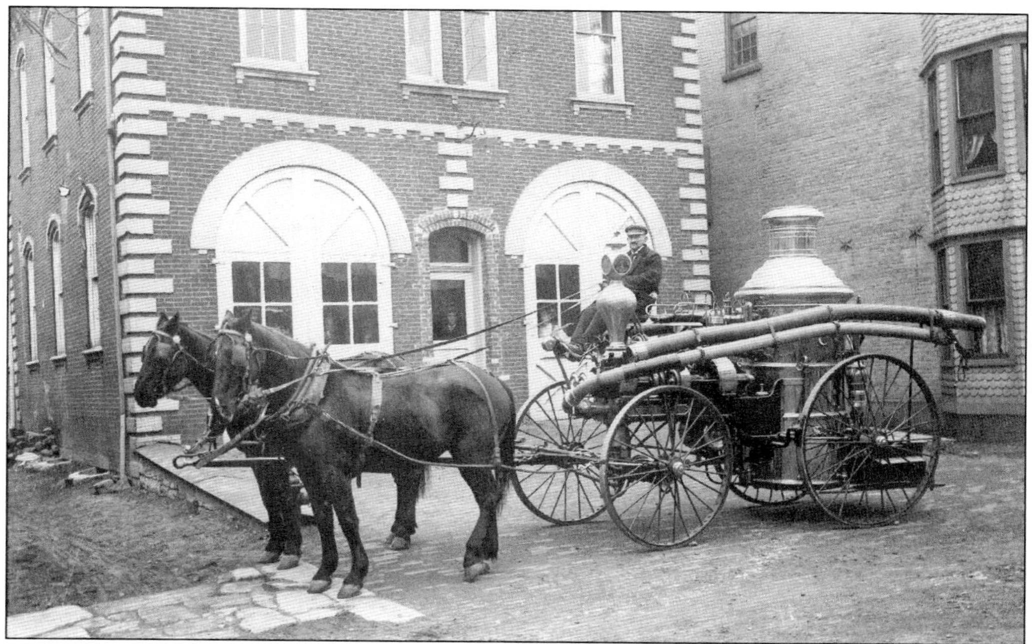

The William Cameron Engine Company's Silsby Steamer was last used in fighting the fire at Bucknell University's Old Main building in 1932. Regularly shown in Lewisburg parades, it is now on display in the company's museum. The original fire hall in the background was razed in the late 1960s. (UCHS 92.9.92.136.)

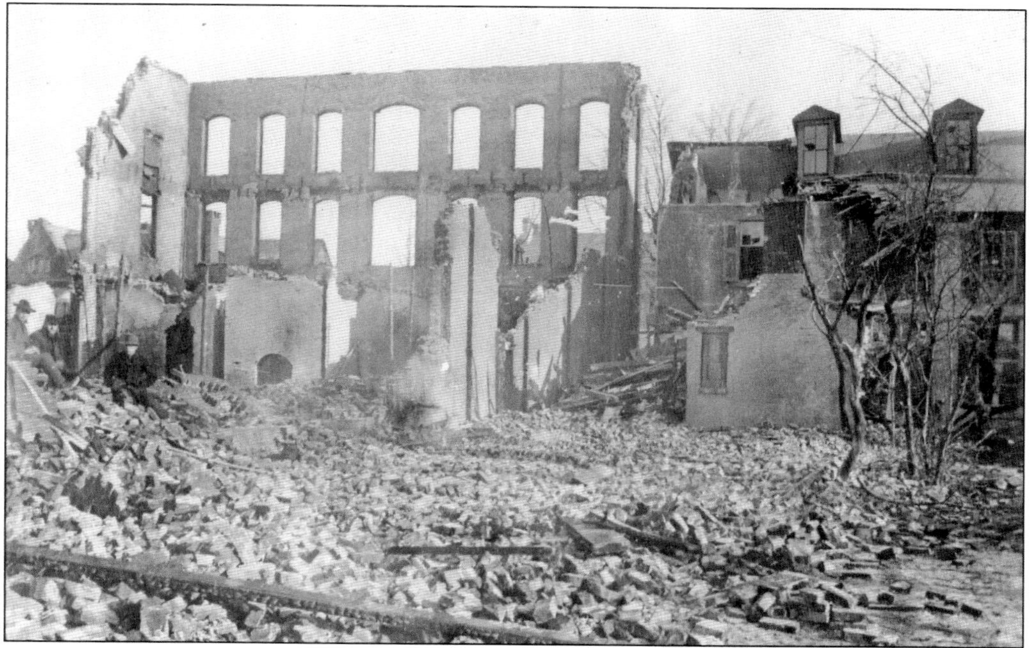

From its original designation as the music hall, the brick structure built by H. G. Swartz in 1869 was renovated and renamed the "Opera House" in 1893. Its glory was short-lived. In 1908, it was gutted by fire and never rebuilt. Later an automobile repair shop occupied the site. Today it is a municipal parking lot, and only a small brick column with a brass plate commemorates the Opera House. (UCHS 89.5.16.3.)

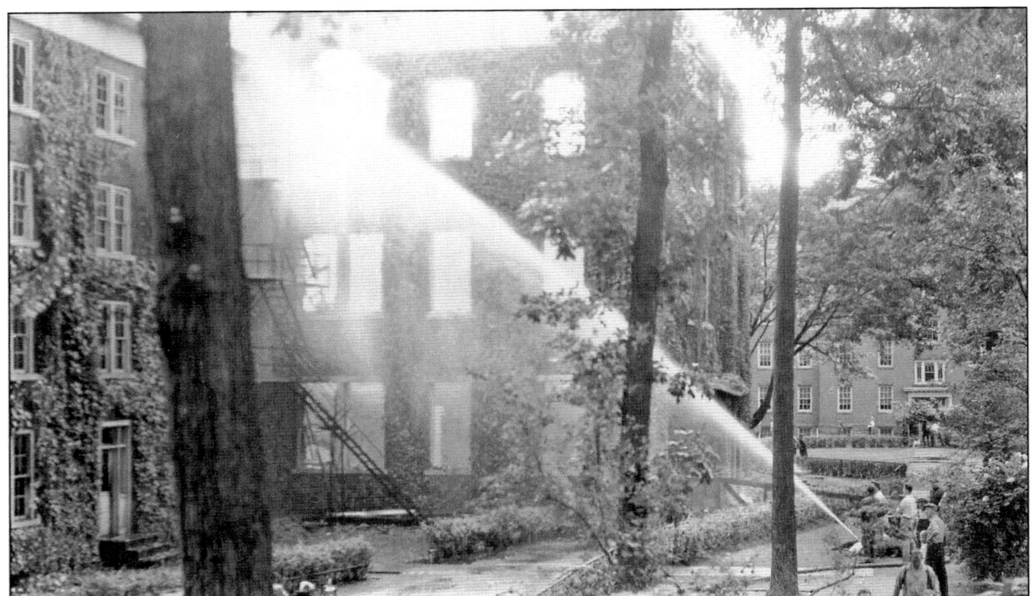

The center portion of Old Main at Bucknell University burned on August 27, 1932. Destroyed in the 4:40 a.m. blaze were the geological and biological collections of Dr. Nelson Davis as well as many musical instruments. Firefighters came to Lewisburg to fight the blaze from Sunbury, Northumberland, Milton, Watsontown, and Mifflinburg. The Lewisburg Silsby Steamer pumped water to Old Main from a fireplug located on the 300 block of Market Street. (Donna Slear.)

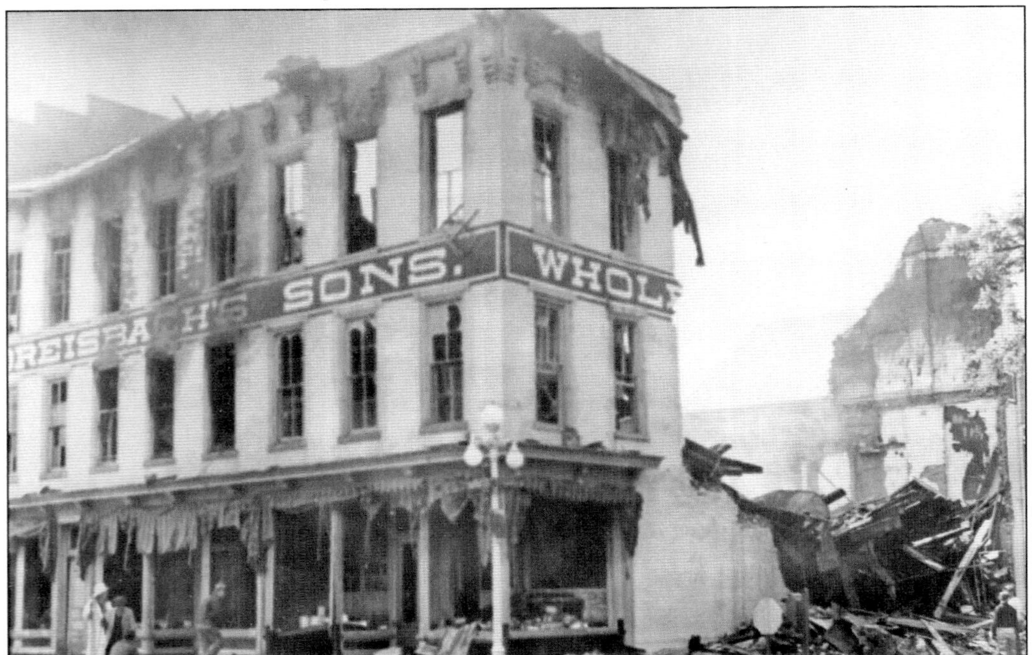

The C. Dreisbach Sons Hardware building went up in flames on May 11, 1941. It took the combined efforts of five fire companies to bring the conflagration under control; two firemen died when a blast blew out a brick wall. The company rebuilt the structure, and it lasted until 1961, after which a succession of businesses used the structure until 2009, when Bucknell University began renovations to move a Barnes and Noble bookstore into it. (UCHS 89.5.16.5F.)

A fire at the Lewisburg Chair Factory on October 30, 1911, started in the Finishing Building. Volatile liquids used in spraying furniture ignited; water sprayed on the fire by local fire companies only made the situation worse, as the fire spread. The building was completely destroyed. When the company rebuilt the structure, firewalls were added to prevent future accidents from again causing so much damage. (UCHS 92.9.92.68.)

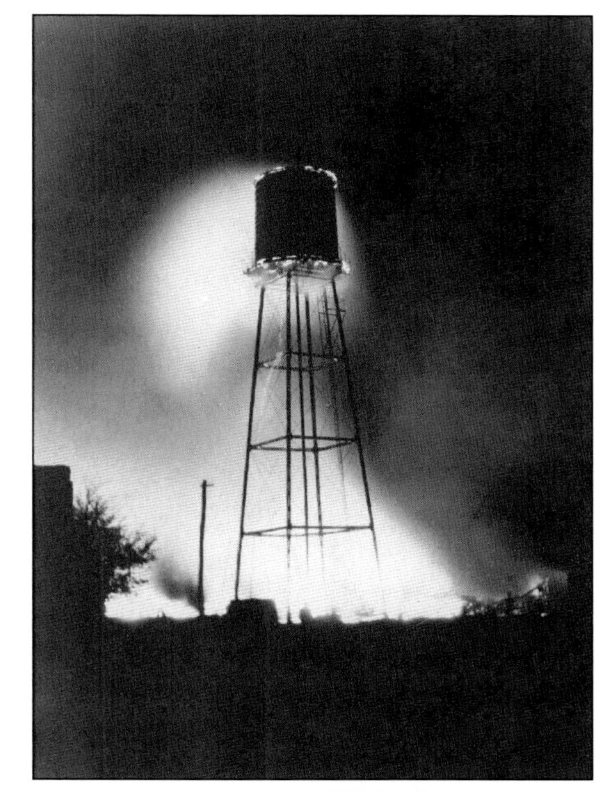

This fire, below, took place on July 2, 1959, in the Byerly Building in the 200 block of Market Street. Quick response by the William Cameron Engine Company kept the fire from spreading and the damage to a minimum. Lewisburg has seen numerous fires over the years, but the borough has avoided large-scale conflagrations such as occurred in nearby Milton. (UCHS 82.4.C59.9.Ec.)

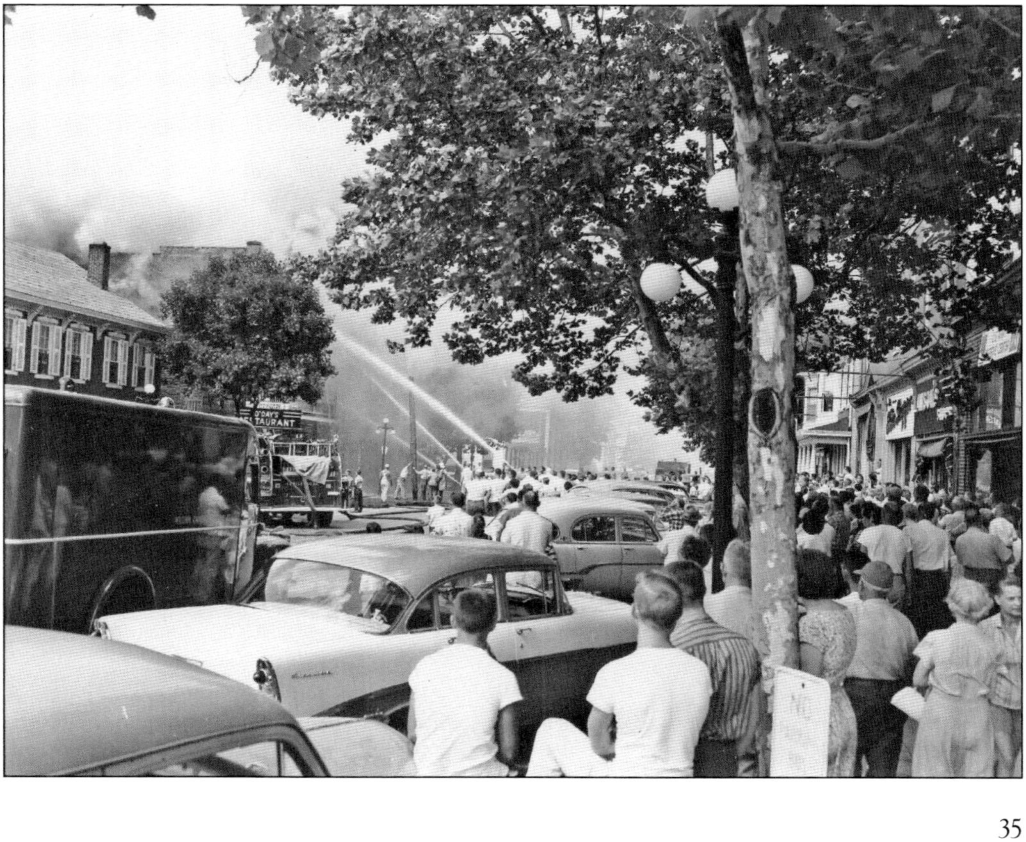

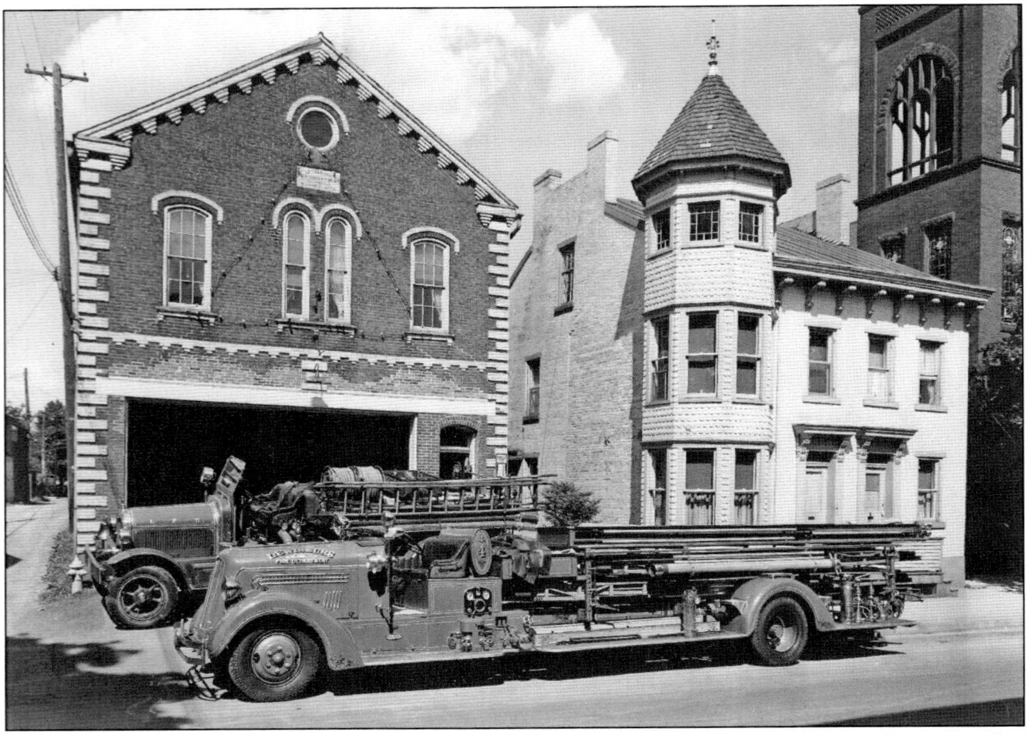

The William Cameron Engine Company's firehouse on South Fourth Street is shown in this image. In front sits a 1936 quad engine, which carried everything but water to a fire, while in the back is a smaller pumper vehicle. The building was renovated to handle these new machines by replacing the old doors with a larger entrance and a poured-concrete floor in place of the old wooden one. (UCHS 83.53.1.)

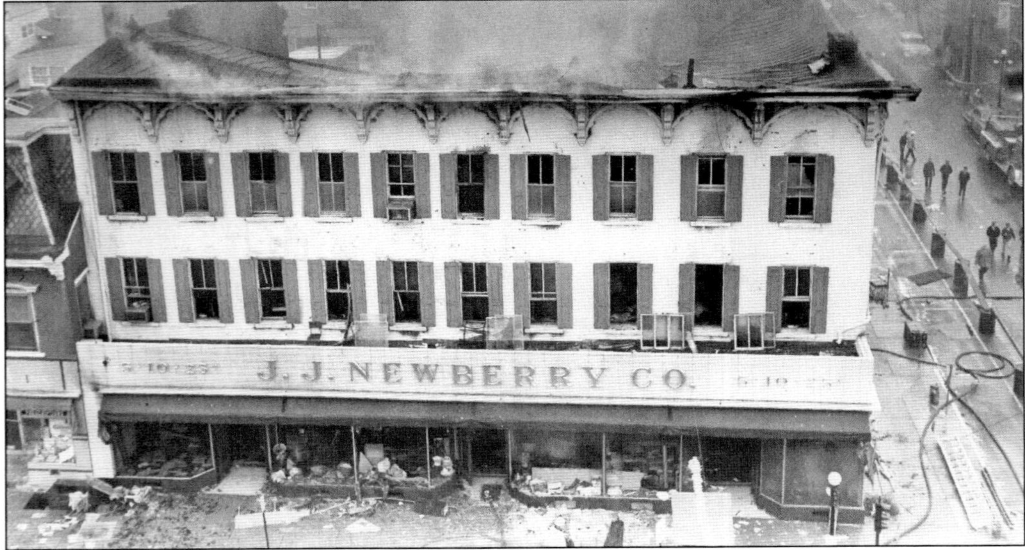

The J. J. Newberry store at the corner of Market and Third Streets burned on December 27, 1959. Investigation revealed that the fire probably started in a pile of flammable Christmas decorations stored in the basement. The store was completely renovated and remained in business into the 1980s. The site is now occupied by a CVS pharmacy. (David Mensch.)

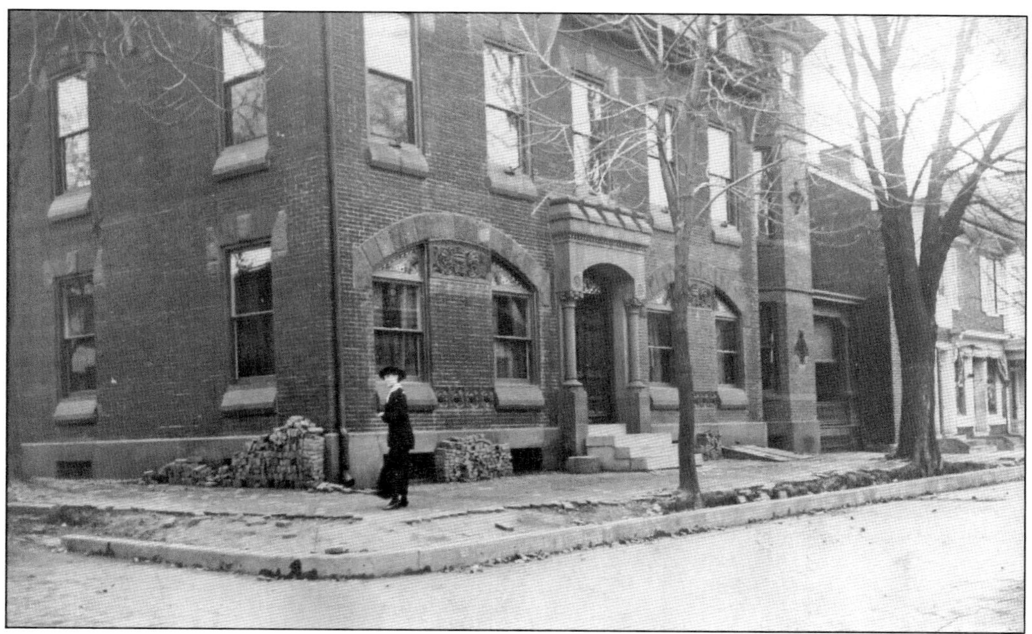

This majestic building was completed in 1840 by William Cameron, brother of Simon Cameron—the future secretary of war during the Lincoln administration. Located at 201 Market Street, it was renovated in 1893 in the Queen Anne style with round towers, multiple gables, and terra-cotta rosettes. Cameron founded Lewisburg's first bank in 1852 in this building; the old safe is still in place. (UCHS 82.4.7.15Tb.)

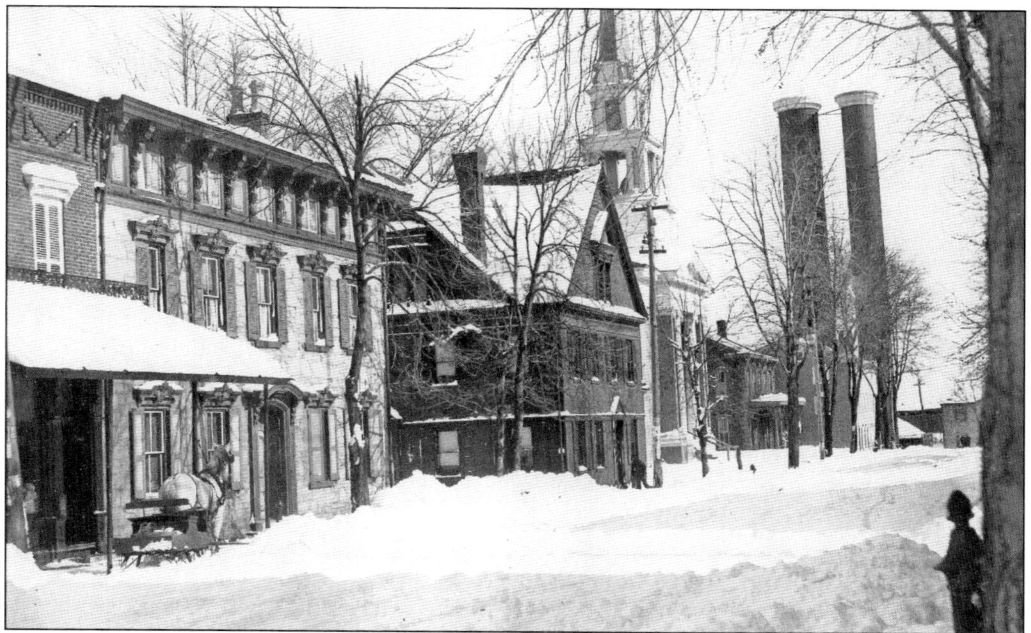

Jonathan Nesbit built the First Presbyterian Church (center) on Market Street in 1856. To its left, the snow-covered Cox-Mount Vernon House, erected in 1868, served as a tavern in the late 1800s and was later converted into apartments. Farther left, the three-story Federal-style house was built in 1819. It was owned for many years by the Halfpenny family, which owned and operated the nearby woolen mills. (UCHS 92.25.1.)

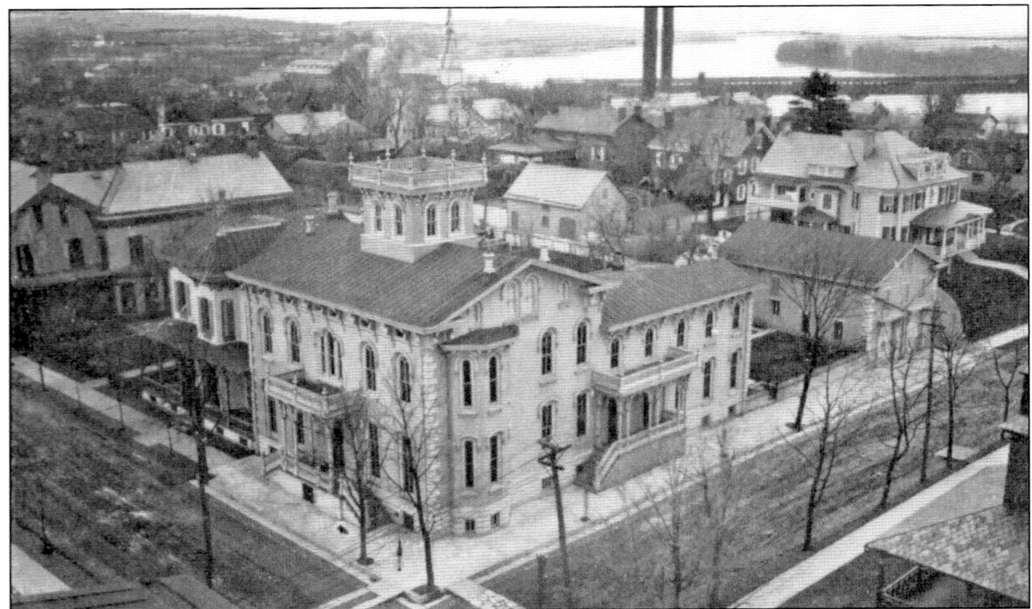

This view looking north from the courthouse shows the covered toll bridge and water pipes in context. In the left foreground is the large Italianate mansion of congressman Benjamin Focht, built in 1860 and now called "Tuscan Villa." To the right is the Burgess Convalescent Home on the corner of St. Louis and South Front Streets, which had once been a fraternity house and is now an apartment building. (PHM.)

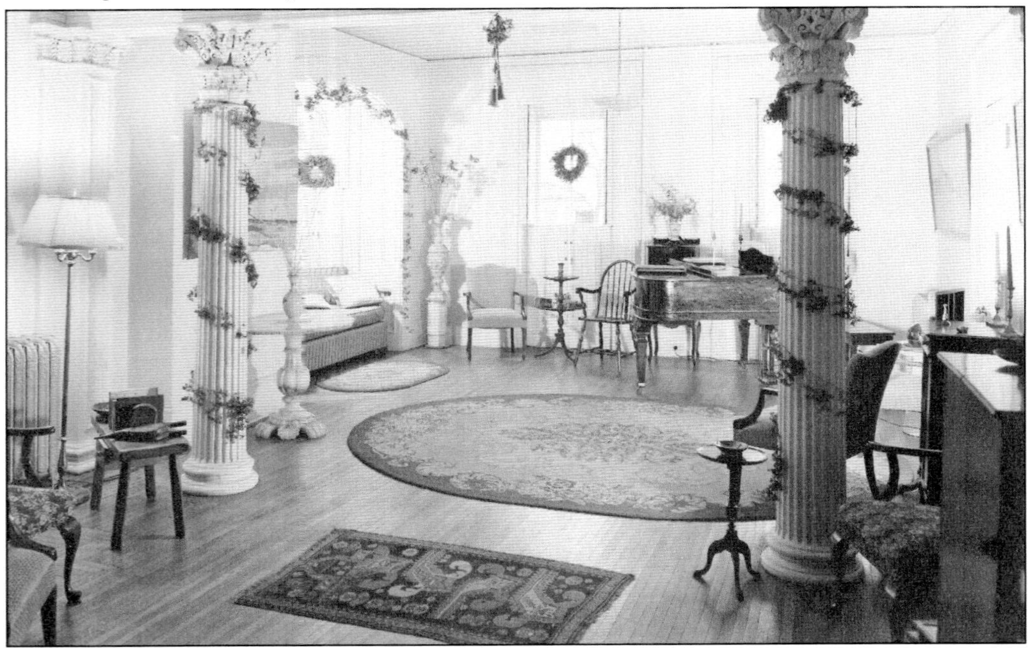

Mary Belle Harris was the daughter of a Bucknell University president. Herself a Ph.D., Dr. Harris worked with Jane Addams at the Hull House in Chicago before a long career in the administration of women's prisons. She retired to Lewisburg in 1941. This photograph shows her formal living room with all the trappings of a successful career, such as a piano, classical columns, and electric lighting. (UCHS P82.4.C41125.16.)

This three-story brick Federal structure at 129 Market Street was built in 1793. It was once a tavern, then the law office of Andrew Dill, and then a millinery shop run by Betsy Maze. The Stoughton family bought the house in 1891 and owned it until 1971. (David Mensch.)

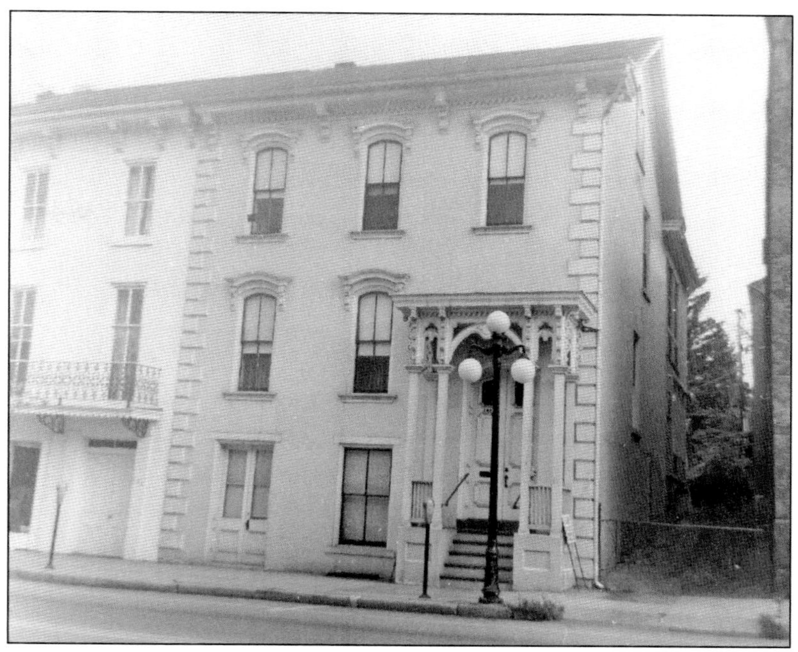

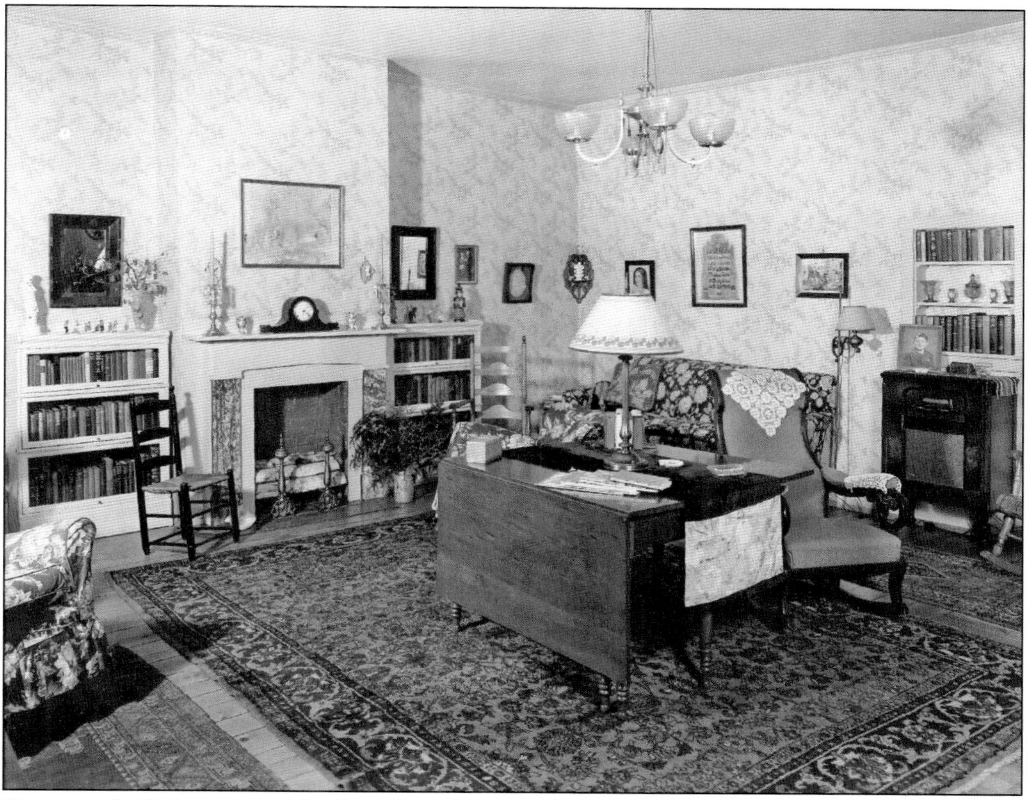

Compare the living room of the Stoughton house to that of Mary Harris on the previous page. Jane Stoughton lived here until her death in 1967. Stoughton was the widow of Christy Mathewson, who attended Bucknell and became the Hall of Fame pitcher for the New York Giants from 1900 to 1916. (UCHS 82.4.C40133.16D.)

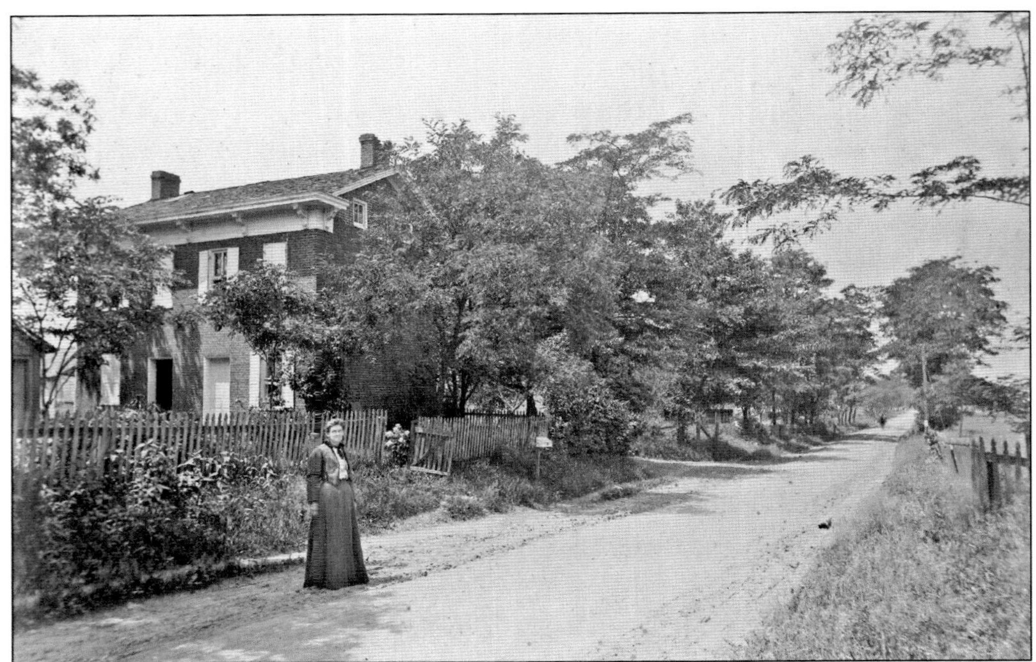

This cabinet card photograph of the Derr homestead on Buffalo Road (modern PA Route 192) shows Lewisburg's rural heritage. This brick farmhouse was built only a mile from the heart of Lewisburg and shows the bucolic splendor that dominated the area in the late 19th and early 20th centuries. (UCHS 2009.22.)

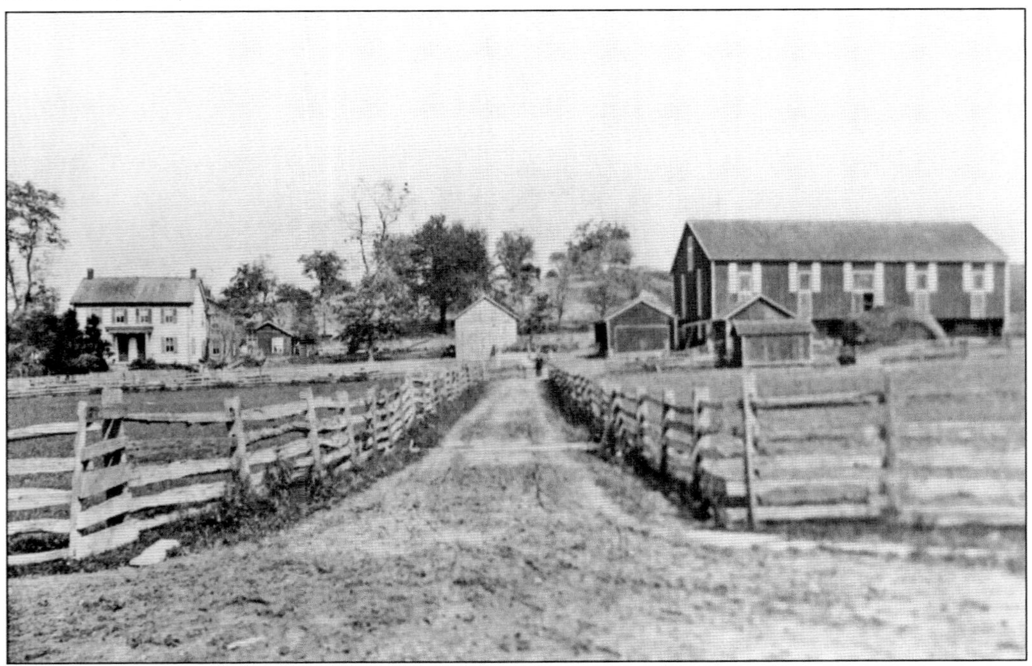

The Hilkert farm, northwest of Lewisburg in Kelly Township, was a typical area farm when this image was taken. A stately farmhouse, several outbuildings, and the large Pennsylvania bank barn all point to a prosperous and hardworking farm family. The rich farms surrounding Lewisburg relied on the town to provide services such as iron tools, groceries, and clothes. (UCHS 89.5.9.12.)

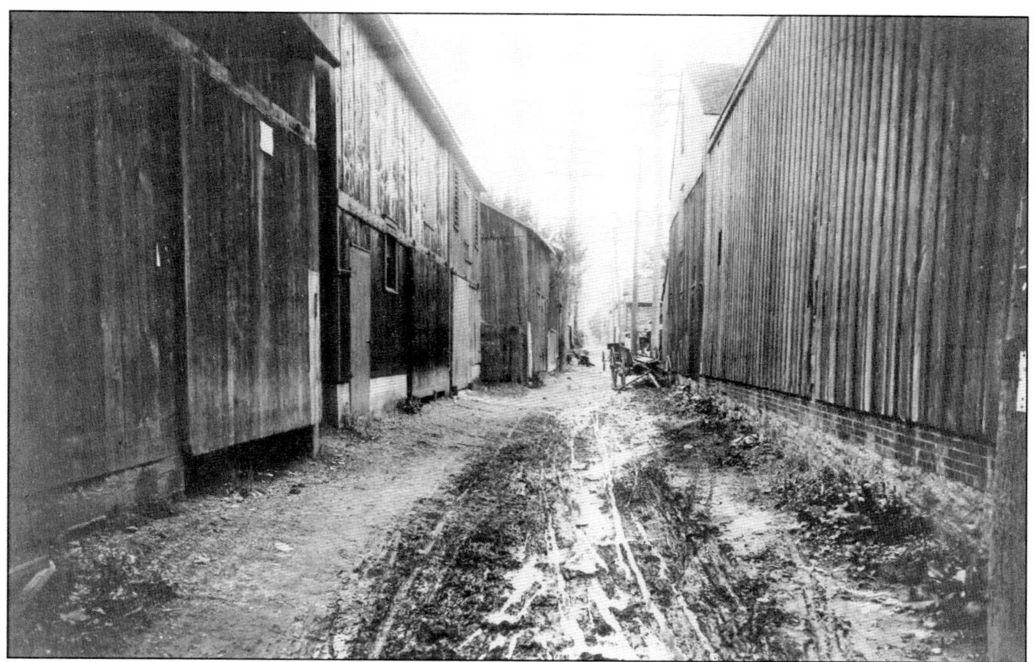

The core of Lewisburg included 77 carriage houses and 29 automobile garages by 1953. Situated at the rear of narrow house lots, most carriage houses owe their survival to conversion to garages. These carriage houses/garages open up into an alley and typically hold one automobile and some household storage. (UCHS 89.5.24.17.)

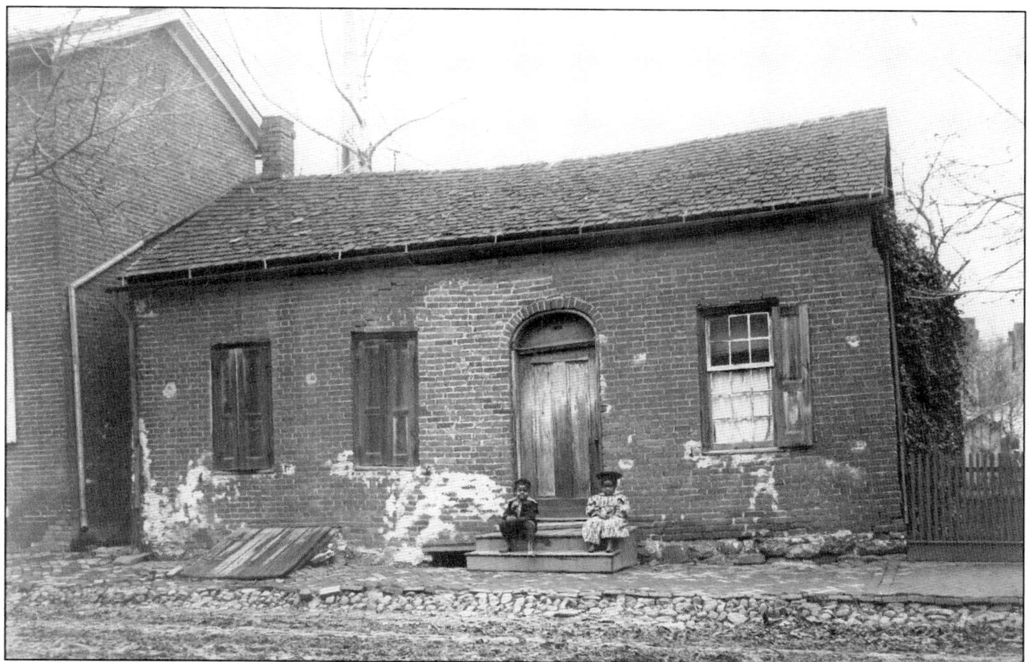

The African American population of Lewisburg has always been very small. As a result, their lives have not been chronicled much at all. This rare image of two African American children sitting on the front steps of their brick home is one of few surviving photographs. The house stood on a side street near the Cameron Hotel at Market and Second Streets. (UCHS 2006.42.2.)

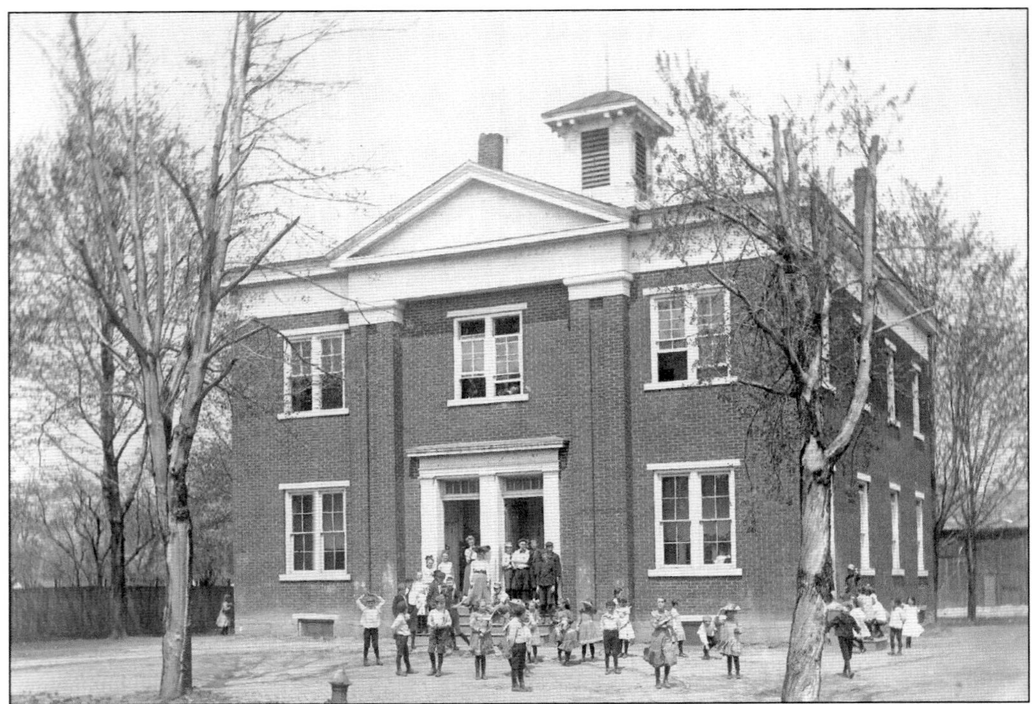

The North Ward School, a two-storied, multi-roomed brick structure, was erected in 1855 on North Second Street. A former early subscription school, established in the first quarter of the 19th century, had once occupied the site. Elementary school grades met in the building until 1985. Today the structure serves as a senior center. (UCHS 80.7.20.)

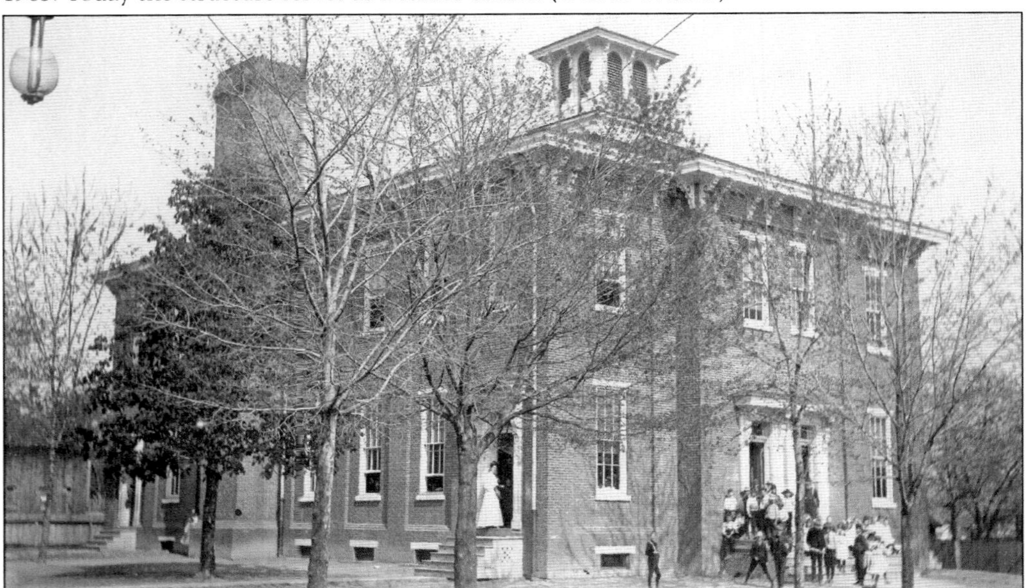

The South Ward School, another two-storied, multi-roomed brick structure, was erected in 1861 at the corner of St. Catherine and South Fourth Streets. The high school was moved to the South Ward building in 1898, when an addition was made to it. A new one-story elementary school for South Ward was erected on the same site in 1950 and used as a school until 1995, and later for school administration until 2004. (UCHS 80.7.20.)

The West Ward School, a multiroomed brick structure, was erected on North Eighth Street in 1869, the third and last in a series of similarly styled schools built between 1855 and 1869. The high school was housed in this structure starting in 1885, until it was moved to the South Ward building in 1898. The structure still stands, having added a third floor with dormers and converted into apartments. (UCHS 80.7.20.)

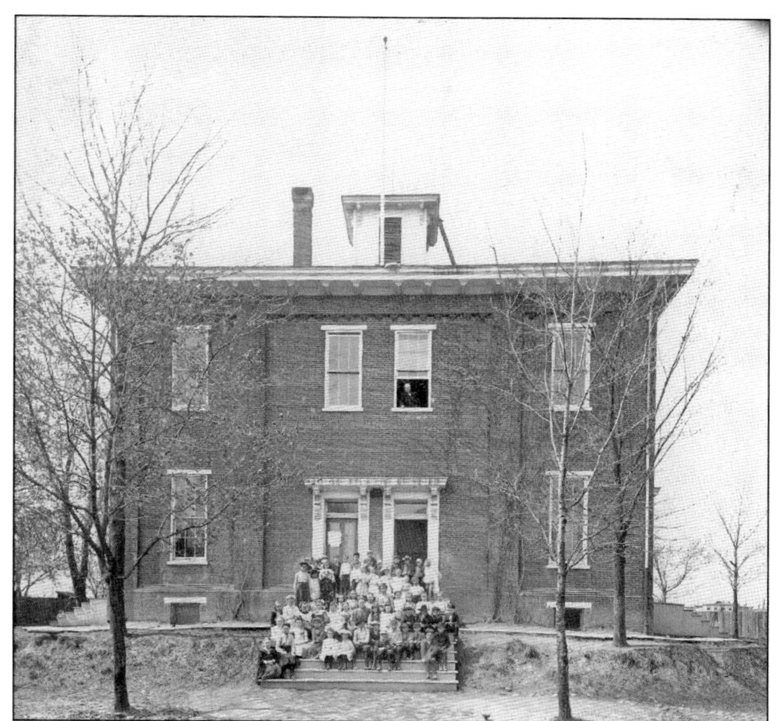

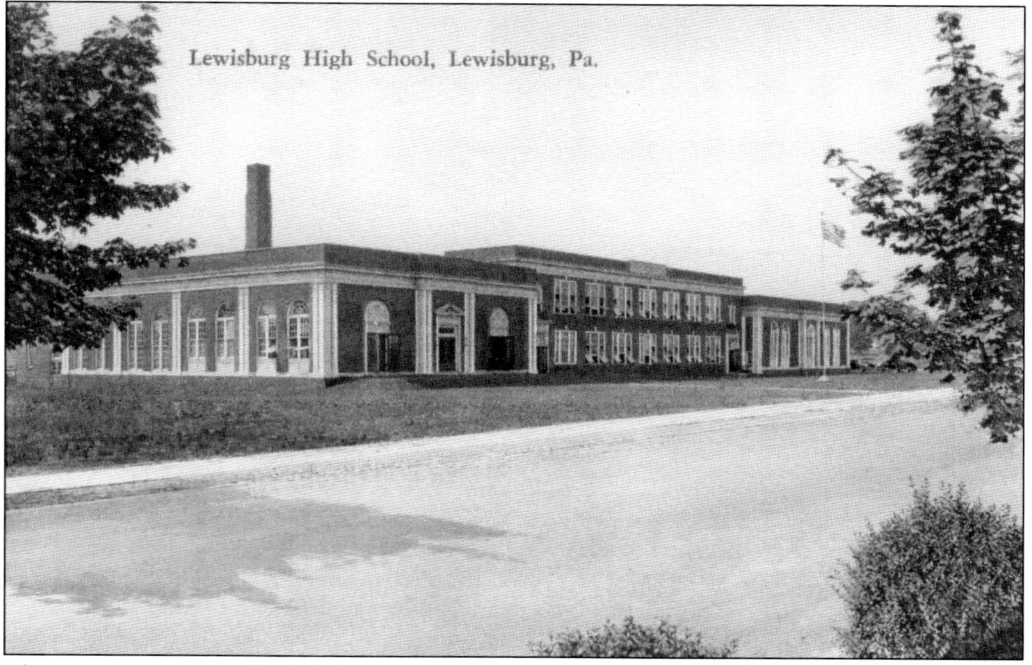

The present Lewisburg High School was constructed in 1927–1929, at the corner of Market Street and Route 15. In the 1960s, the Lewisburg Area School District was created, which included the borough and townships of East Buffalo, Kelly, and Union. Students living in the eastern end of Buffalo Township were allowed to attend Lewisburg until 1974, when all students in Buffalo were sent to Mifflinburg. (UCHS 82.2.82.)

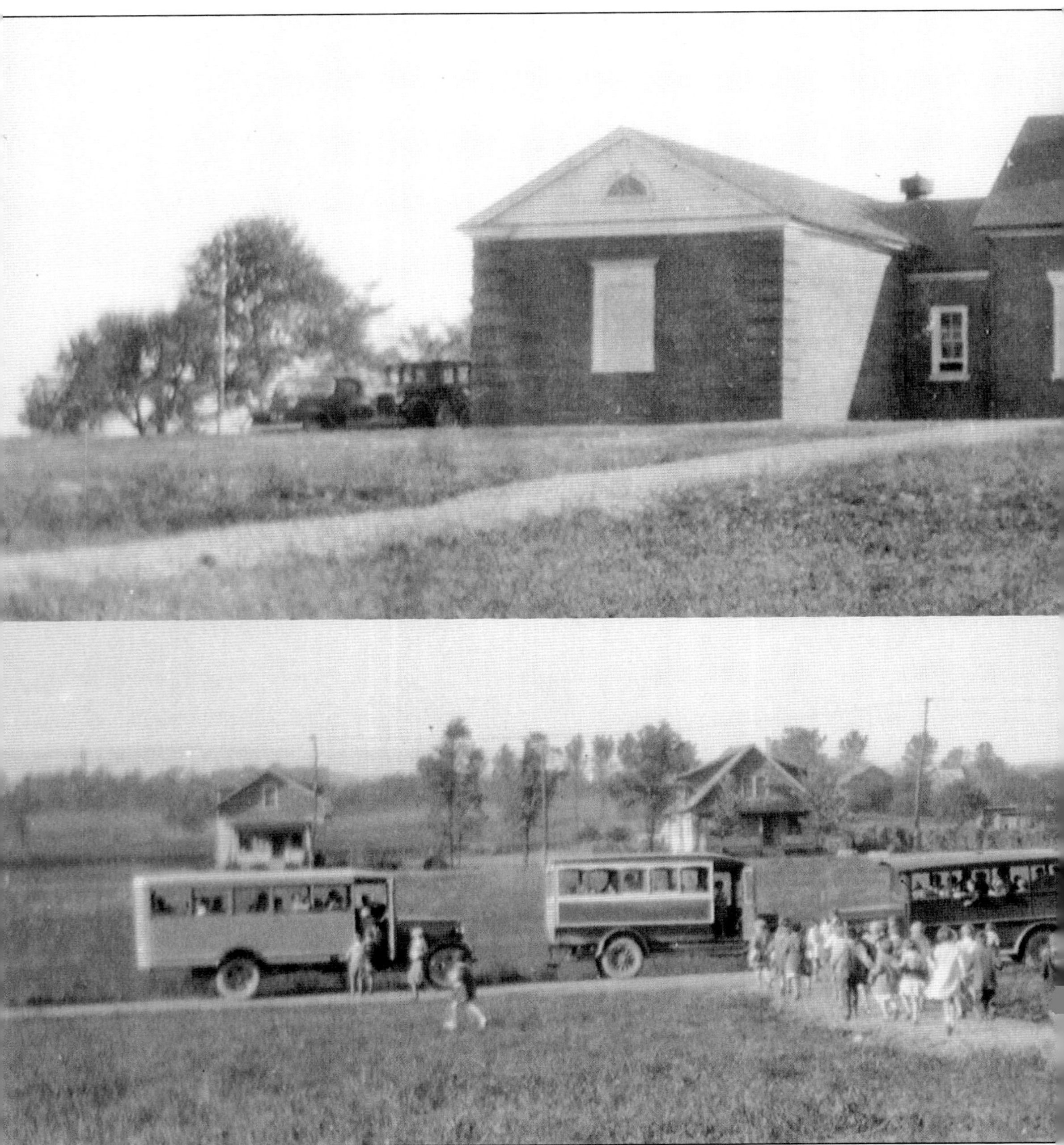

Built in 1934, the East Buffalo Consolidated School was located on Washington Avenue in a development known as Linntown. This was an elementary school that enabled township officials to close three smaller schools and thus centralize education. Shown here are early school buses that brought children to and from schools; most families in rural areas even close to Lewisburg

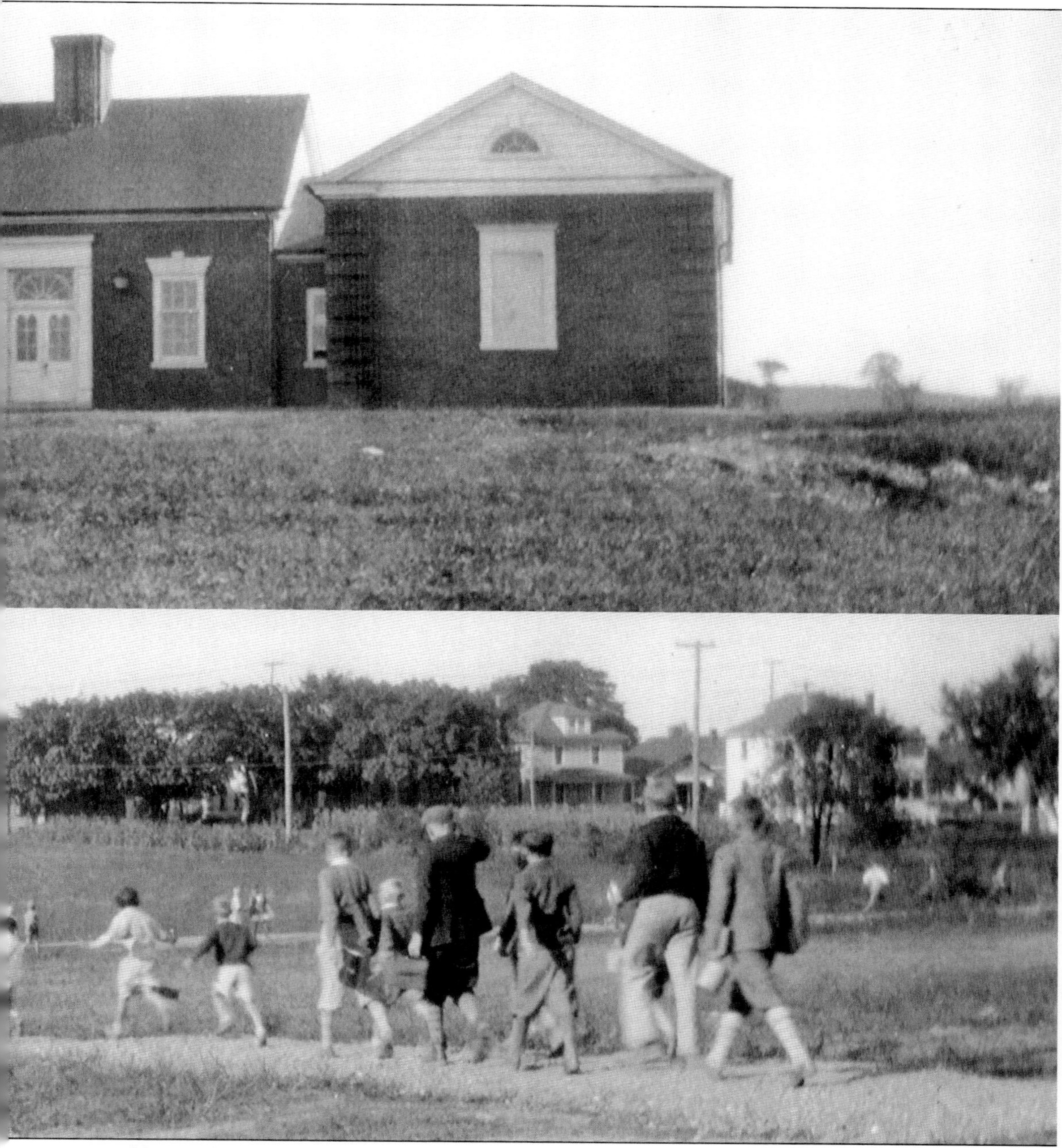

were unable to take their children to a more distant school, thus creating the need for buses. The school building shown here was enlarged as an elementary school in the 1950s. In 2004, the Lewisburg School District offices were moved into this structure. (UCHS 80.7.20.)

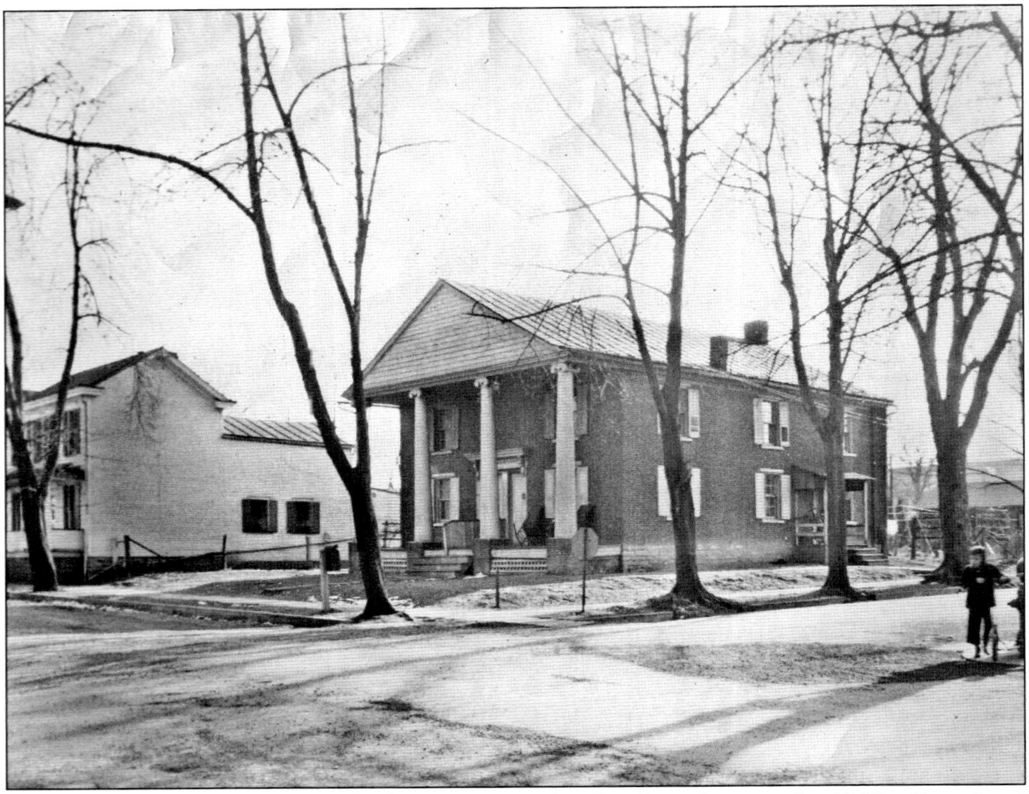

The Lewisburg Academy flourished as a private school in Lewisburg in the 1800s. Completed in 1839, the redbrick building on the corner of North Front and St. Mary Streets was erected in the classical revival style with a front portico. Also known as the Brick or Randolph Academy, it continued for about 15 or 16 years under headmaster John Randolph. The building was razed in 1976. (UCHS 89.53.17A.)

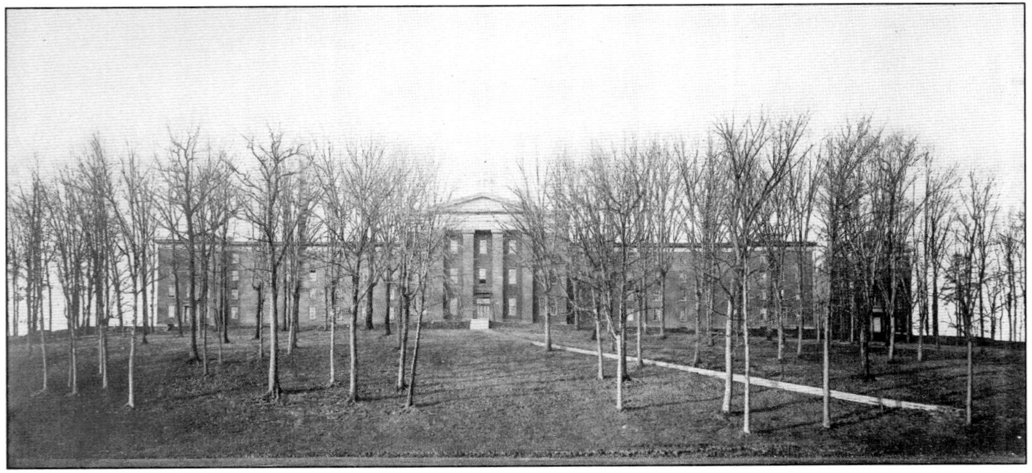

Construction of Old Main was completed in 1858. Thomas Ustick Walter (1804–1887), the architect of the University at Lewisburg, designed the building with its classical Greek style. The center part contained recitation rooms, a chapel, a library with 3,500 volumes in 1865, meeting rooms for two literary societies, and a commencement hall on the third floor. The wings contained study rooms and dormitories. (UCHS 80.7.20.)

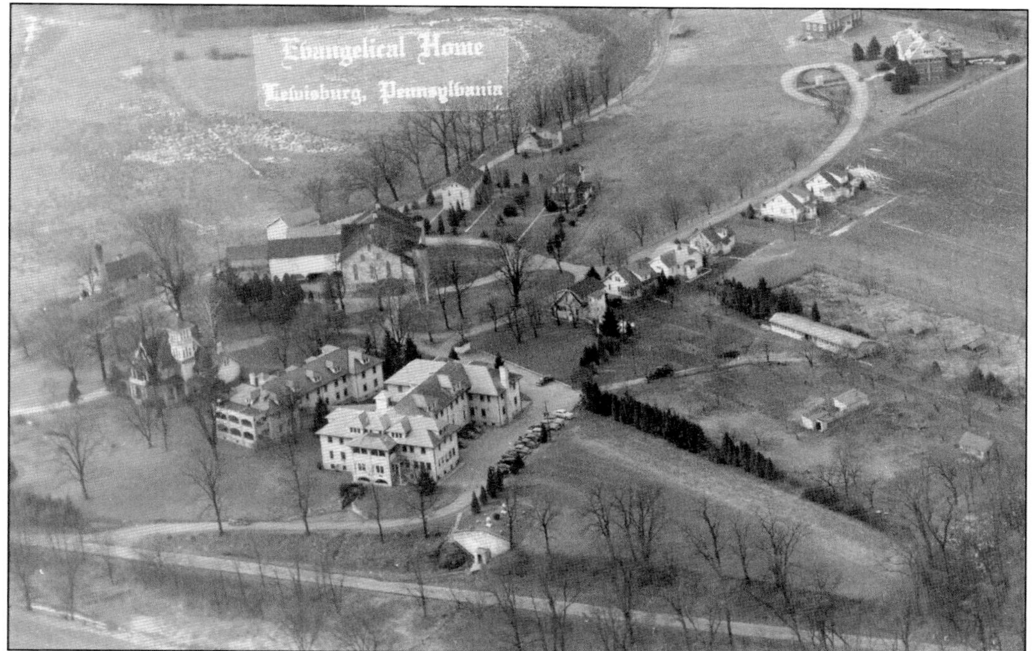

In 1916, the Evangelical Church opened a retirement home in the Victorian home once owned by Eli Slifer, the building with the cupola to the lower left in this photograph. An orphanage (upper right) opened in 1921, and a hospital opened in 1926, located to the right of the Slifer House. River Road can be seen on the bottom of this postcard image. (UCHS 82.2.8.)

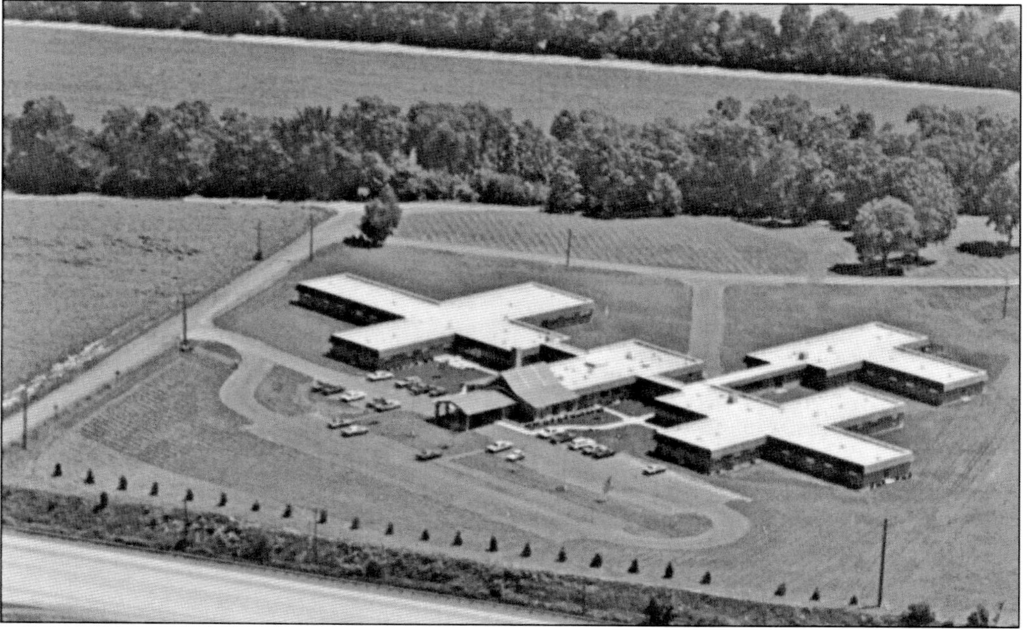

The Evangelical Home closed its hospital in 1953 and its orphanage in 1959. The complex became Lewisburg United Methodist Homes in 1970 and continued to grow, adding a number of retirement cottages, a skilled nursing center, and other buildings. In the late 1990s, the organization became Albright Care Services, with the Lewisburg facility renamed RiverWoods Senior Living Community. (UCHS 84.59.3.)

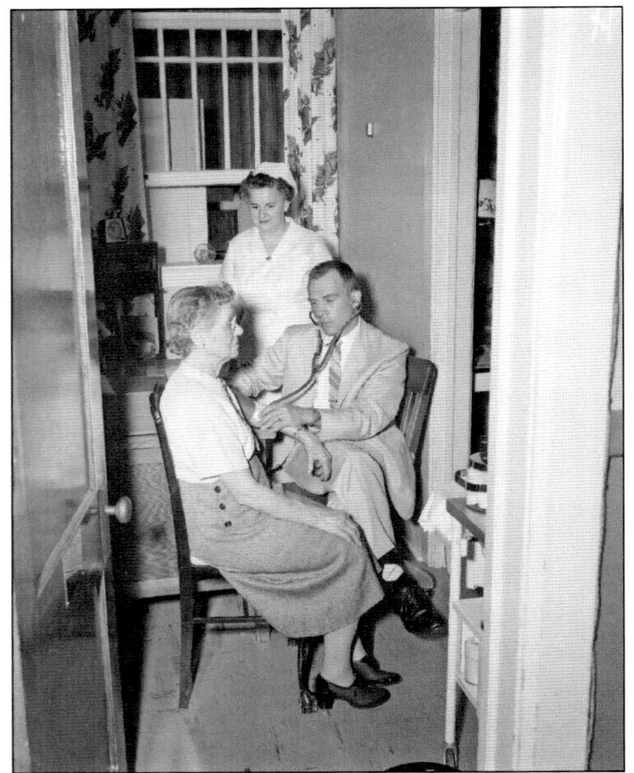

Although a new hospital opened in 1953, residents of the Evangelical Home still needed care. This image shows Mifflinburg physician John Purnell visiting the home and checking a female patient. Nurse Helen Heim stands behind the doctor. The doctor's office was reserved for visiting physicians and thus was limited in space. Any patients needing more intensive care would be sent to Evangelical Community Hospital. (UCHS 82.4.C60.15.)

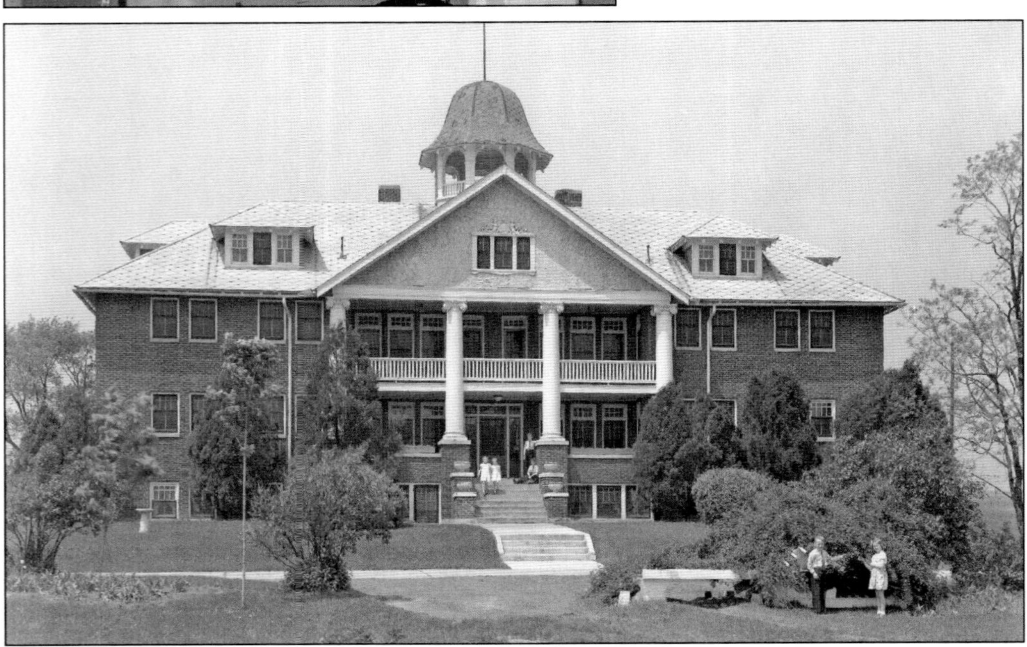

This May 7, 1945, photograph shows the Evangelical Orphanage. From its opening in 1926 to its closing in 1959, more than 250 children found temporary homes here. In 1976, this building reopened as the Gamber House Retreat Center, named in honor of Hattie Gamber, who retired as matron of the orphanage in 1959. Today it is known as the Gamber Office Building. (UCHS P82.4.C45.15Sa.)

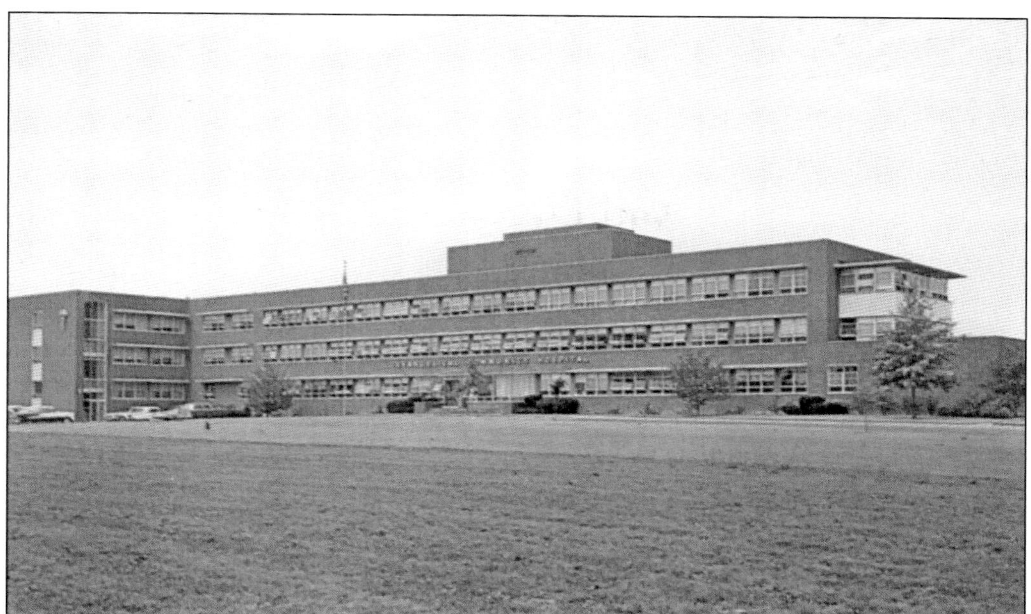

The present Evangelical Community Hospital is so named because the Evangelical Church sold the land on which it sits for a token fee. Adjacent to Route 15 just north of Lewisburg in Kelly Township, the hospital opened in March 1953. The hospital has added buildings to accommodate physician offices, and in the early years of the 21st century, it underwent an extensive modernization and renovation. (PHM.)

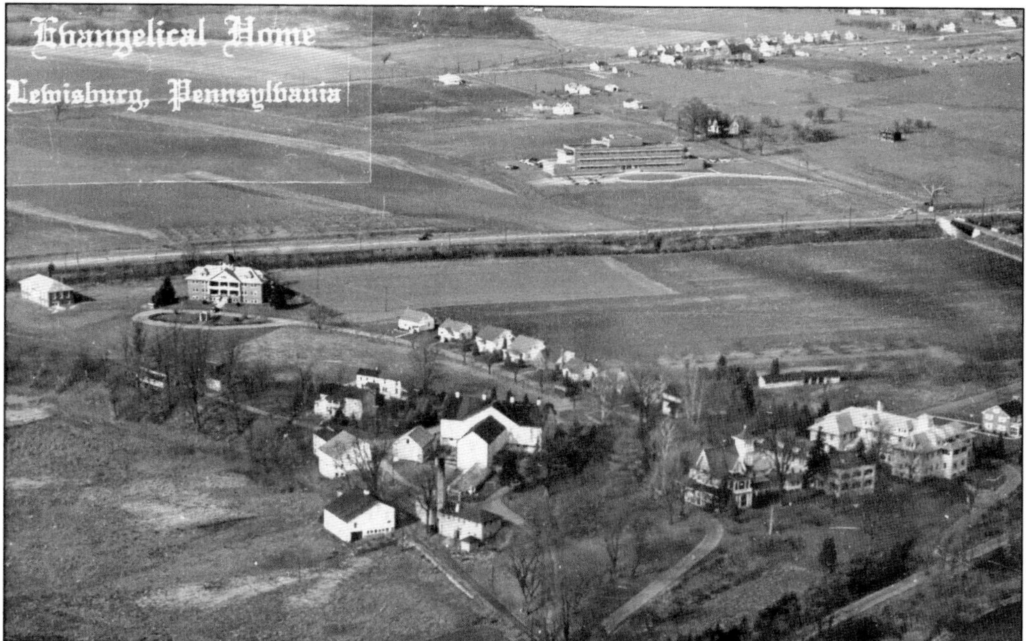

An aerial shot taken sometime after 1953 shows the rural nature of the Lewisburg area. At top is the recently opened Evangelical Community Hospital. The structures at the bottom collectively make up the Evangelical Home and Hospital. Route 15 is still only two lanes. Today the space west of the four lanes of Route 15 is filled with shops, restaurants, and a much larger hospital complex. (UCHS 95.1.3.)

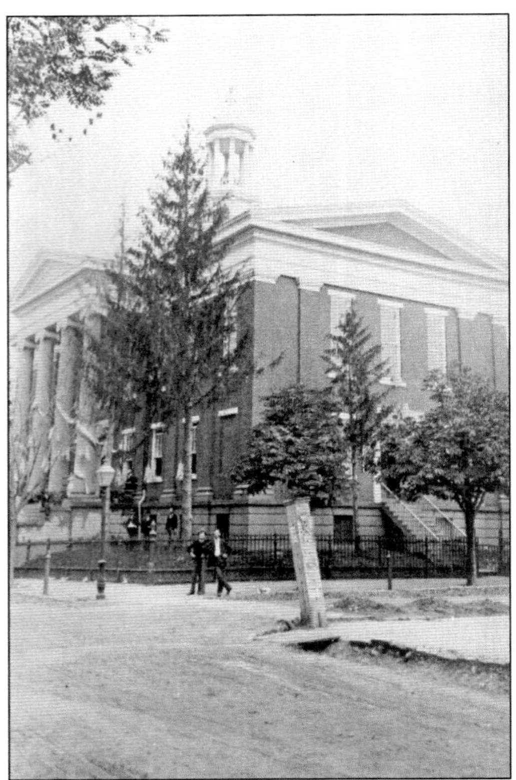

After several prominent Lewisburg residents succeeded in bringing the county seat to Lewisburg in 1855, construction of a new county courthouse commenced. The new structure was dedicated in 1857, when Simon Cameron presented a bell for the cupola. This is how the courthouse looked during the 1885 centennial. The entire building was renovated, and a new wing was added in 1971–1973. (Tiffini Scott.)

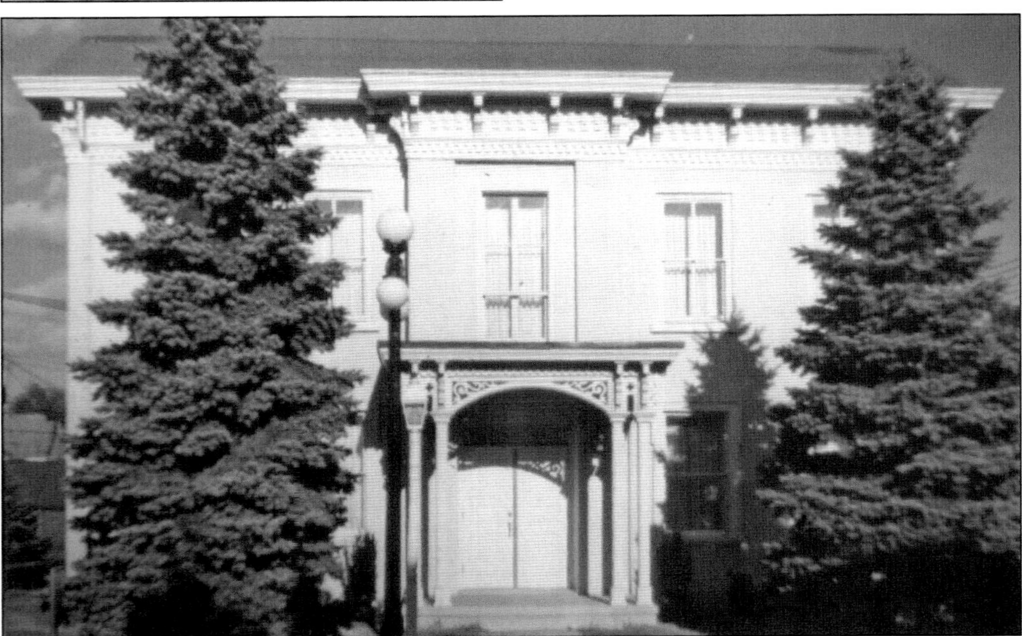

William Frick had this house built at 28 North Front Street in 1860. Together with Eli Slifer, Frick owned a canal boatbuilding business a short distance away, among his many business dealings. His house combined classical and Victorian styles. In 1961, the Charity Lodge No. 144 Free and Accepted Masons purchased the house as their headquarters. The lodge has been in Lewisburg since 1844. (PHM.)

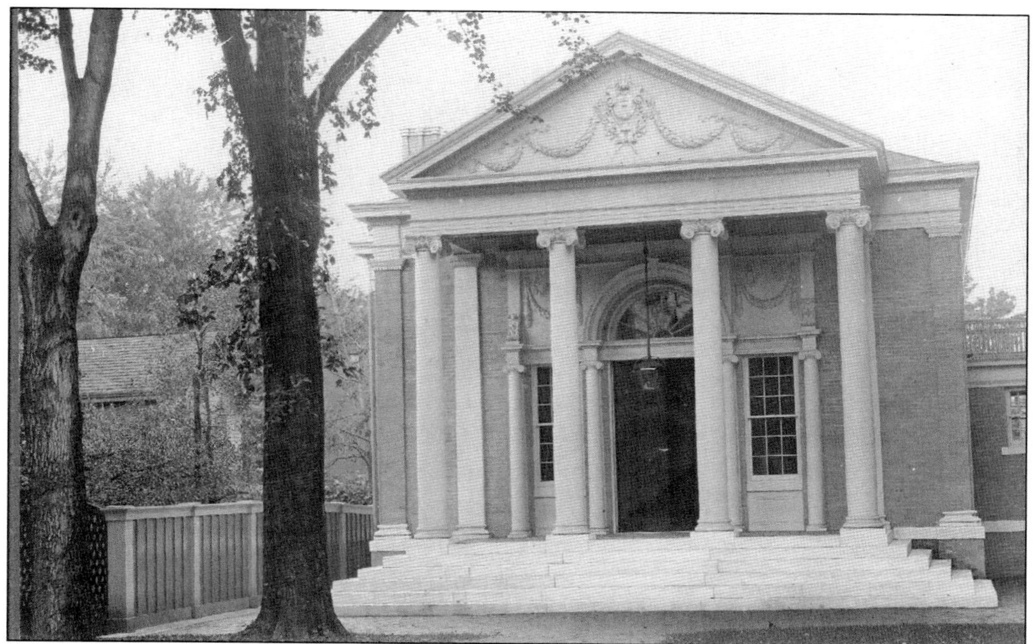

When noted businessman William D. Himmelreich passed away, he left $15,000 for the construction of a library for Lewisburg. The small but magnificent building was dedicated on November 7, 1902. Located adjacent to the First Presbyterian Church on Market Street, the Himmelreich Memorial Library functioned as the town's library until 1989, when the Public Library for Union County opened in East Buffalo Township. (UCHS 79.481.13.)

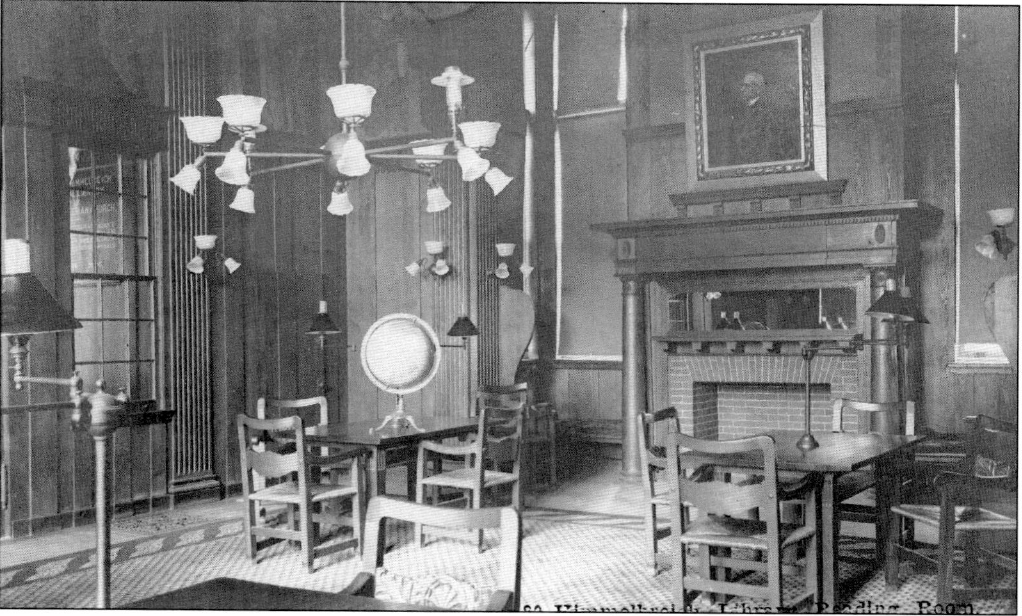

Shown here is the ornate main reading room of the Himmelreich Memorial Library as it appeared in 1907, complete with fine wood paneling, heavy tables and chairs, and works of fine art. Thanks to a long fund-raising campaign by library friends, the basement was renovated to include a children's room that opened in 1956. Today the library is known as the Himmelreich Christian Resource Center. (Donna Slear.)

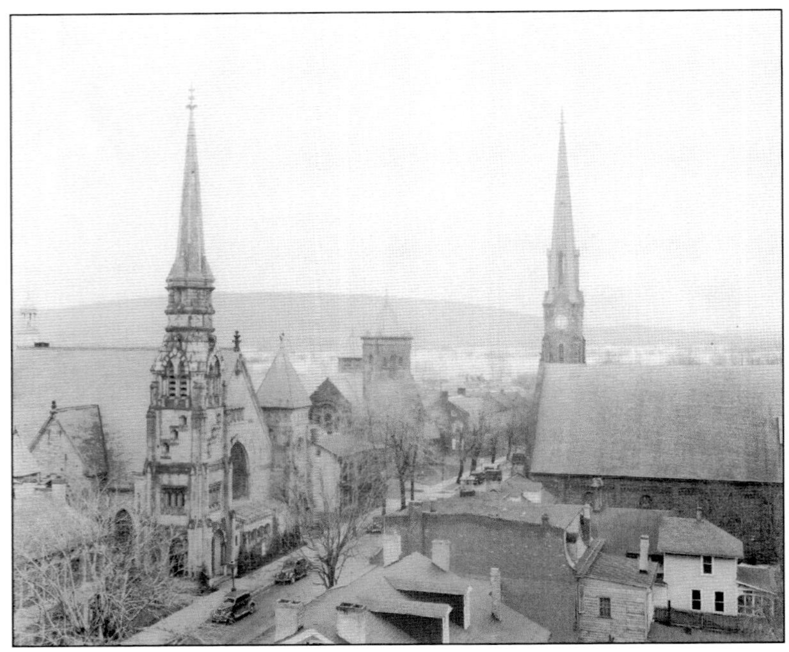

Three large church edifices are clustered on the corner of Third and St. Louis Streets: Beaver Memorial United Methodist, First Baptist, and Christ's Evangelical Lutheran. This photograph was taken in 1936, and in the background one sees the waters of that devastating flood. (UCHS 79.481.7.2.)

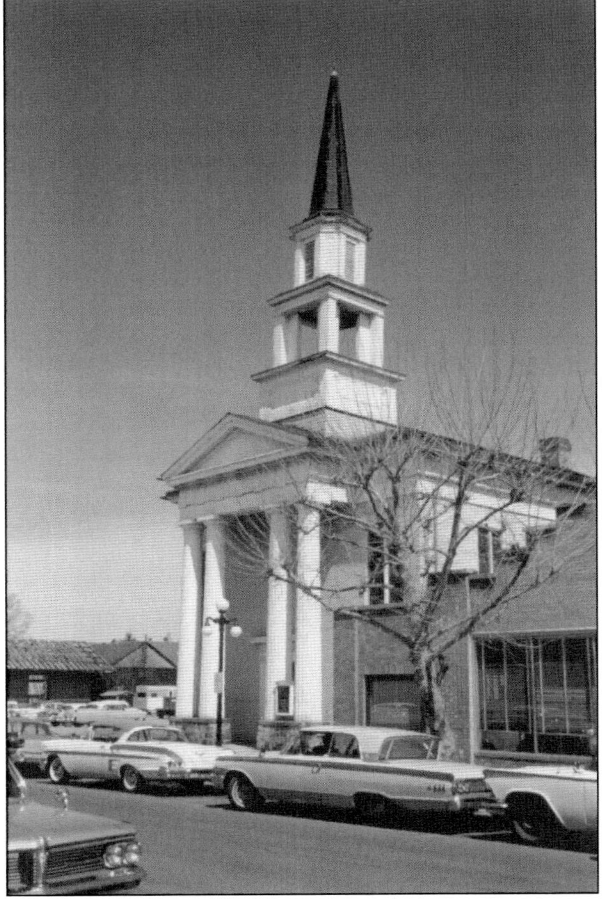

The Christian Church on North Third Street was built in 1854. This neoclassical building housed an active congregation for decades. In 1957, the church merged with others to form the United Church of Christ, which used the church across the street. The structure pictured at right was demolished in May 1963 to make way for part of the parking lot for the new Weis Markets store, then under construction. (UCHS 89.5.2.3.)

The sharply sloped steeple of the First Baptist Church on South Third Street is an unmistakable Lewisburg landmark. Erected in 1870, the basement of the church building housed the earliest classes of the University at Lewisburg, now Bucknell University. Justin Loomis, president of the university, shingled the original spire. (UCHS 98.40.5.)

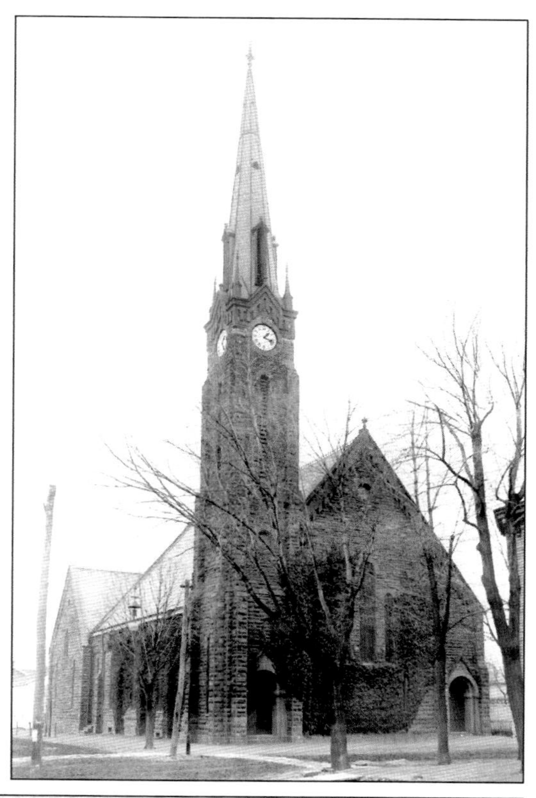

The simple building of the German Reformed Church could be found on North Third Street. The first congregation of this faith in Lewisburg was organized in 1826. As membership rose, the building pictured below was erected in 1848 and remained in use until replaced by a more modern, larger structure in 1902–1903. (UCHS 2006.42.2.)

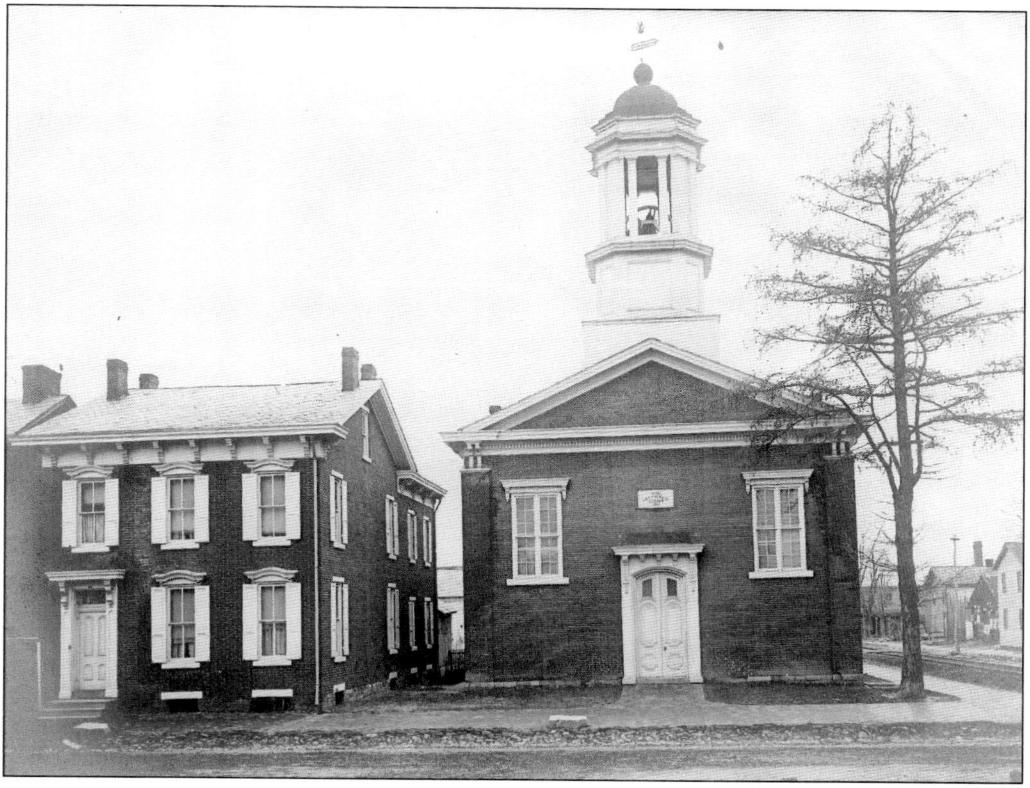

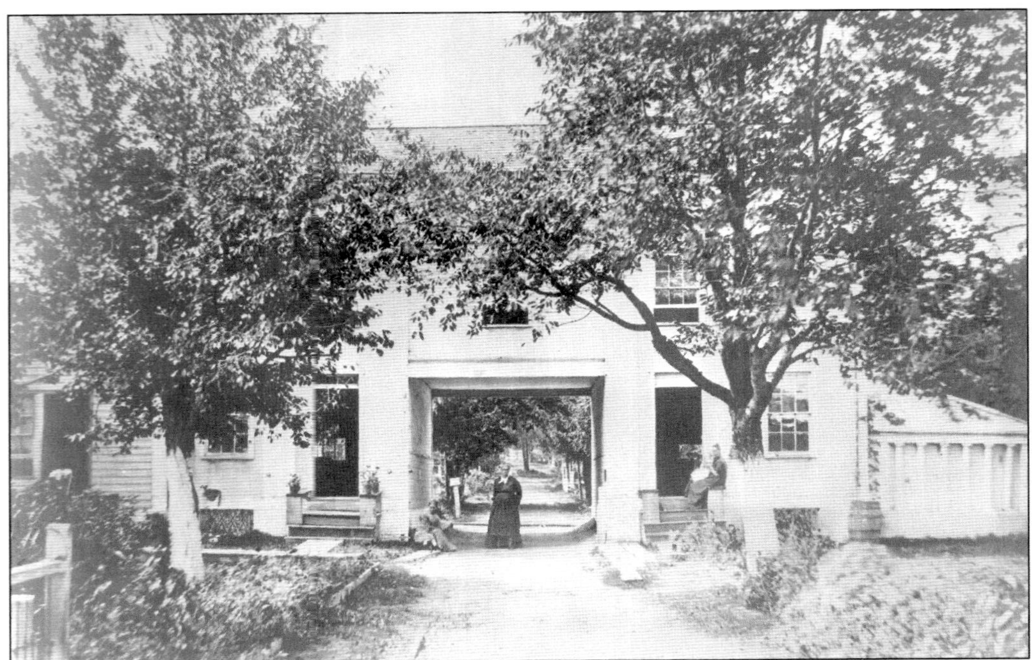

Few early images of the Lewisburg Cemetery have survived since the cemetery was formed in 1848 on ground purchased from the John Chamberlain farm. Then came the morbid process of removing bodies from the individual church cemeteries scattered across town. This image shows the cemetery entrance as it looked in the late 1800s. The house was moved in 1892 to 304 South Seventh Street. (UCHS 89.3.7.124.)

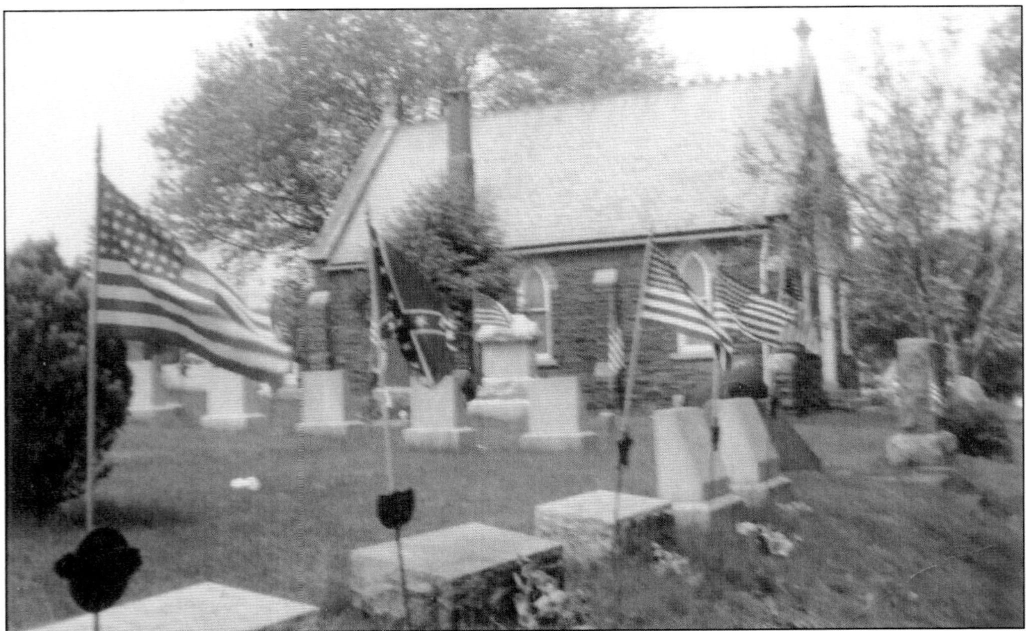

Here in the midst of the Grand Army of the Republic (GAR) burial plot is the grave of John W. Jordan, Company I, 5th Virginia Cavalry, marked by a Confederate flag. Jordan was a traveling salesman and died in Lewisburg in 1867. Local Union veterans in the GAR buried him. In 1948, the United Daughters of the Confederacy marked his grave. (UCHS 65.16.216.)

Two

Working

Lewisburg, from the beginning, was the home of family businesses, often big enough to have a number of employees and small enough to know almost all of their customers' needs and eccentricities.

Some work was hard and dangerous. After steering large log booms down the river to Harrisburg, workers then walked back with their pay in their pocket, only to do it again with another boom. Farming, always dependent on the weather and not without its own dangers, was the backbone of the community. Farmers brought their produce to town, and grain mills sold flour in large sacks, sometimes for cash, but often for exchange of goods and services. Wagons hauled wheat or corn and sacked ground grains, and buggies were built for those who could afford them. Blacksmiths shod horses that pulled these vehicles, until the car made its debut in numbers. Repair shops, tire dealers, and gas stations sprang up in the 1930s on street corners, and road construction almost never stopped, both in town and on the new Route 15 on the west side of Lewisburg.

Resources for businesses evolved as needed. The post office grew out of its early structure and moved into the stately Federal Building. Banks opened, several of them, each changing management and names until one would need a genealogical chart to remember which had been which. Evangelical Community Hospital and the Northeast Federal Penitentiary in Kelly Township became two of the area's largest employers, as did Bucknell University, straddling both Lewisburg Borough and East Buffalo Township. These institutions contributed to the uniqueness that is Lewisburg. Other industries began, thrived, and ceased, each adding a chapter to the working life and wealth of the area: the Lewisburg Woolen Mills, Pennsylvania House, Moore Business Forms, International Paper, and JPM among them.

Steady, challenging work is a gift of the community to itself. Lewisburg benefits greatly from its easy accessibility. It is ultimately connected to big cities and industrial giants, but when Lewisburg workers and small business and industry owners go home, they live as neighbors beside or near each other.

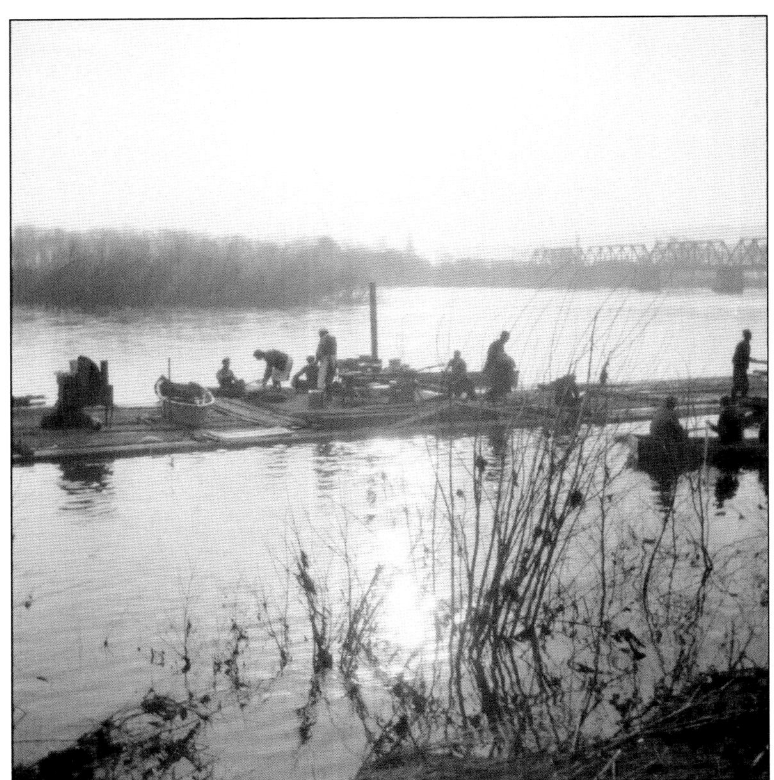

For about 30 years (1850s–1880s), rafting was popular on the Susquehanna River, as lumbermen exploited the rich forests of north central Pennsylvania. Rafters managed the thousands of logs that were floated down the Susquehanna River from Williamsport each spring, when the water level in the river was at its highest. In 1934, veterans of the trade manned a ceremonial "last raft," seen here at Lewisburg. (UCHS 89.5.26.5.)

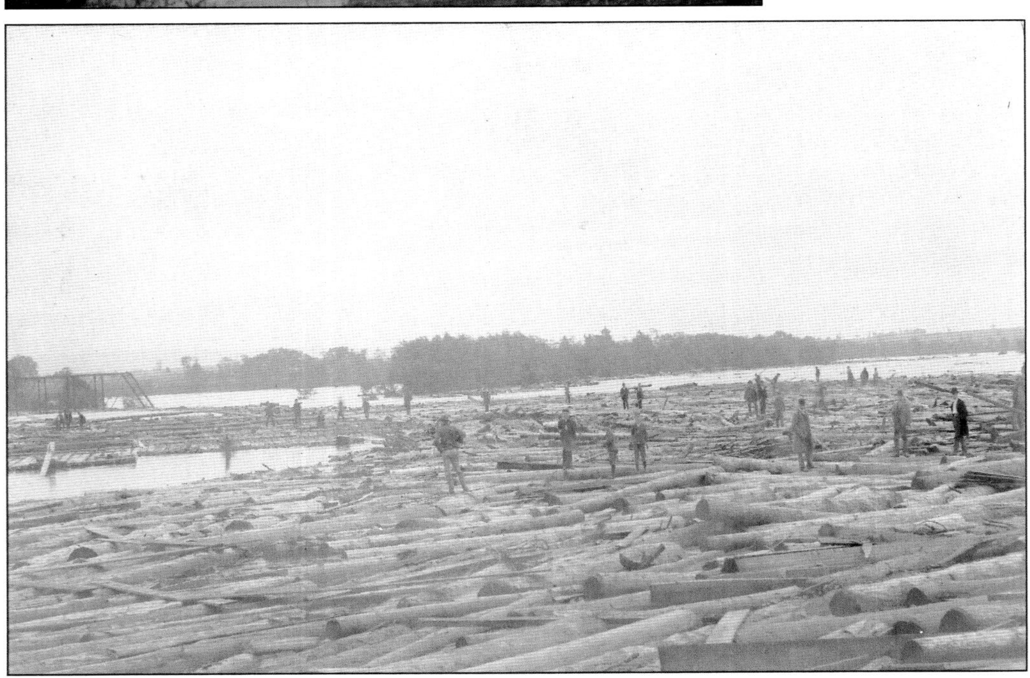

This photograph, taken on May 21, 1894, shows a logjam on the north side of the covered bridge over the West Branch of the Susquehanna at Lewisburg. Though logging had already peaked by this time, it was still a profitable business; the rich homes in Williamsport's "Millionaire's Row" attest to the fortunes that were made by lumber barons of this era. (UCHS 79.4.81.5.2.)

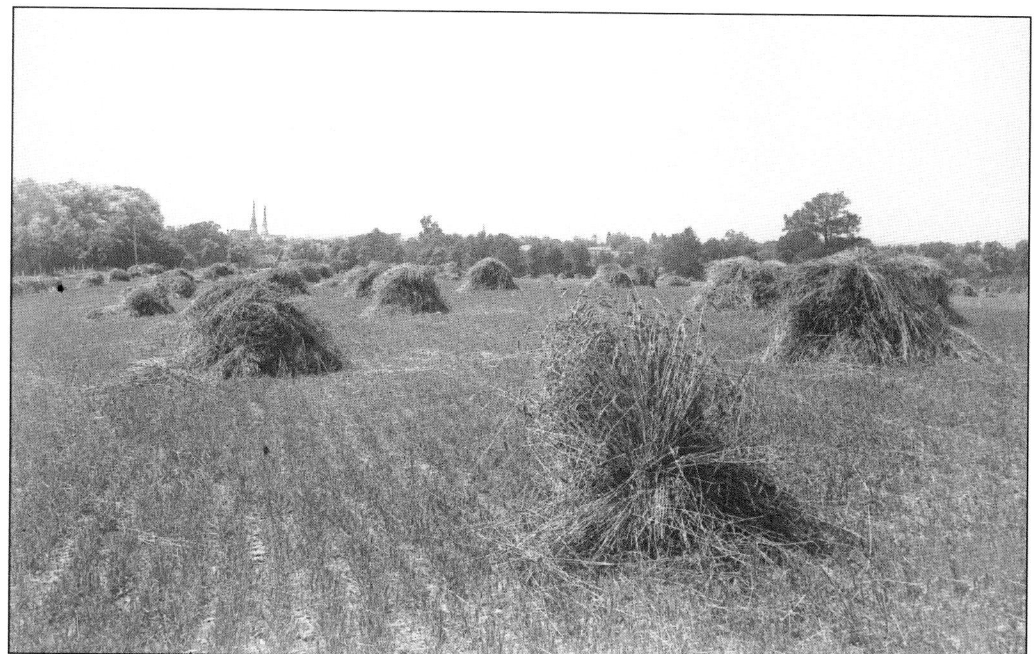

This early-20th-century view of Lewisburg speaks to the town's importance as the center of a thriving agricultural area. Looking north toward town across a newly harvested wheat field, one can see the spires of the Baptist and Methodist churches on Third Street (left), the Presbyterian spire on Market Street (center), and to the right, Bucknell University. (PHM 1987.03.46.)

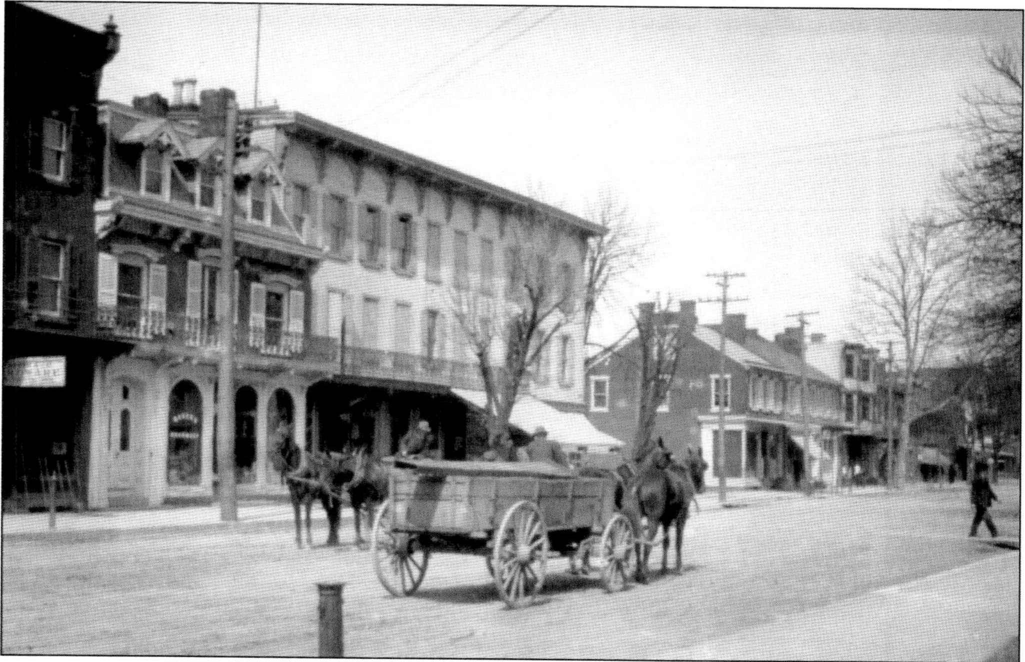

Farmers and their horse-drawn vehicles were a common scene in Lewisburg as late as the 1930s. Here is a driver steering his two-horse team east along Market Street. Baker's Pharmacy is in the building on the left; the large structure in the center of this image would later become home to Newberry's for many years. (PHM.)

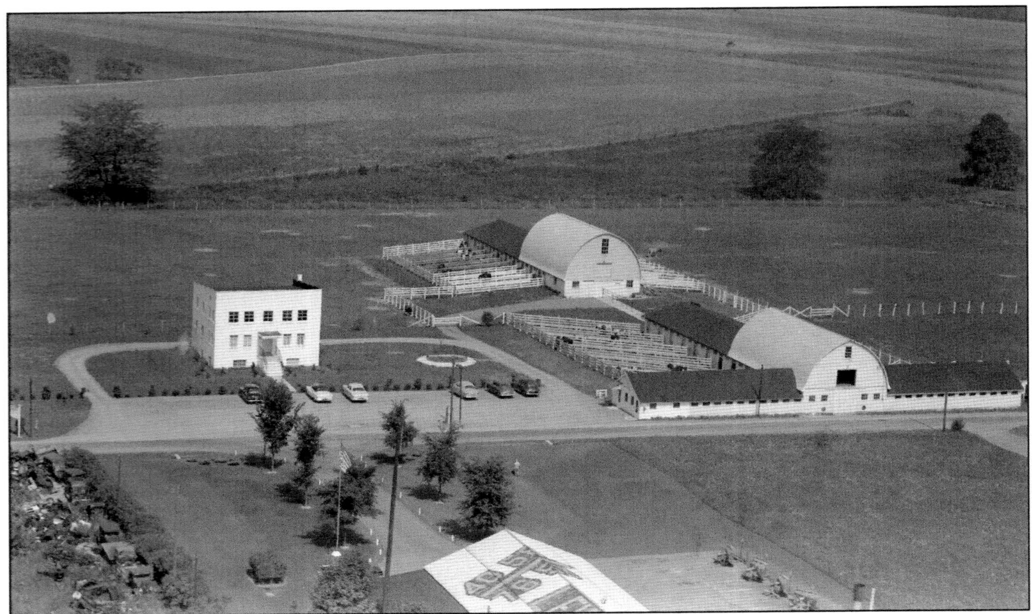

The Pennsylvania Breeders Cooperative was formed in 1942 to develop an artificial breeding system that would enable farmers to use registered "sires" to upgrade their herds. With the help of artificial breeding, farmers were able to increase average milk production and obtain cows with known classification. The present East Buffalo Township Municipal Building on Fairground Road originally housed the Pennsylvania Breeders Cooperative. (UCHS 82.4.C51.4QQe.)

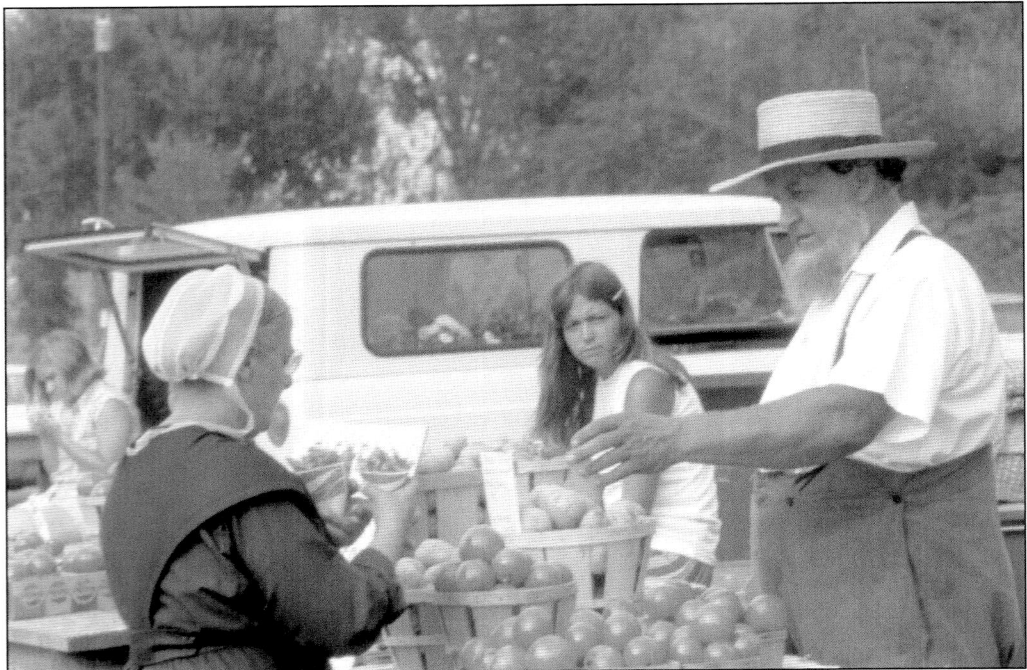

The Lewisburg Farmers Market began as a produce auction, and many residents still refer to it as the "auction." Local farmers, including many Amish and Mennonite families, have been directly selling their produce at the market since the 1950s. Situated on the former site of the Union County Fair, the farmers market draws large crowds every Wednesday. (PHM.)

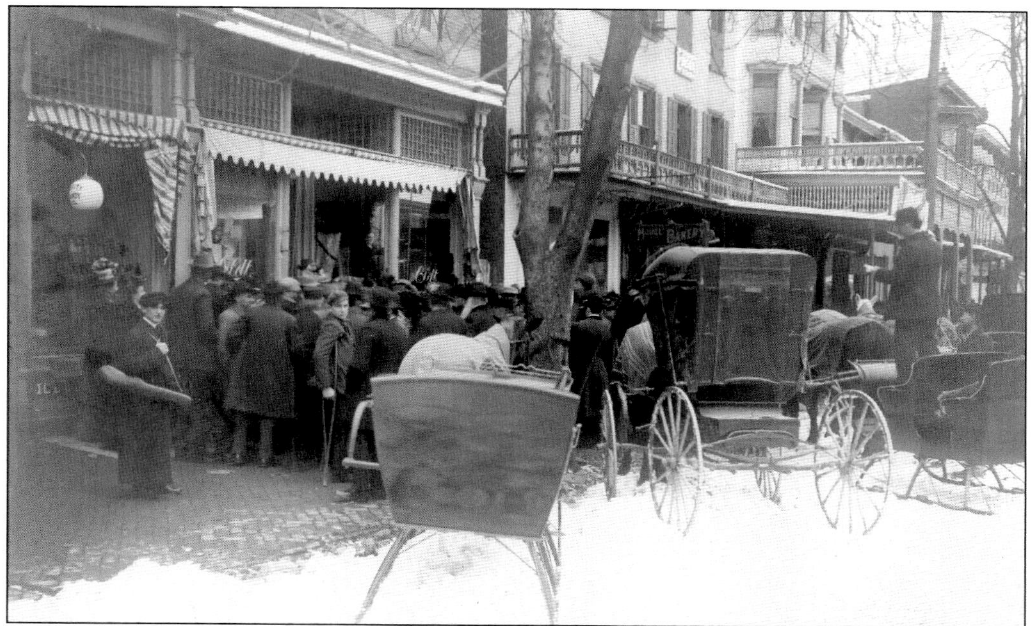

This was the scene on a snowy day at 332 Market Street, at the Oldt Dry Goods store, dated sometime between 1893 and 1913. The small white globe on the left signifies the entrance to Purity Candy Company. The event is possibly an auction of some kind, and it surely has drawn a crowd. On the left is a young man with a violin case, and another man is on crutches. (PHM.)

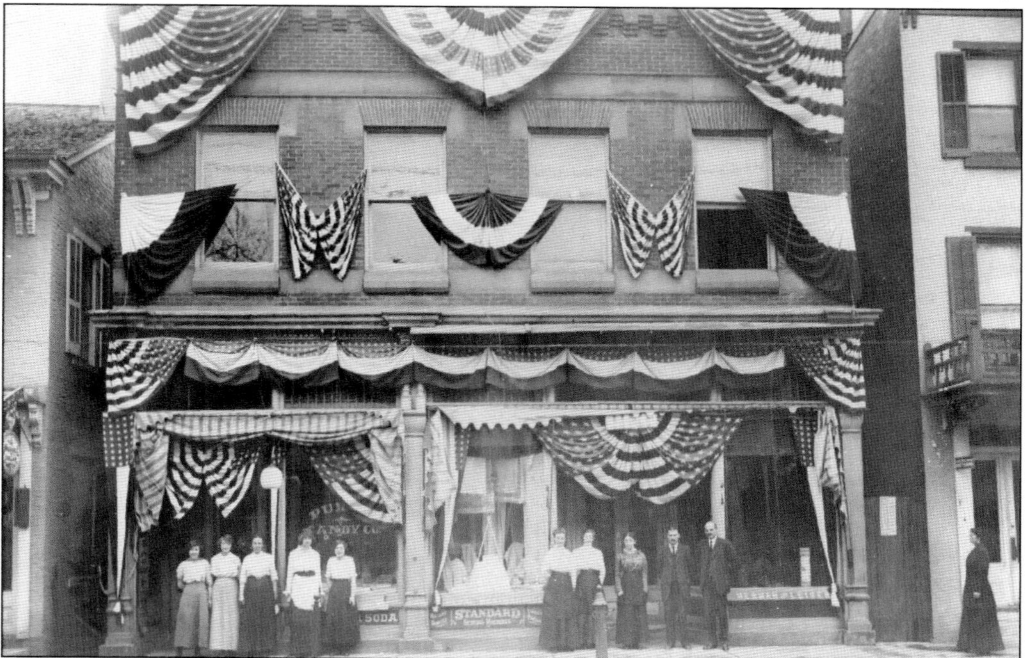

The Oldt Dry Goods business changed ownership in 1913 after the death of C. Willard Oldt. The new owners, Herman and Leiser, are seen here (farthest right) in an image taken perhaps during World War I. They pose in front of their store together with their clerks. On the left is the staff of Purity Candy, which opened in Lewisburg in 1907 and is still going strong in Lewisburg. (UCHS 89.5.15.32.)

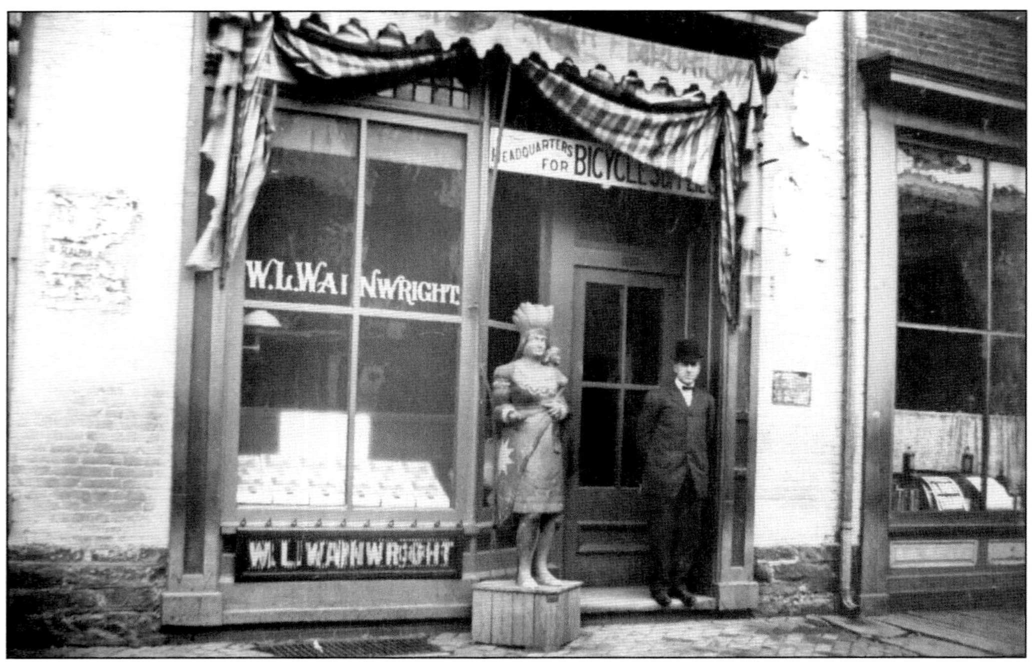

An undated view of 234 Market Street focuses on a wooden Native American standing outside of Wainwright's Tobacco Emporium. Wainwright's was a long-standing local business that catered to tobacco users but branched out into bicycles and other items of leisure. In later years, it became primarily a pool hall popular with teenagers and older men alike. (PHM.)

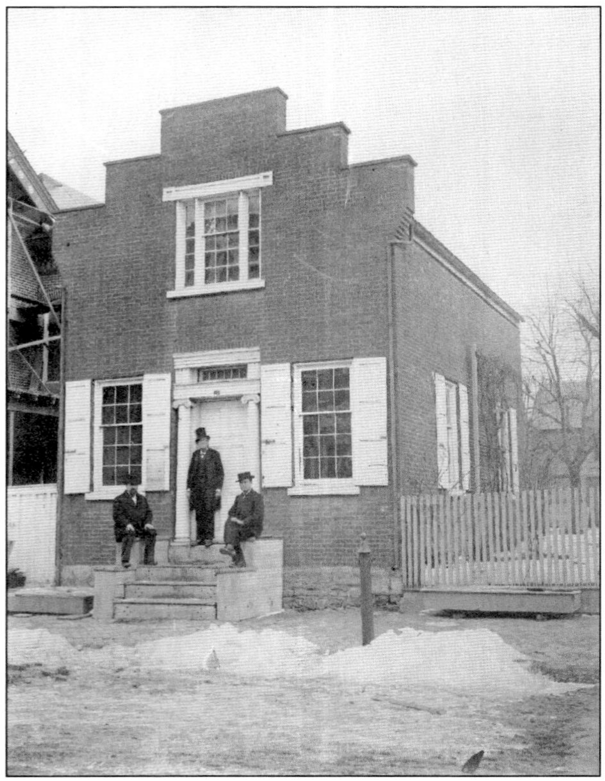

George F. Miller (1809–1885) was a member of the U.S. House of Representatives, serving in the 39th and 40th congresses. Admitted to the bar of Union County in 1833, Miller practiced law in Lewisburg in this brick structure. He was a charter member of the board of curators of the University at Lewisburg (now Bucknell University) from 1846 to 1882. (PHM 2005.03.)

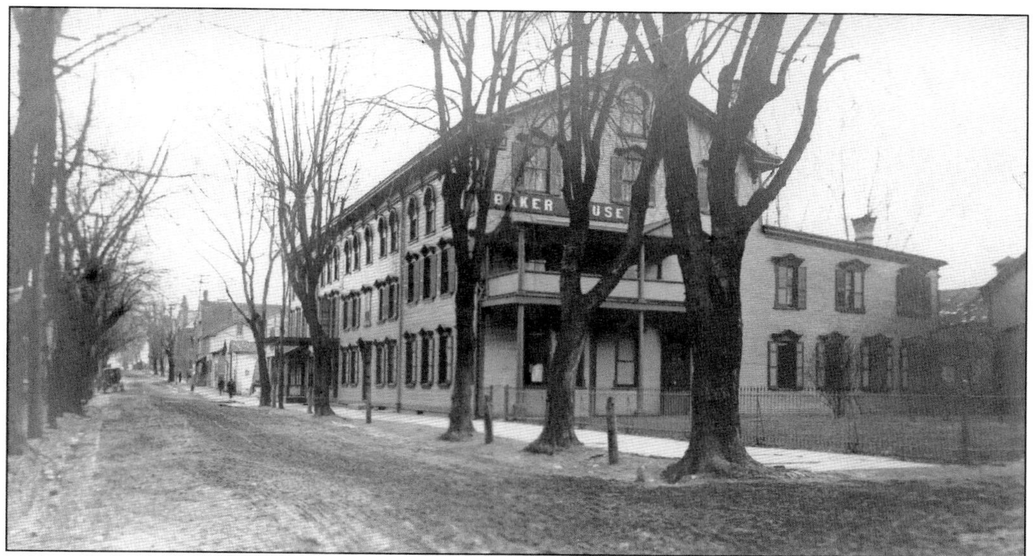

The Baker House Hotel, located on North Second Street, was one of Lewisburg's largest hotels from at least the 1880s until 1918, when it was sold and converted into apartments. The building was demolished in January 1962 in preparation for the construction of a Weis Markets store on part of the site. (UCHS 92.9.91.48.)

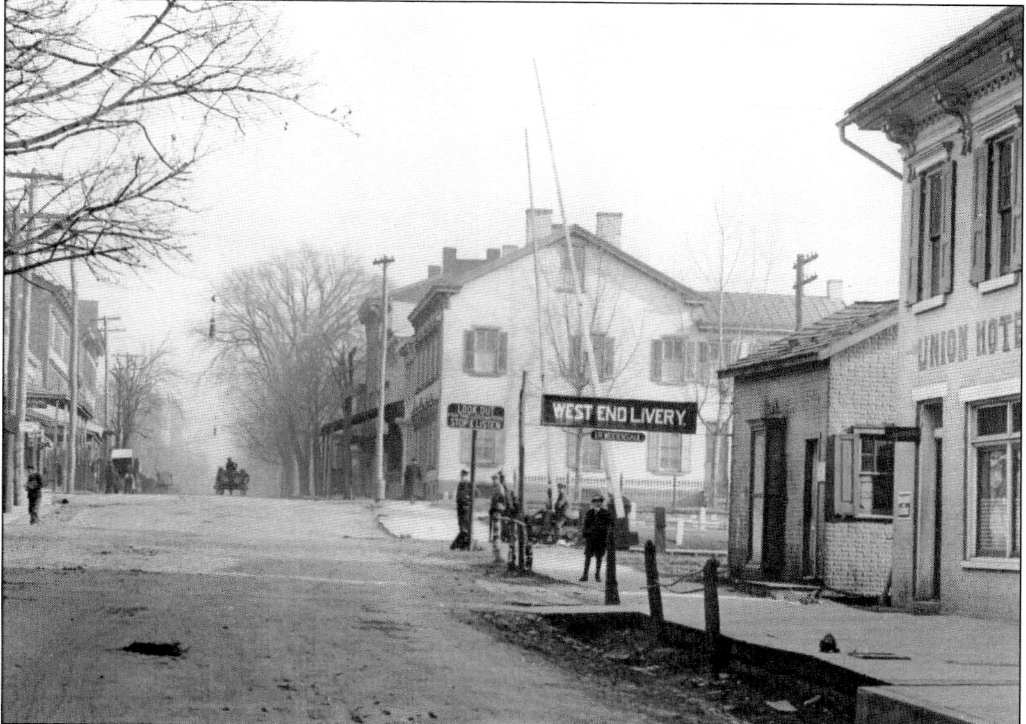

This view looks east down Market Street. On the right is the Union Hotel, erected in 1861 as the business district expanded west on Market Street. The tracks of the Reading Railroad cross Market Street just past the West End Livery. The large building on the right background was constructed by architect William Palmer in 1857; it now houses the Pineapple Inn Bed and Breakfast. (Nada Gray.)

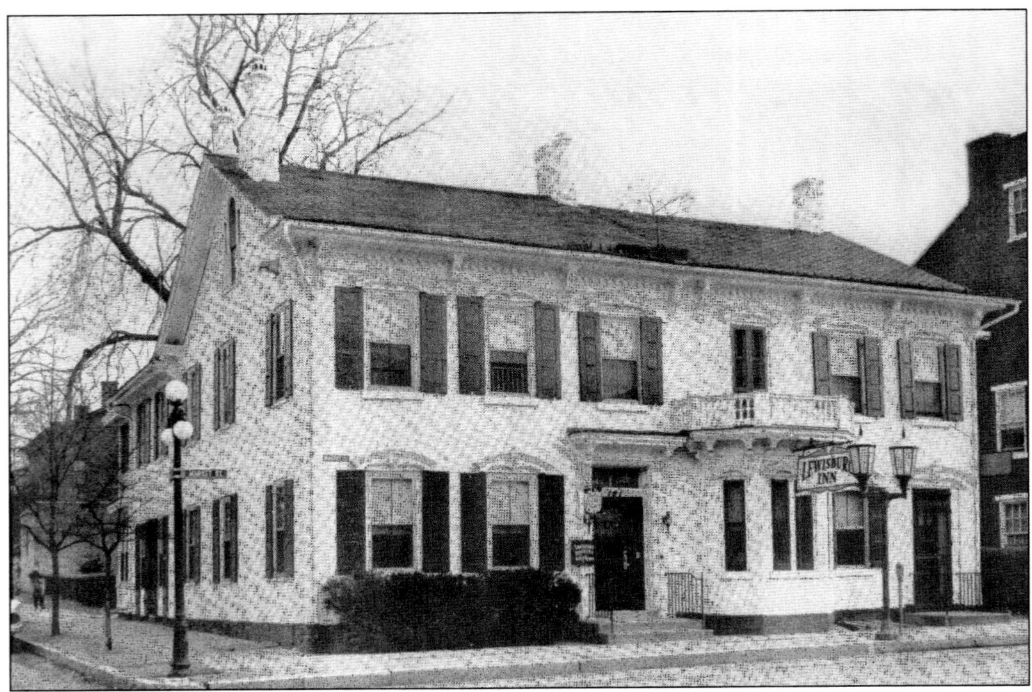

Attorney James F. Linn built this fine house on Market Street in 1827. It remained in the Linn family until 1931, when it was sold to Rhoda Berg and Sara Ritter, who converted it into the Lewisburg Inn. Since the inn went out of business in 2001, a succession of new owners have tried their hand at keeping a restaurant in this historic building. (PHM.)

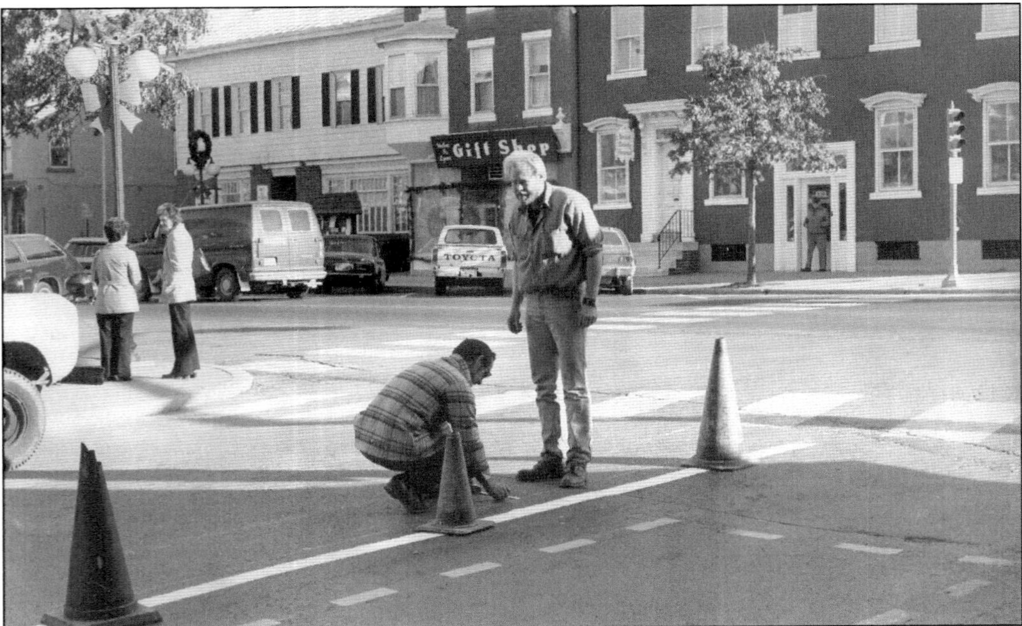

Robert L. Richard (kneeling) and George (Buck) Stump (standing) measure and mark the street surface at the corner of Market and North Fourth Streets. Taken in the early 1970s, the photograph shows the former Borough Building, Helen Lyons Gift Shop, the *Union County Journal* office, and the Nesbitt Building. (UCHS 89.5.24.8.)

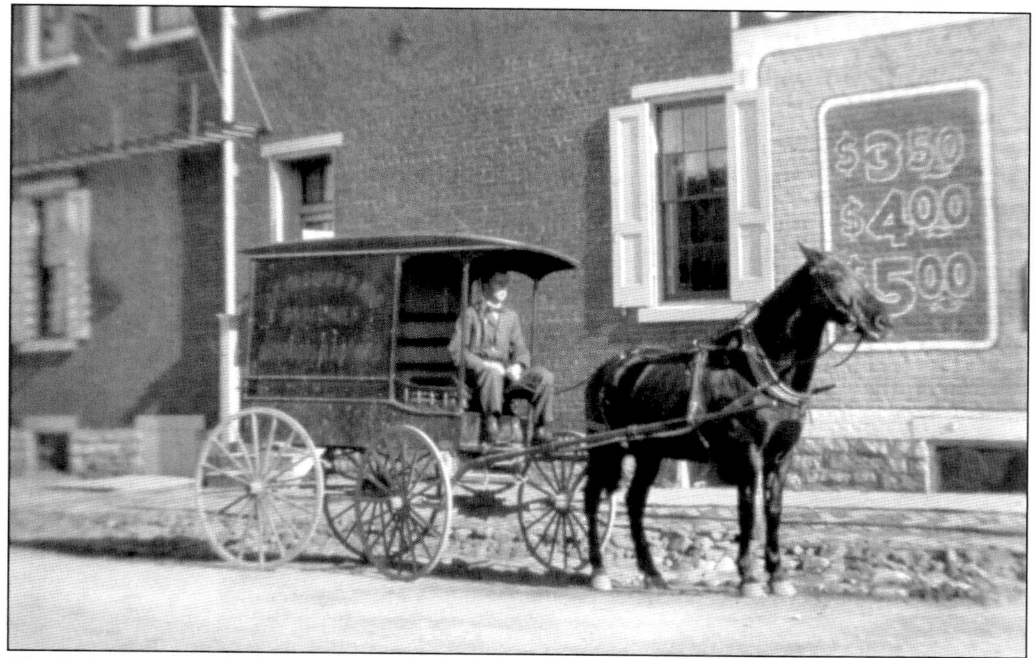

Obediah Groover sits on the Groover store's delivery wagon on a side street in Lewisburg. In the days before modern transportation enabled quick and easy delivery of goods to stores and customers, drivers of horse-drawn delivery wagons were the norm in small towns and big cities alike. Everything from ice, dry goods, and groceries were delivered to regular customers. (PHM.)

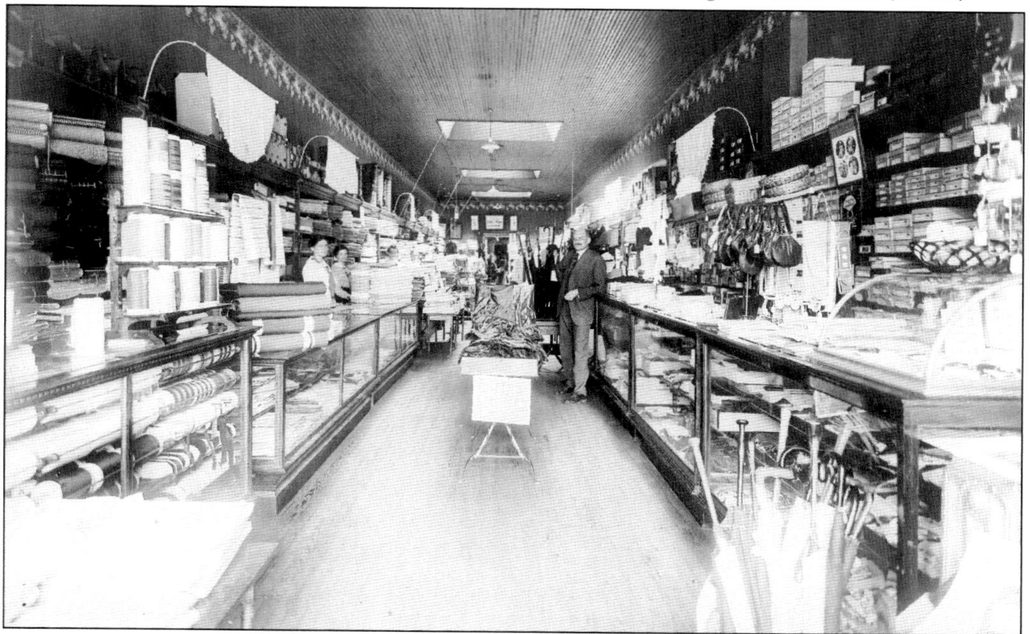

This undated view shows the interior of the Herman and Leiser Drygoods Store at 332 Market Street. Herman and Leiser replaced the earlier owner, C. Willard Oldt, in 1913. Here one can see the high wooden ceiling with electric lighting. A plethora of dry goods can be seen, including umbrellas and walking sticks, purses, fabrics and sewing accessories, and other items necessary to run a successful household of the time. (UCHS 92.9.69.2.)

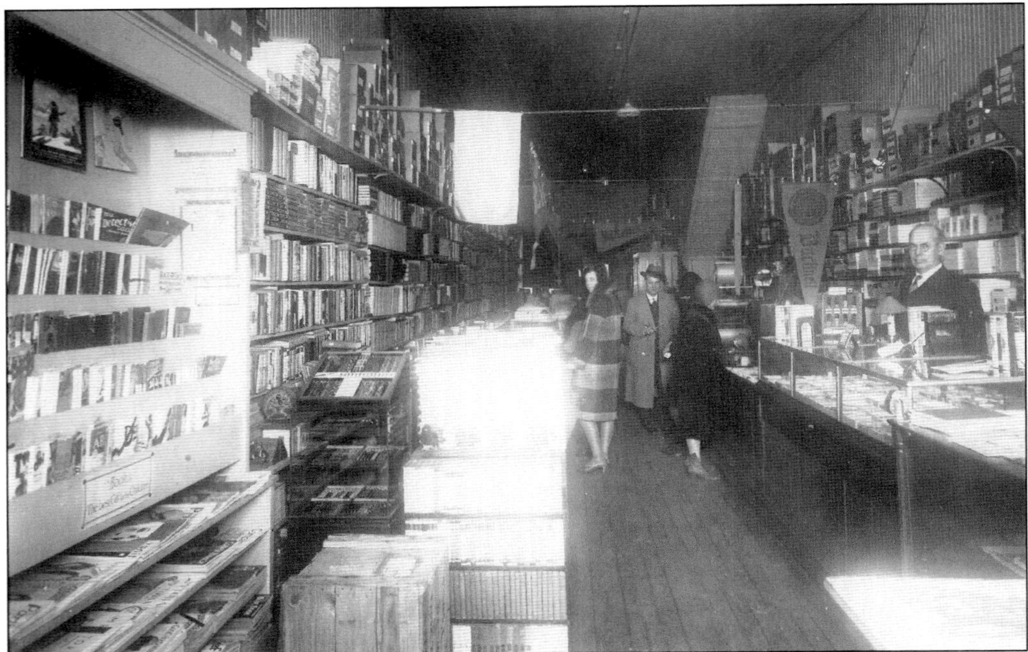

Joseph M. Wolfe's store on Market Street is pictured sometime during the 1920s. Wolfe provided a range of stationery supplies such as folders, ledgers, tablets, and writing utensils. He also sold books, newspapers, and magazines. The proud owner of this establishment stands behind the counter on the right of this image. (UCHS 83.39.3.)

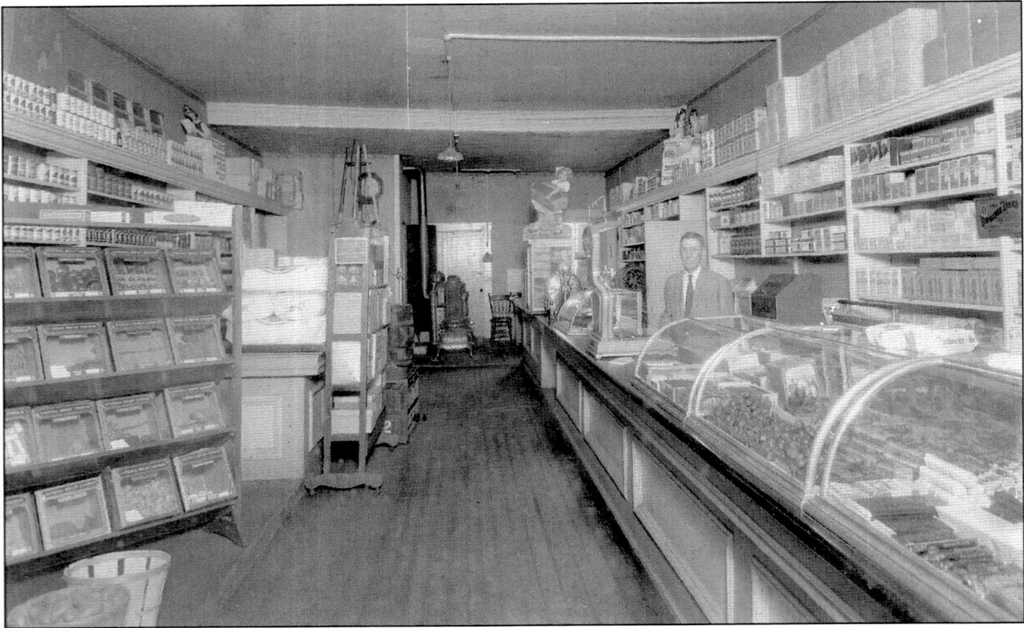

Yet another Lewisburg business shows off its interior in this undated view of the M. Halfpenny and Company store. Mr. Halfpenny carried a complete line of groceries. One can see bread and rolls in the cases on the left, with rows of canned goods behind, stacked as high as a person could reach. The rounded glass cases on the right seem to contain sweets and penny candy. Boxed grocery items line the shelves behind the glass cases. (UCHS 89.5.15.39.)

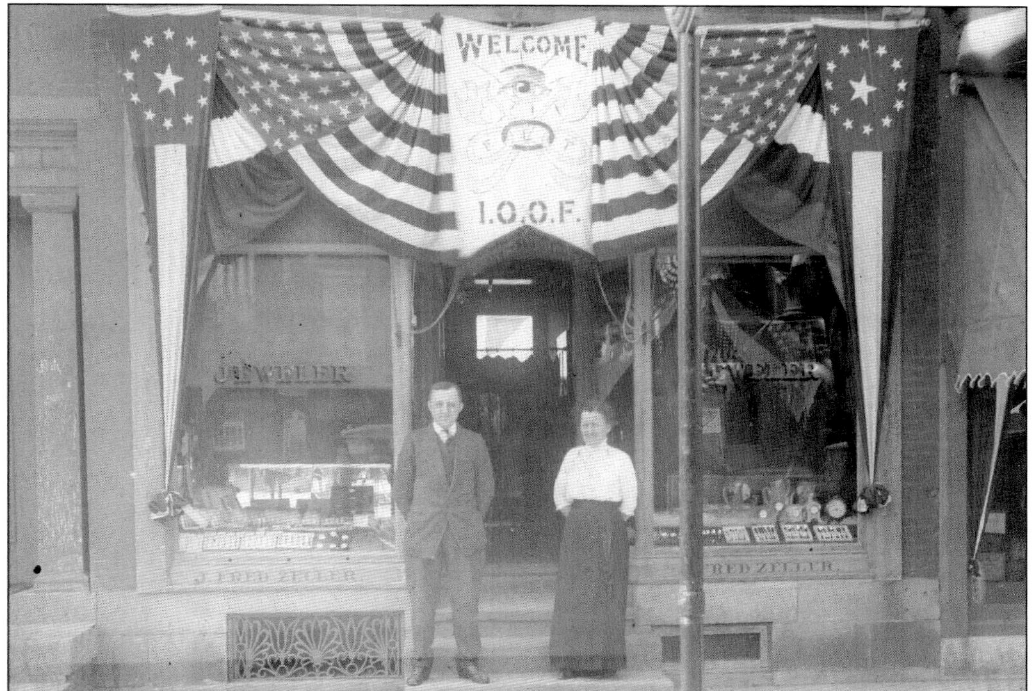

J. Fred Zeller and his sister Alice stand in front of Zeller's Jewelry Store at 318 Market Street around 1910. The building was earlier owned by Bran Thomas and operated as a men's clothing store. Fred Zeller purchased the building in 1906. It was remodeled in 1933, when the floor was lowered and the steps leading into the store were removed. (UCHS 2010.11.1.)

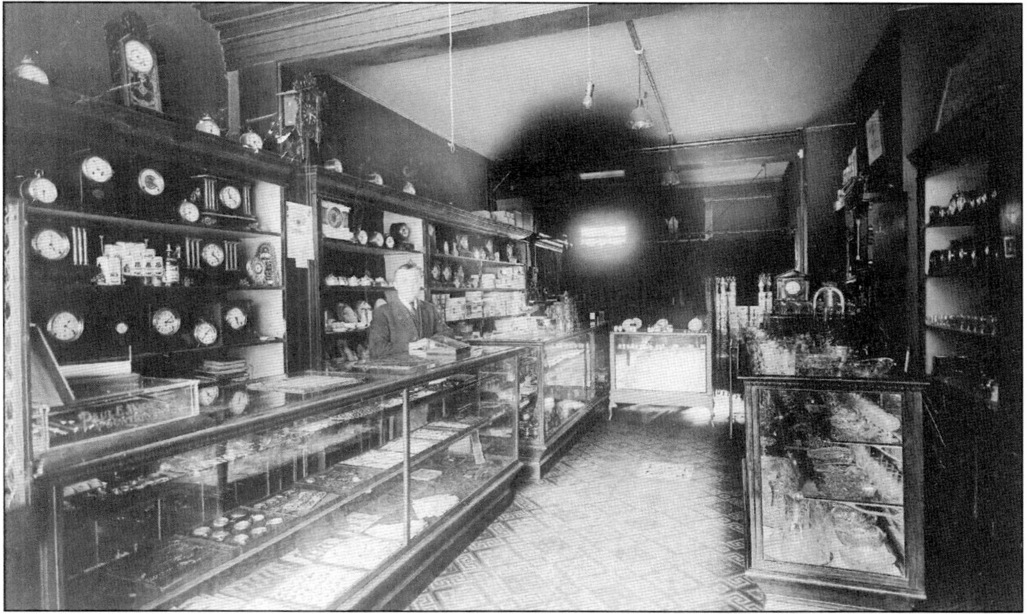

Fred Zeller stands inside the Zeller Jewelry Store. Two apartments were made on the second floor and two store rooms on the first floor. The store closed in the 1960s. Zeller, who died in 1959, was the father of John Zeller, former vice president for administration and legal counsel at Bucknell University. (UCHS 2010.11.2.)

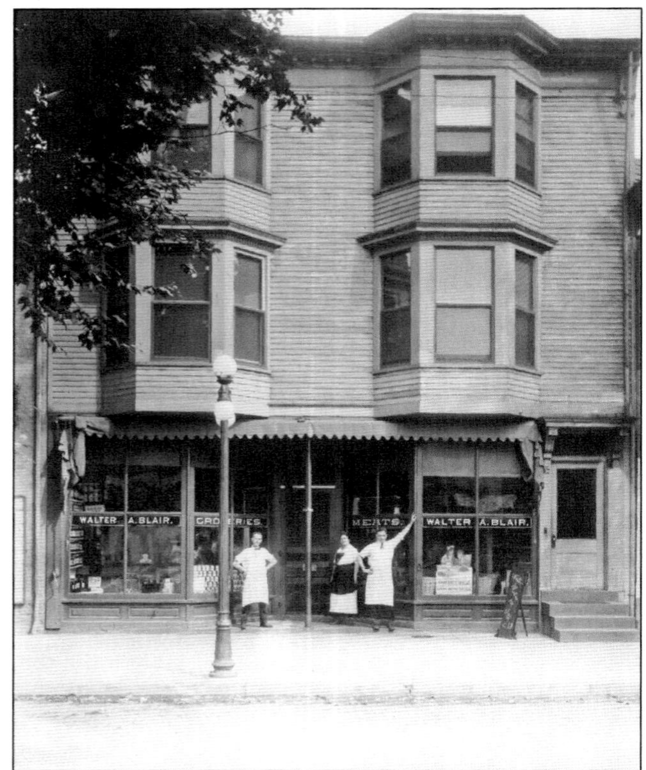

Walter A. Blair sold groceries and freshly cut meat in his store at 230 Market Street. Blair (1883–1948) played professional baseball with the New York Highlanders (1907–1911) before coming back to Lewisburg to coach Bucknell University baseball. He then operated this store as well as an insurance agency. (James Mathias.)

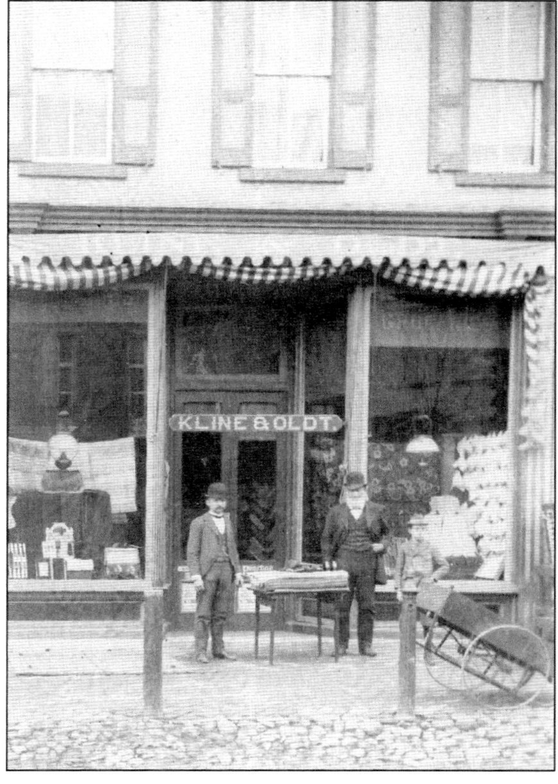

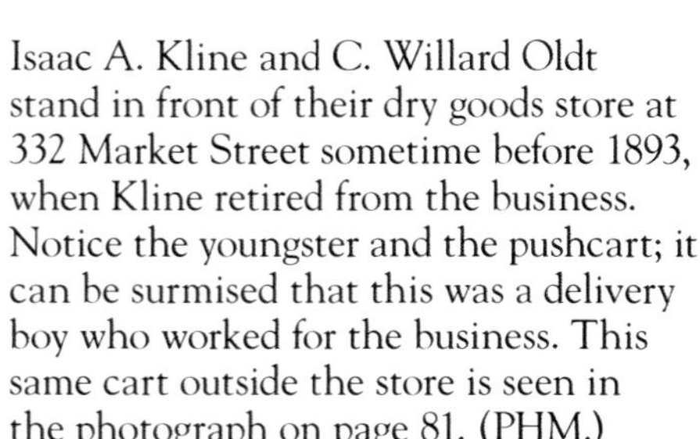

Isaac A. Kline and C. Willard Oldt stand in front of their dry goods store at 332 Market Street sometime before 1893, when Kline retired from the business. Notice the youngster and the pushcart; it can be surmised that this was a delivery boy who worked for the business. This same cart outside the store is seen in the photograph on page 81. (PHM.)

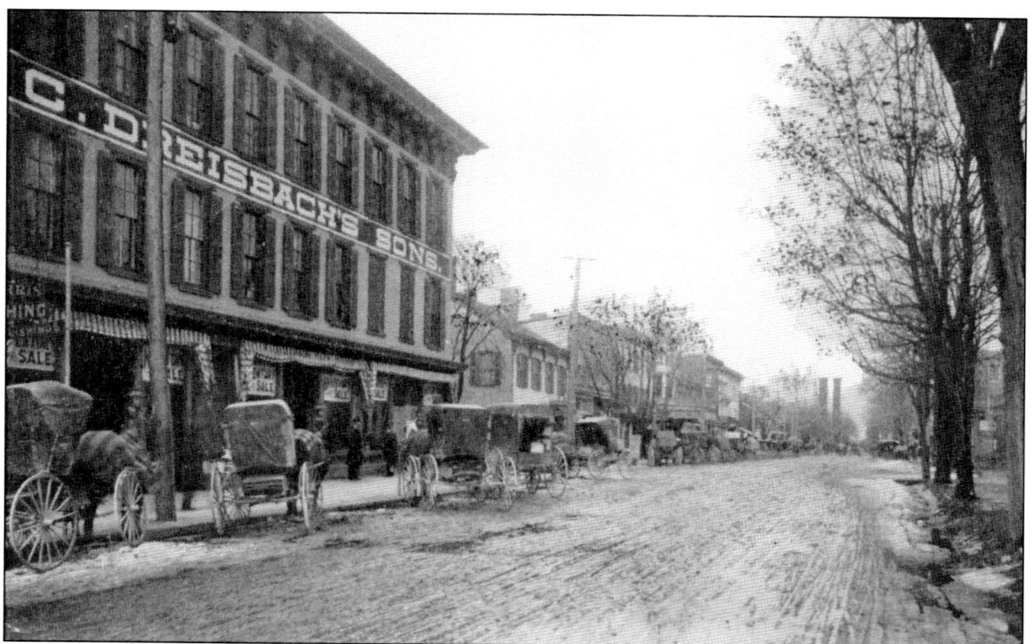

A year after the Panic of 1873 threw the United States into an economic depression, Cyrus Dreisbach quit farming and moved to Lewisburg, where he started a hardware company that remained in business until 1961. This postcard shows a "century sale," dating the scene to 1900. Cyrus made his sons partners in 1891 and changed the name of his store to Dreisbach's Sons. (PHM.)

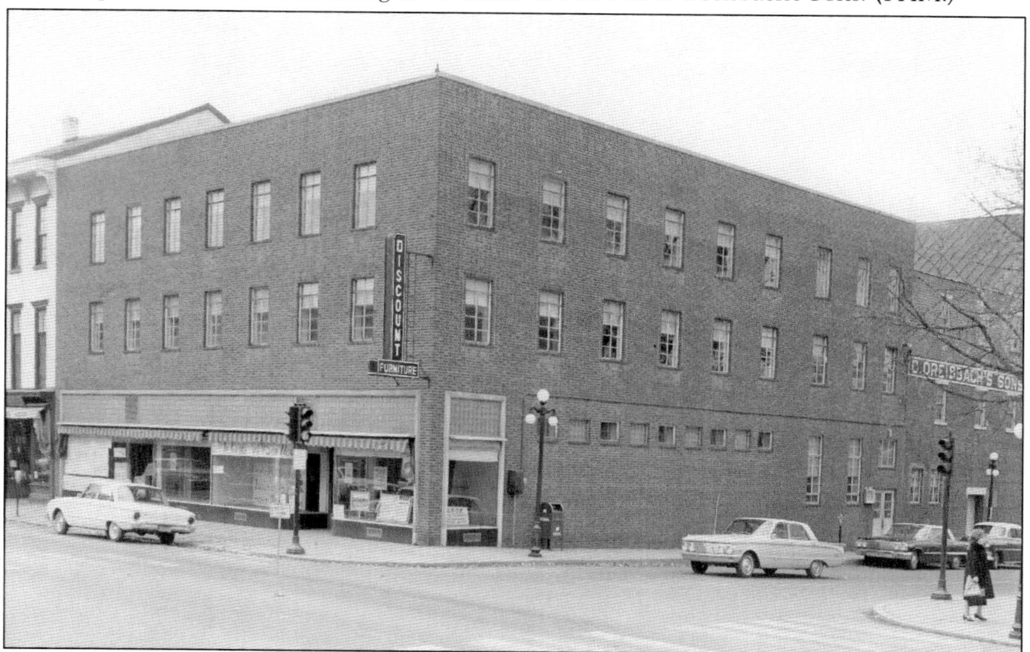

Reconstructed in 1941 after a severe fire, this building, at the northwest corner of Market and Fourth Streets, was home to the C. Dreisbach Sons Hardware business until it closed in late 1961. This image shows a discount furniture company occupying the site. Brozman's women's store opened in the old Dreisbach building in the 1970s, selling "First Fashions First For Young-in-Heart Women." (David Mensch.)

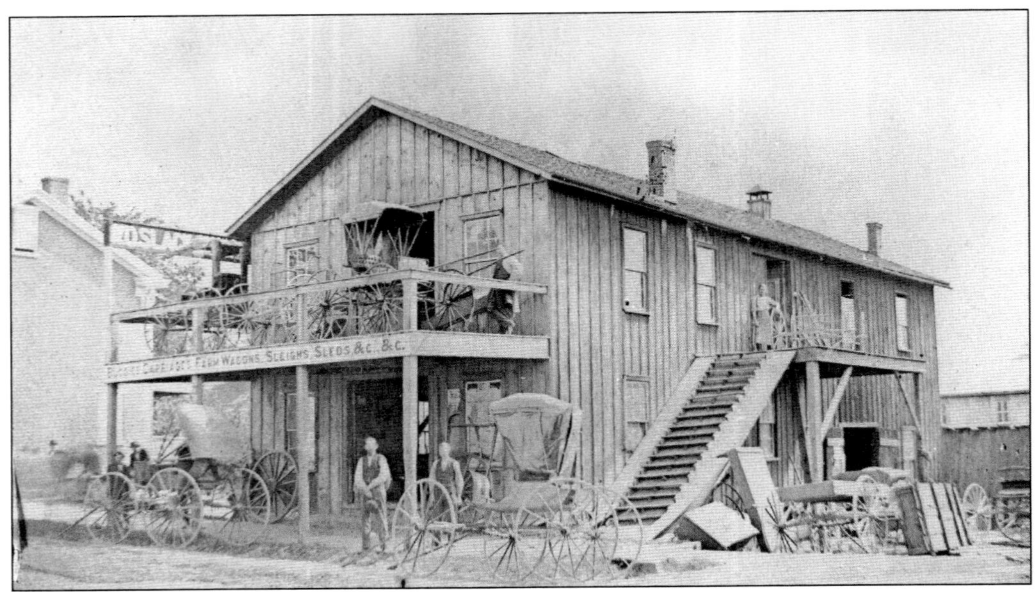

This 1877 image shows the W. D. Slack Buggy Works, located at Sixth and Market Streets. The firm made farm wagons, sleds, and other conveyances. However, the center of buggy making in Union County was 9 miles away in Mifflinburg; in the 1870s, there were at least 10 buggy makers working there. (UCHS 89.5.11.20.)

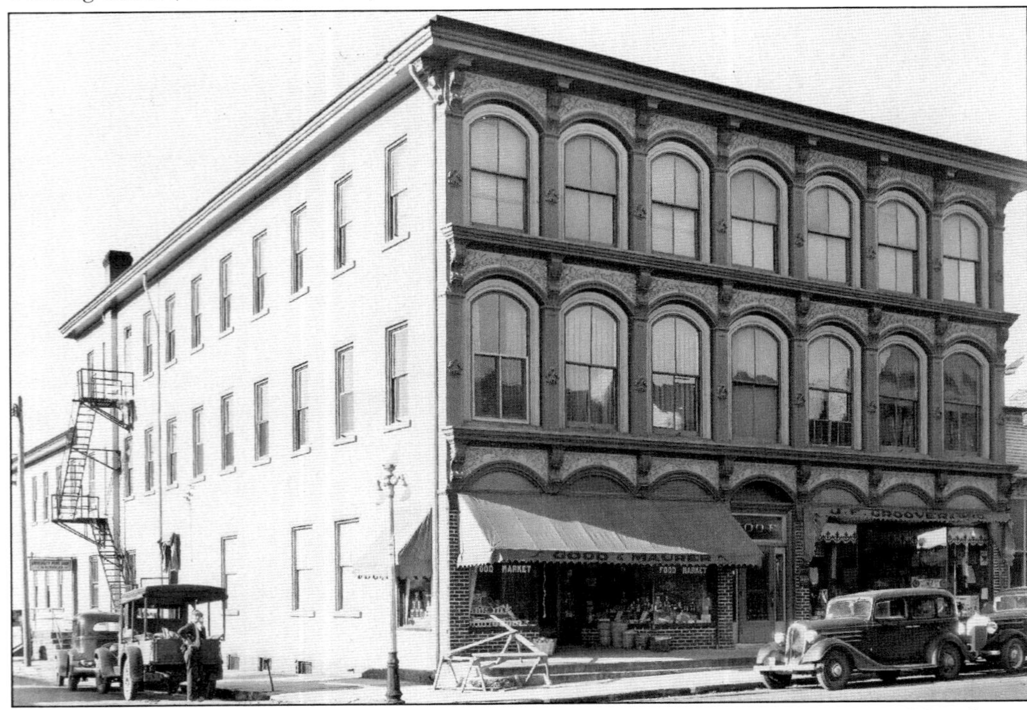

The three-story, iron-front Chamberlin Building was constructed in 1855. Its principal facade was composed of cast iron over brick. For many years, the building accommodated the Independent Order of Odd Fellows and housed offices of the Red Cross and County Welfare above the ground floor. The Groover's hardware store and later the Reish Brothers electrical supply store were on street level. (UCHS 89.5.25.2.)

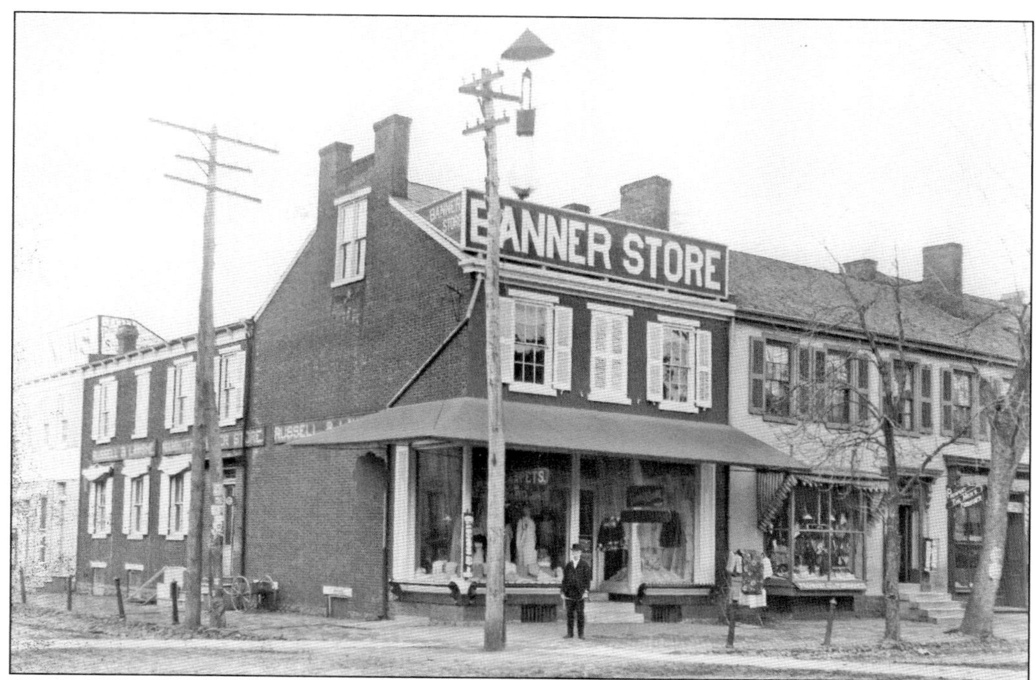

The owners of the Banner Store, Russell and Lawshe, advertised general merchandise, dry goods, and "pretty and useful articles suitable for Christmas presents." The Georgian-style brick building seen above was erected in 1835 at 238 Market Street and at times was home to a jewelry store, a drugstore, and the Banner Store. Throughout much of the 20th century, two menswear stores occupied it. (UCHS 82.4.7.4GGGa.)

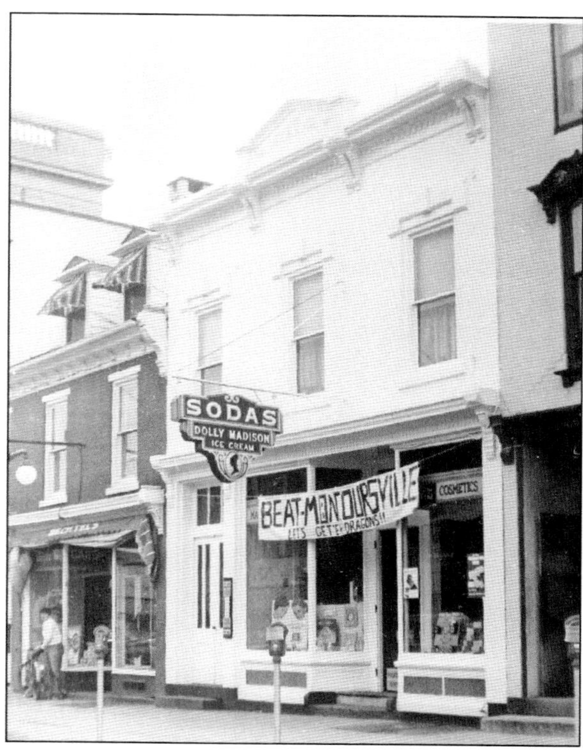

The left side of this 1945 photograph shows Bechtel's Dairy Restaurant before it moved out along Route 15. Next to it is the Bennett and Moyer Drugstore. In addition to dispensing prescriptions, Bennett and Moyer had a small ice cream counter, sold a line of general goods such as cosmetics, and developed camera film. The banner hanging across the storefront supports the Lewisburg High School football team in an upcoming game against rival Montoursville. (PHM.)

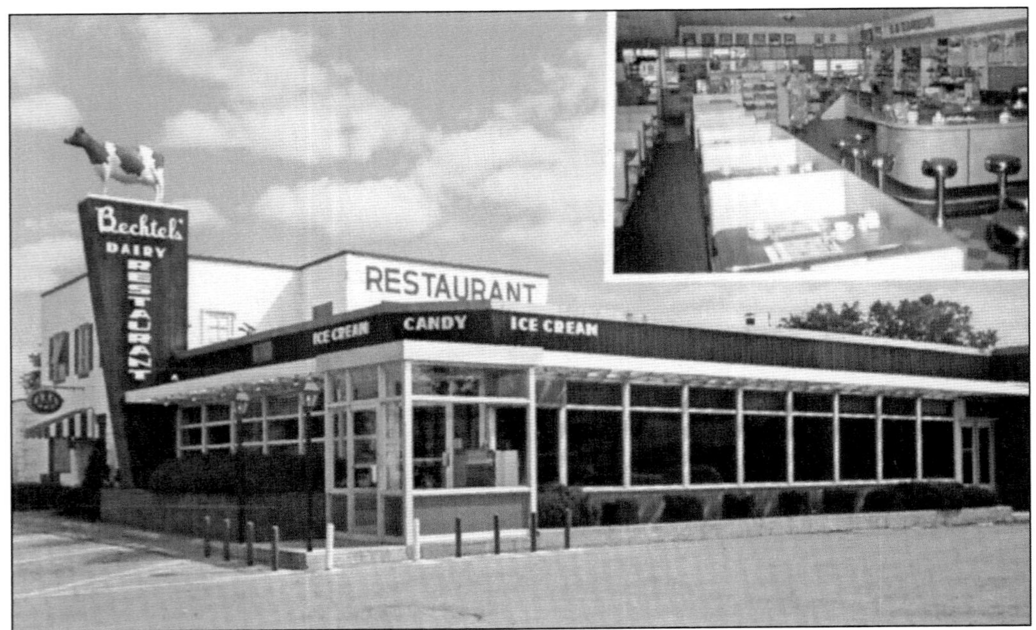

Lott Bechtel began the Citizens' Milk Company in 1923, making home deliveries of dairy products to customers in the Lewisburg area. He soon opened a restaurant, which was on Market Street until 1955, when it moved out along Route 15. The restaurant with the cow on top was a local landmark until it closed in 2006. On one occasion, a Bucknell fraternity absconded with the cow; it later appeared in that year's homecoming parade. (PHM.)

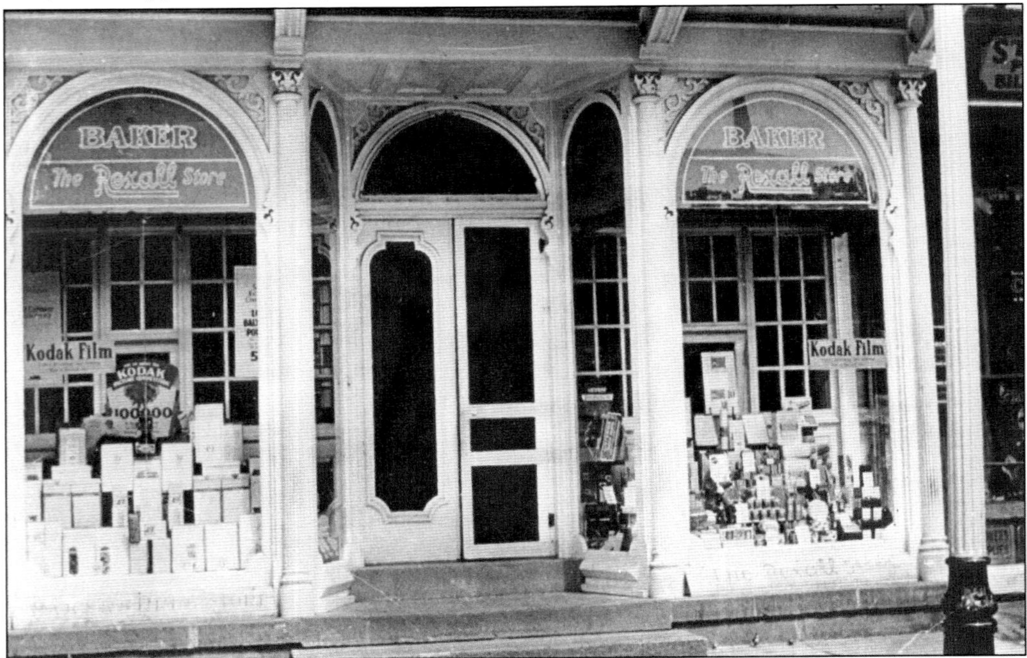

Baker's Pharmacy in downtown Lewisburg was a typical small-town drugstore. In addition to its primary capacity as a center for prescriptions and associated merchandise, Baker's sold and developed Kodak film and various sundries. Baker's was "The Rexall Store," independently operated, but affiliated with the national chain selling Rexall brand products. (UCHS P82.4.9.41a.)

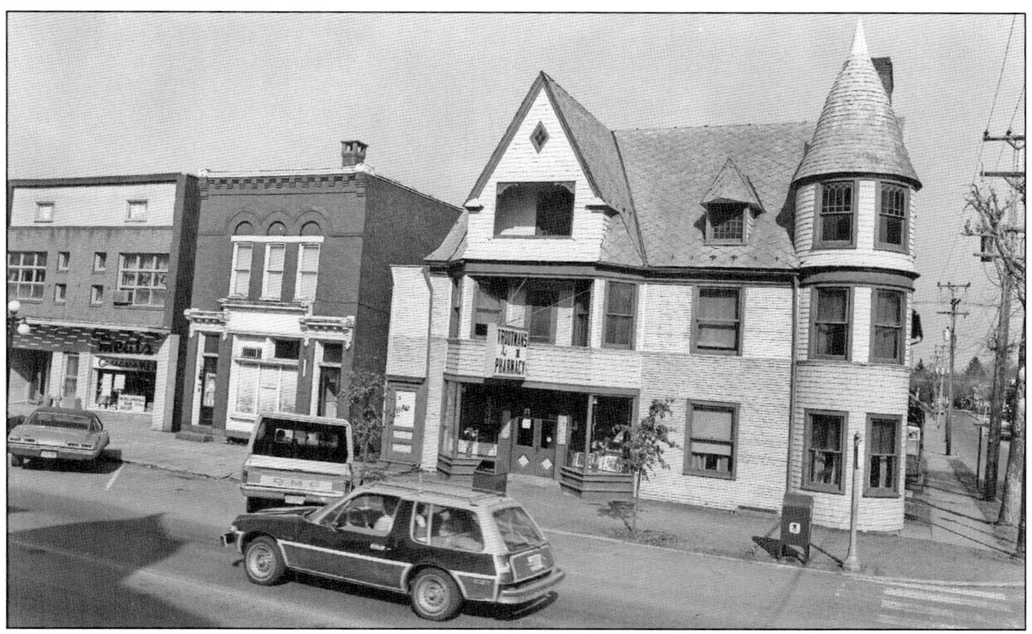

The building at 202 Market Street was a frame structure erected in 1811 and then converted into its present Queen Anne style in 1890. There was a pharmacy in this building from 1841, when Jonathan Wolfe started the town's first such business, until 1992. The pharmacy here was considered to be the longest-lived pharmacy in the same building in the entire United States. (UCHS 89.5.15.35.)

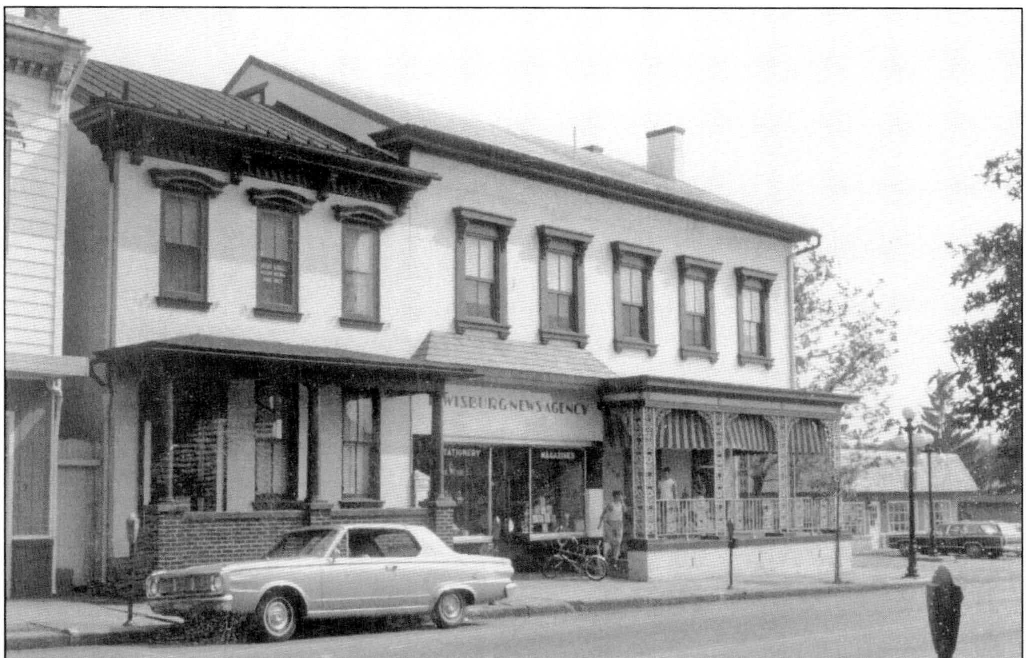

Another long-lived Lewisburg business is seen here in the 1960s. The Lewisburg News Agency opened in 1896 and survived until 2001. It was a small social center, where regulars came to buy newspapers, magazines, and paperbacks, together with nicotine products, candy, and bread. The building has been remodeled and is home to the Pineapple Inn Bed and Breakfast. (PHM.)

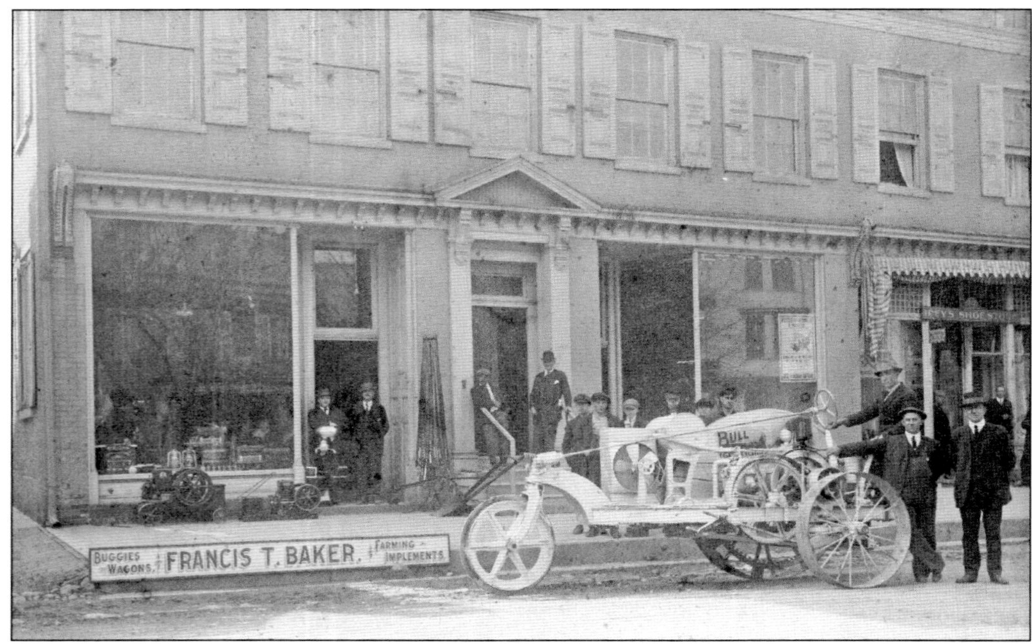

The first gasoline-powered tractor in Union County is shown here in 1913, parked in front of Francis T. Baker's farming implements store on Market Street in Lewisburg. Charles S. Zeller, the owner, spent $585 for the machine; he is the man on the right side of the door. His son Clarence sits in the tractor's seat. (Michael McWilliams.)

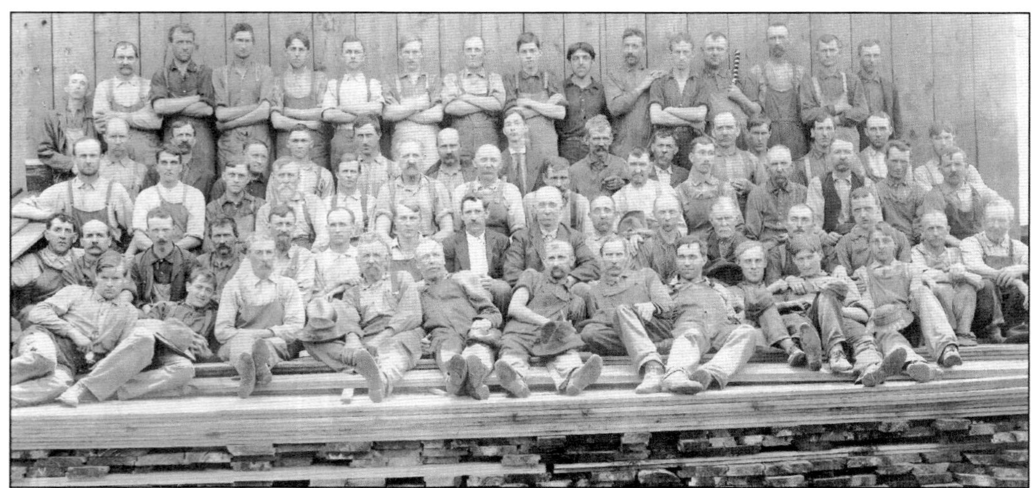

In 1897, Monroe Kulp started a lumbering business in the forest-covered mountains at the western end of Union County. His logging railway brought carloads of freshly cut wood to his sawmill located on North Fifteenth Street in Lewisburg. This *c.* 1905 photograph captures images of the sawmill's employees, ranging from seasoned veterans to inexperienced youths. (UCHS 80.8.3.)

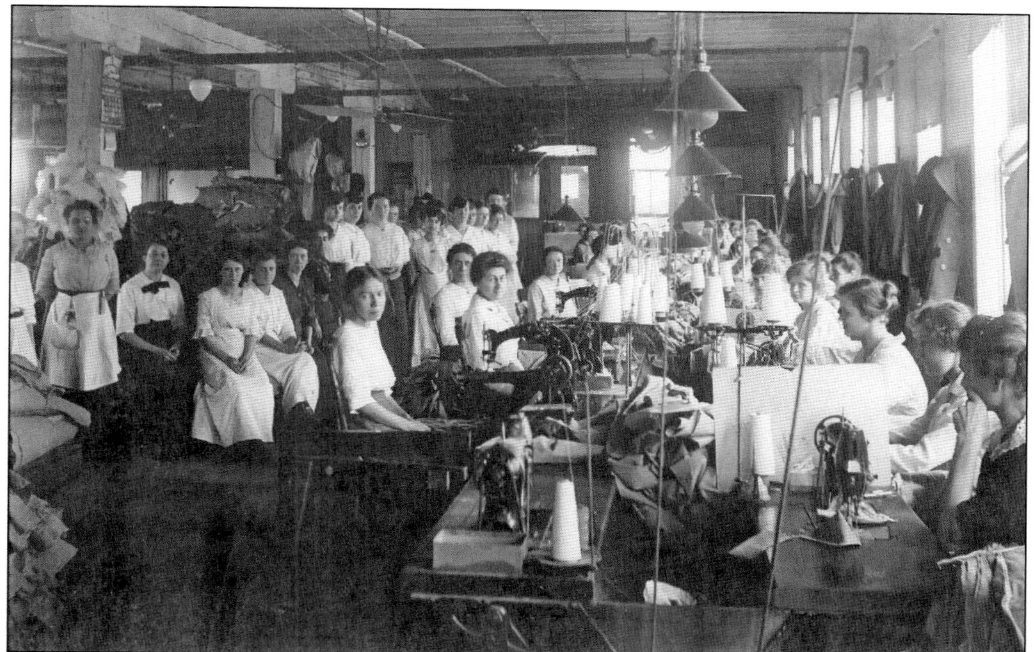

Here are the women who worked in (Joseph) Mussers Knitting Factory on North Fifth Street. When this business opened in 1880, it employed 25 people. This view, taken sometime around 1910, shows at least twice that many women. The factory was still humming in the early 1930s. The site was later occupied by the warehouse for a local plumbing company. (UCHS 1995.10.3.)

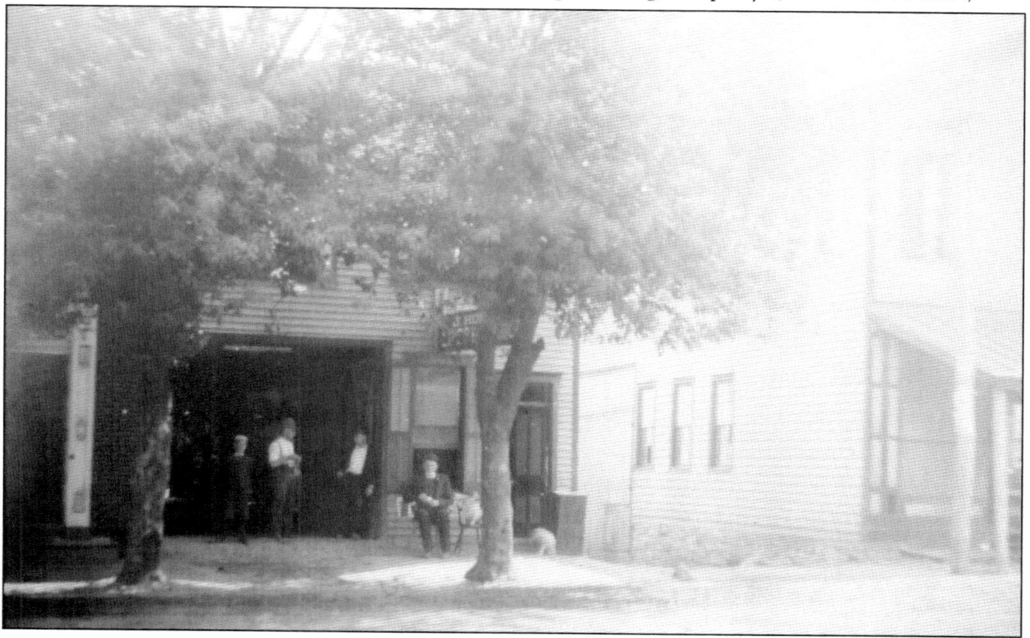

This photograph was taken on December 17, 1906. It shows Jacob Horam's livery stable on North Second Street where the Reliable Furniture Store was afterwards located; a law office now occupies the site. Livery stables were often located near hotels; Horam's was across the street from the Baker House. These stables rented out horses and carriages to hotel guests and local residents alike. (PHM.)

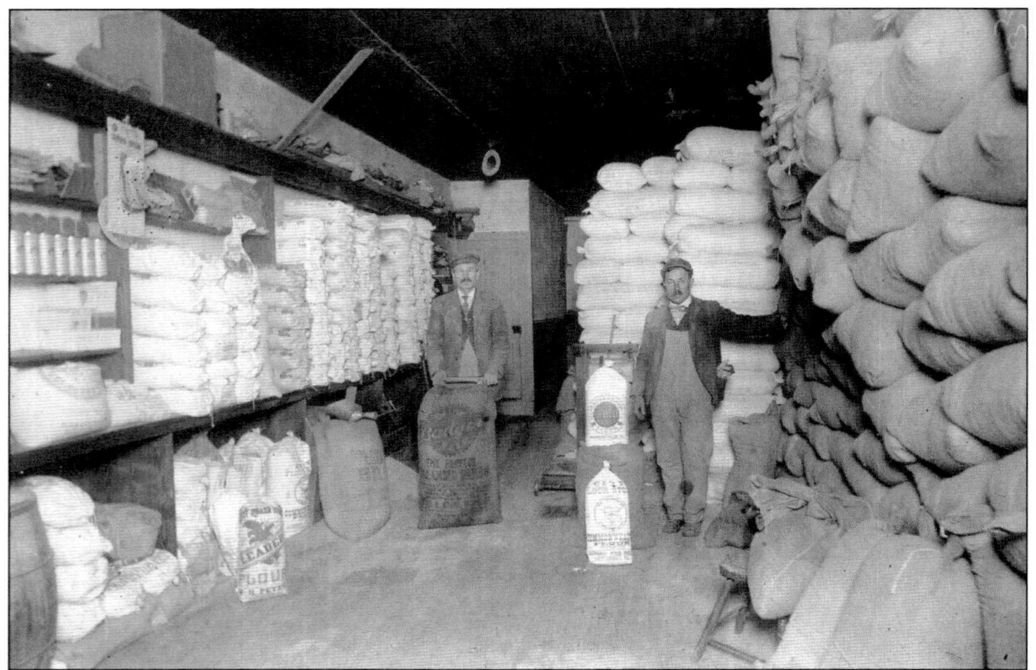

Taken in the mid-1930s, this scene shows the interior of Ed Noll's Feed and Farm Implements store, located near the present Campus Theatre. Noll is on the right with a man known only as "Foster" holding a bag of cow feed. Noll operated his business from the 1920s until 1955. (Charlotte and Robert Smith.)

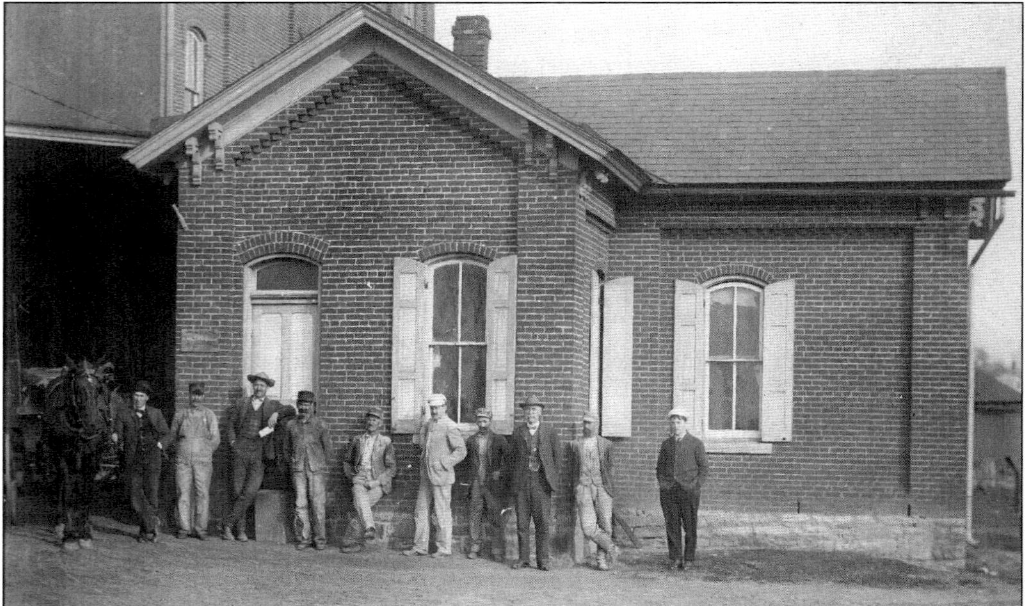

In 1883, shortly after the Shamokin, Sunbury, and Lewisburg Railroad (a subsidiary of the Philadelphia and Reading) came to Lewisburg, Cyrus Hoffa started the Buffalo Mills near the intersection of this new rail line with the Pennsylvania Railroad in Lewisburg. Hoffa's mill remained in the family until 1927, when the Dietrich and Gambrill Mills of Frederick, Maryland, acquired the business. This view shows the offices of the milling establishment. (UCHS 89.5.6.8.)

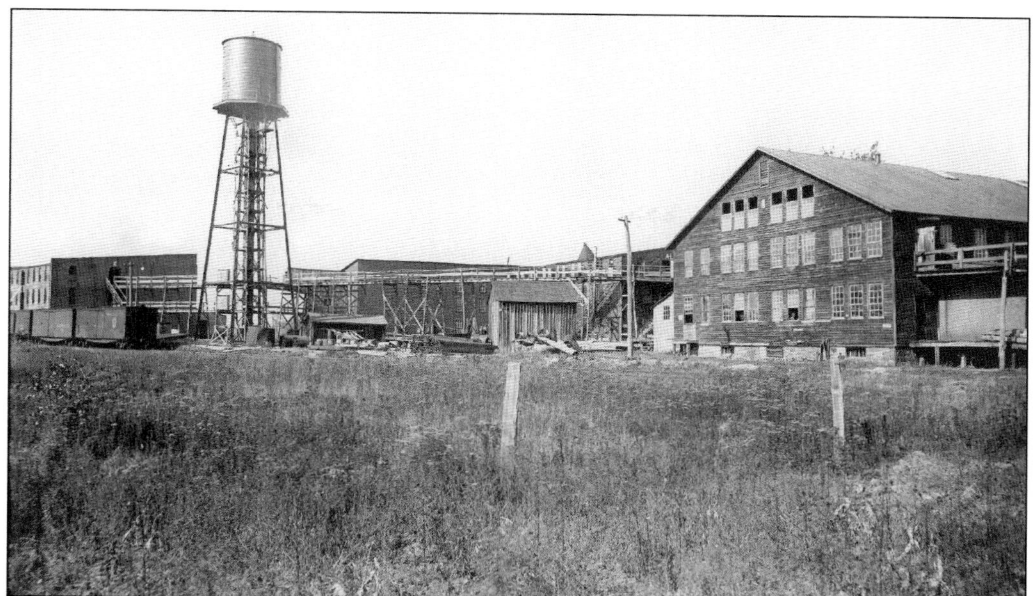

The Lewisburg Nail Works began operations in 1884 and was located along the Lewisburg and Tyrone Railroad, a subsidiary of the Pennsylvania Railroad. In 1886, it produced 300, one-hundred-pound kegs of nails each day. Products were sent all across the country. The Nail Works occupied the site later taken over by Pennsylvania House. (Nada Gray.)

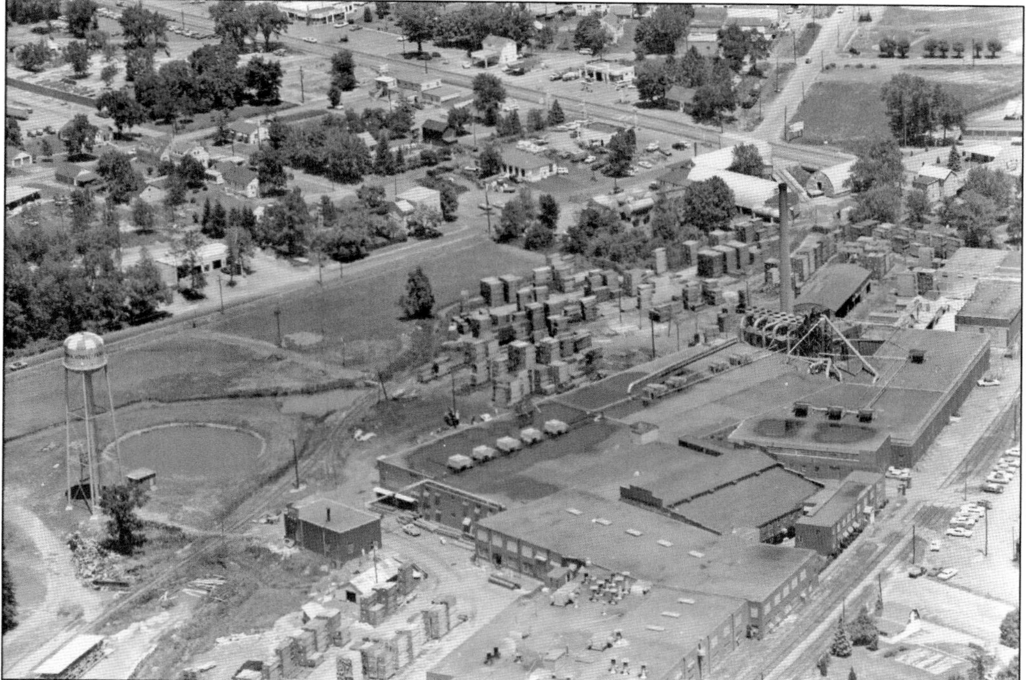

The aerial view here shows Pennsylvania House sometime in the early 1960s, with the modern finishing building at the bottom. A series of fires throughout the company's existence were the result of flammable liquids used to finish the company's fine lines of furniture. The old Lewisburg Chair Company became Pennsylvania House in 1961 and continued in business until 2004. The company was one of Lewisburg's largest employers. (UCHS.)

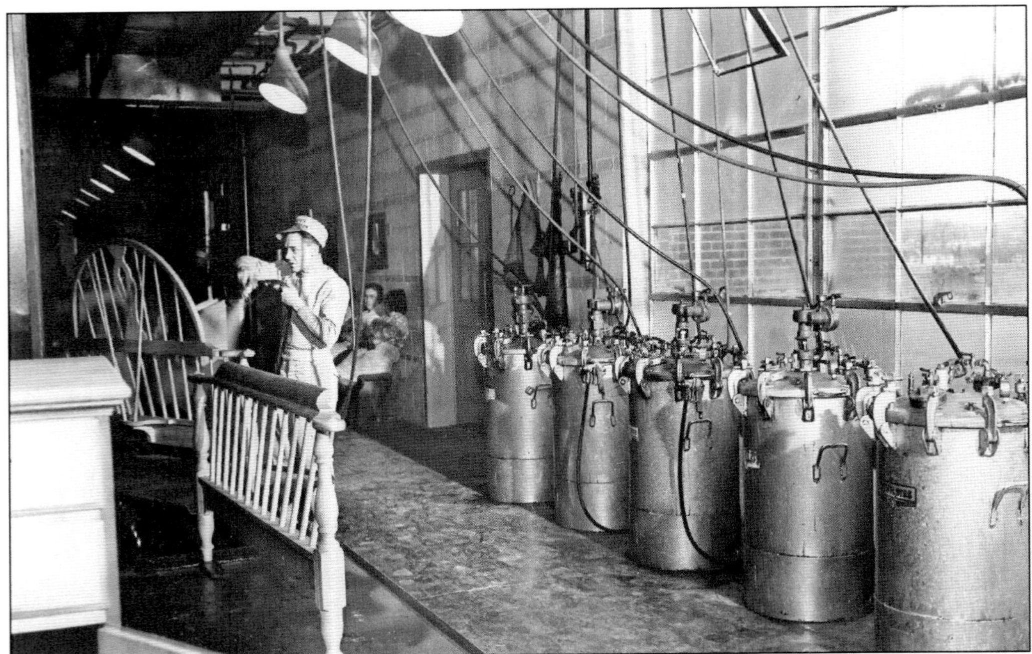

A Pennsylvania House worker in the finishing room sprays a piece of furniture that is on a moving track. Workers applied a pre-finish stain to even out the grains, then sprayed on a stain, hand wiped this coat, and then sent the piece to an oven. A final coat of finish spray followed by a lacquer completed the piece, which was then baked yet again. (UCHS.)

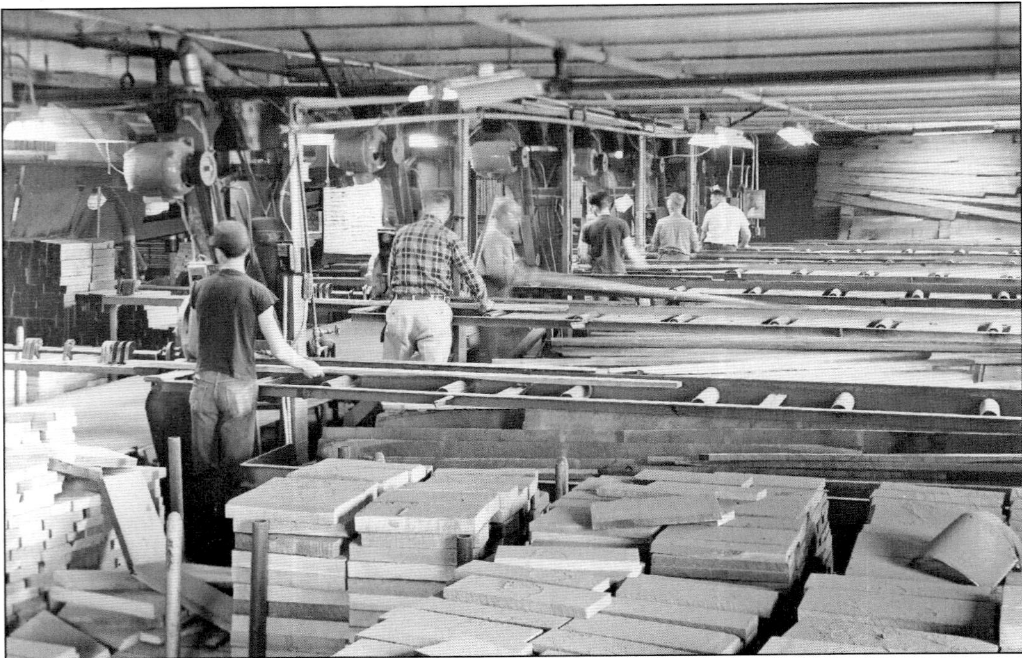

This scene shows the interior of the lumber mill building of Pennsylvania House. In the background is a stack of lumber destined to become furniture. The men shown here are sawing the wood into measured pieces that will be assembled into whatever order has come in to be filled. The foreground shows piles of these cut pieces. (UCHS.)

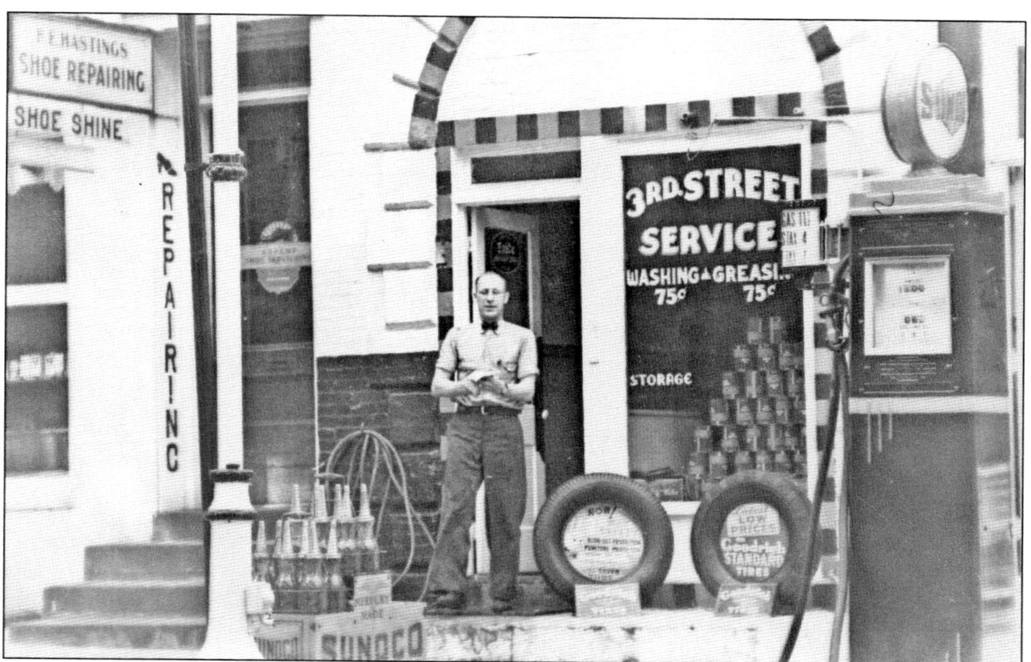

After the Opera House burned in a fire in December 1908, enterprising business owners reused the part of the building that survived along South Third Street. On the left is the F. F. Hastings Shoe Repair, while the owner of the 3rd Street Service Station stands in front of his shop entrance. (UCHS 94.27.13.)

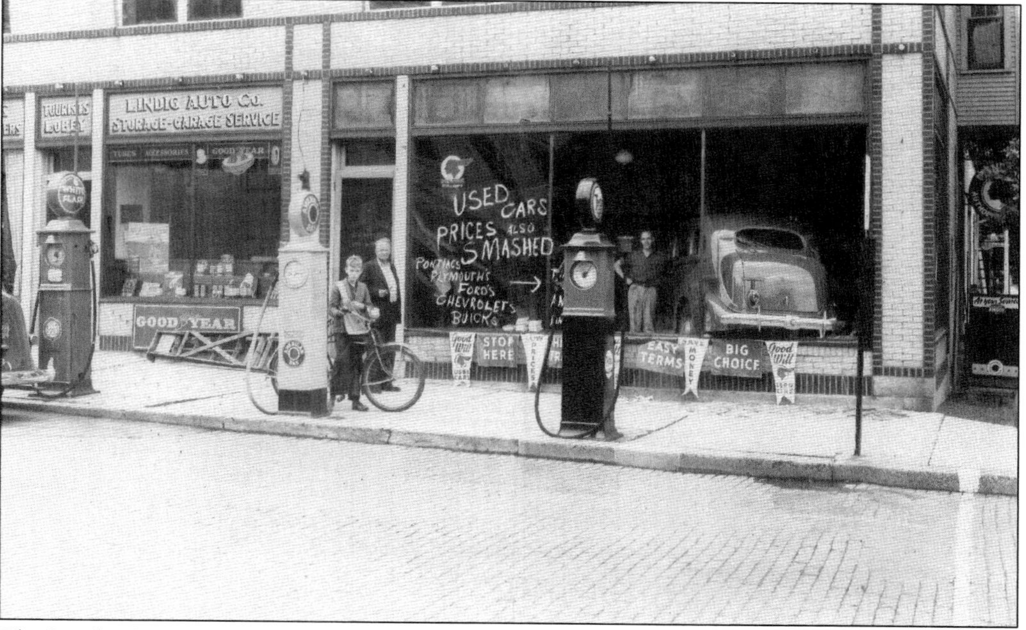

The Lindig Auto Company was literally built over the small stream known as Bull Run, which flowed under Market Street near its intersection with Sixth Street. This full-service business dispensed gasoline and provided a full line of supplies for automobiles; a garage in the rear of the building contained repair space. Note the brick-lined Market Street in front of the store. (Harold Walters.)

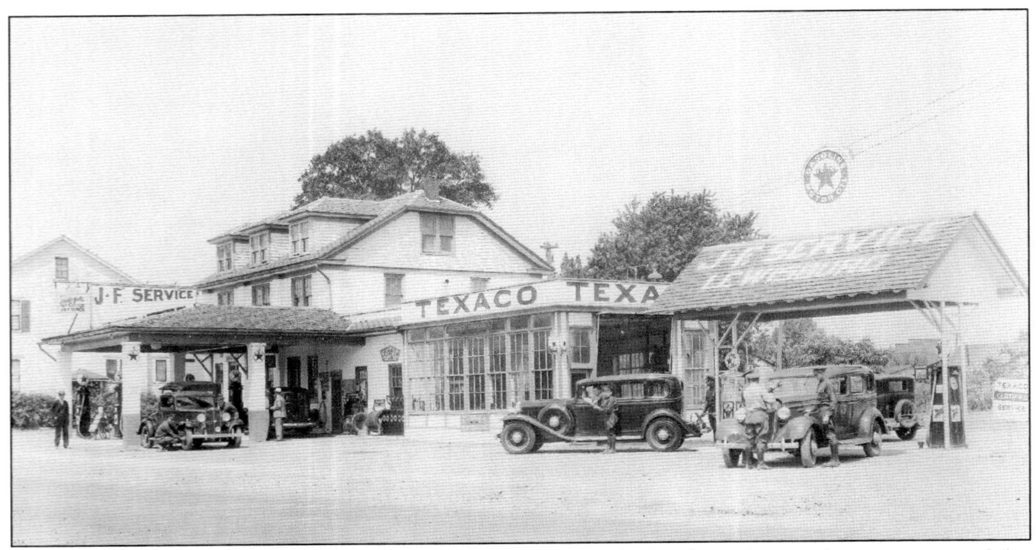

Robert Johnson and Harry Fegley's "J. & F. Service" was located on the northwest corner of the intersection of Market Street with Route 15. It was a full-service automobile station dispensing Texaco gasoline and selling all sorts of auto products such as new tires, oil, and windshield wipers. This Donald Ross image captures the work on a busy day. Shorn of its service station trappings, the building is now home to a beer distributor. (UCHS.)

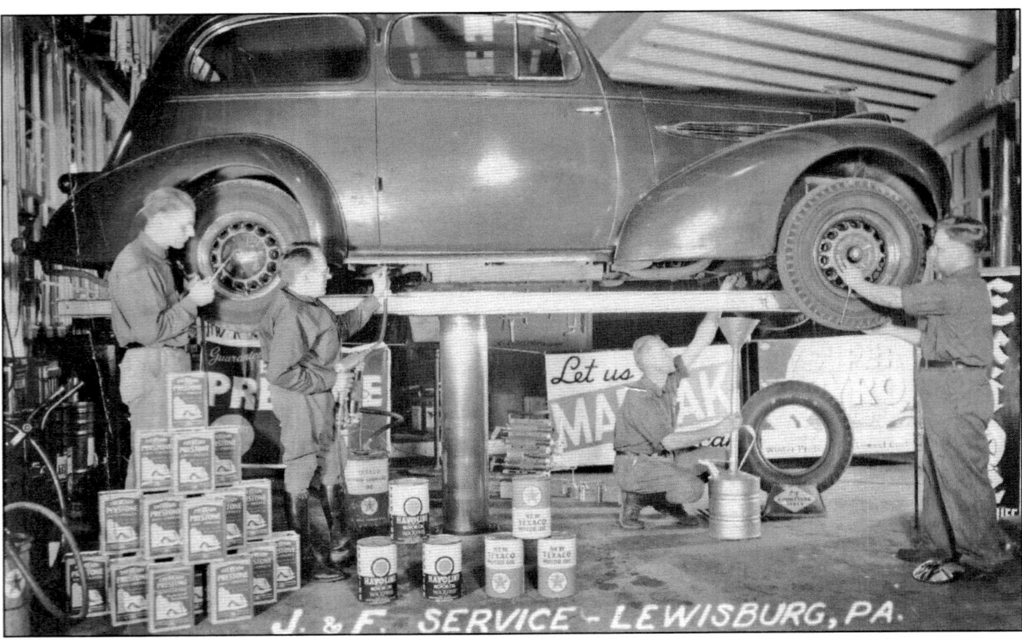

This is the interior of the Johnson-Fegley automobile service station pictured above. The increasing availability of automobiles led to a corresponding increase in service stations. As Route 15 became busier, stations such as Johnson-Fegley's became popular and profitable. One can see piles of the latest automotive supplies and a crew of trained mechanics for a car's every need. (UCHS 2002.6.1.)

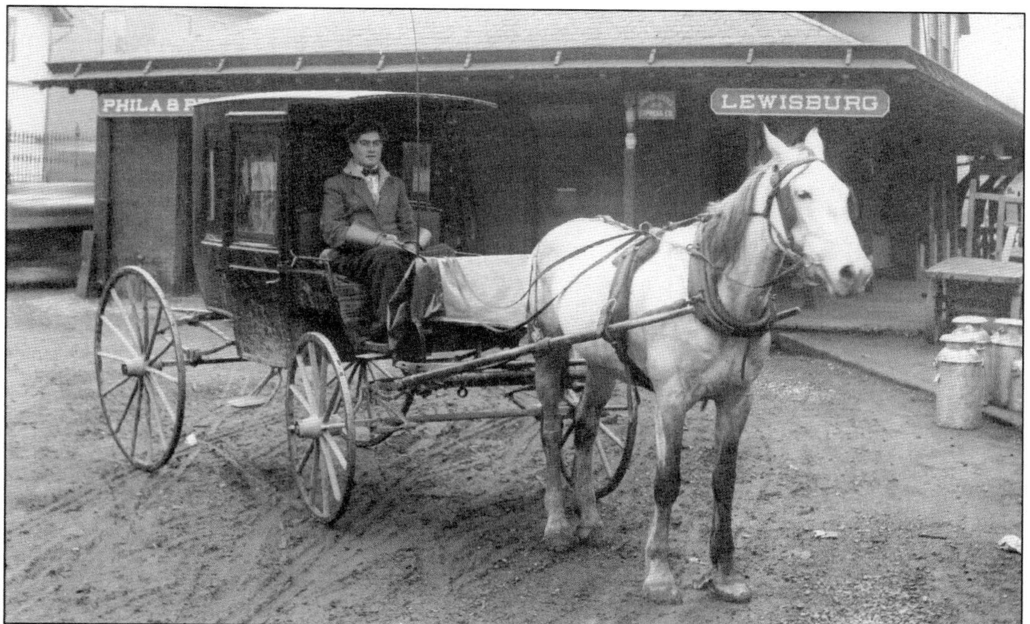

Frank W. Himmelreich advertised his "freight drayman and baggage transfer" business that served Lewisburg and vicinity. His advertisement asked customers to either call him or leave orders and checks at Baker's Drugstore. He is seen here with a delivery vehicle at the Reading Railroad station. In essence, Himmelreich's business was a combination of express delivery and taxi services. (Dorothy Reish.)

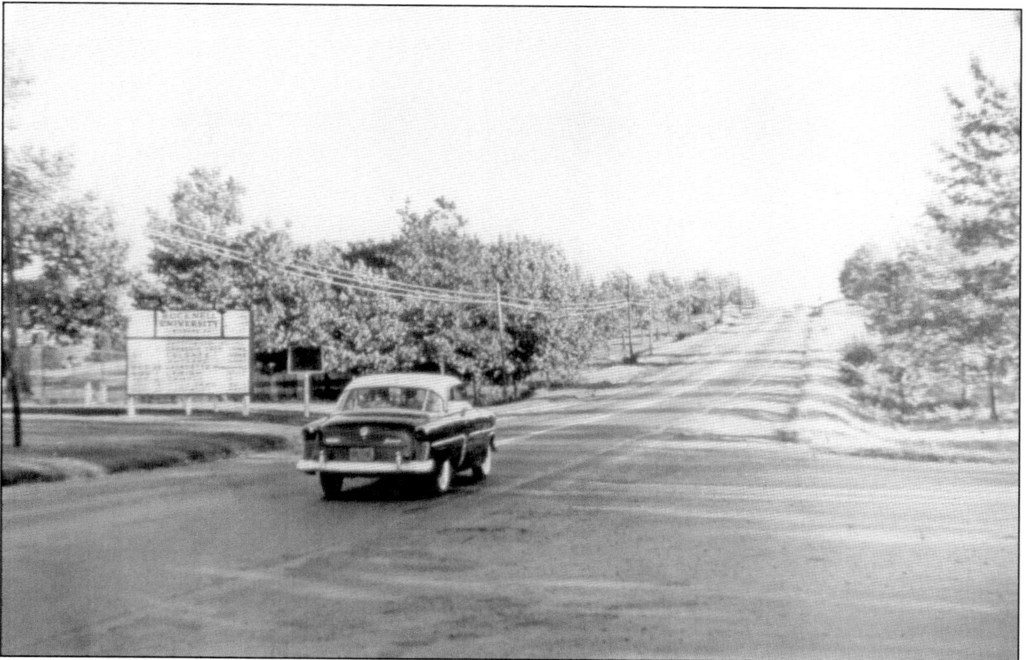

The entrance to Bucknell University, off Route 15, is shown here in this 1950s view. Route 15 was still a tree-lined, two-lane road. As both the university and traffic steadily grew, Route 15 was widened to four lanes with additional turning lanes and a blinking yellow light installed to warn drivers to be careful. Then came a traffic light that better controlled this busy intersection. (PHM.)

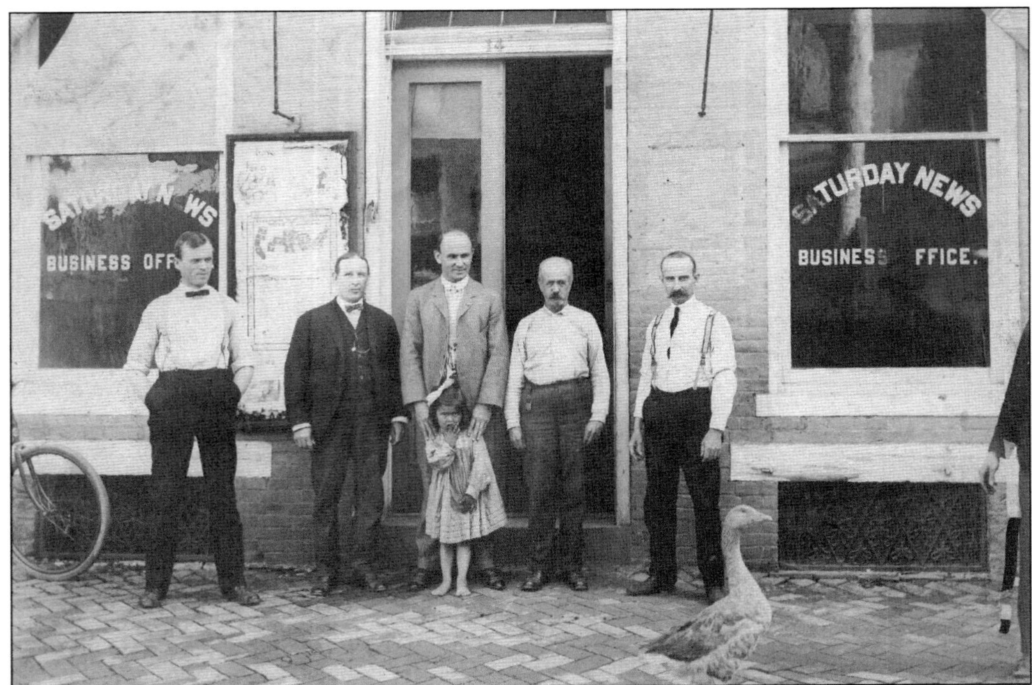

The staff of the Lewisburg *Saturday News* poses in front of the paper's Market Street building. Editor Samuel Wolfe stands in the middle. The goose was a familiar sight in Lewisburg. Post office employee John Reamer daily pushed his mail cart from the post office to the town's two railroad stations to bring mail from the trains. His pet goose always followed him. (UCHS 70.9.13.)

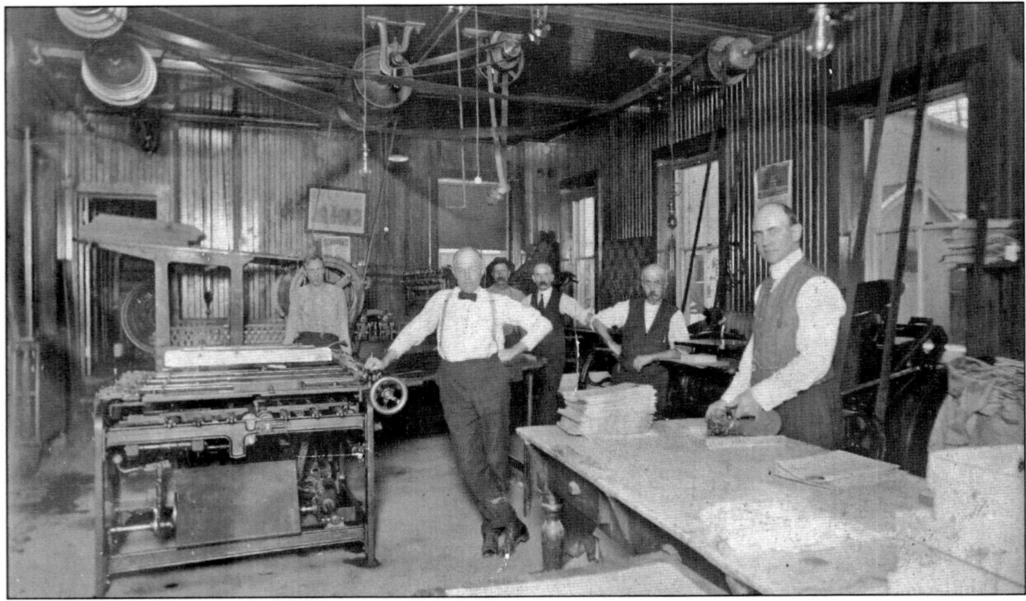

In 1882, Benjamin K. Focht started a newspaper in Lewisburg. At first called the *Local News*, the paper's title changed to the *Saturday News* and lasted until 1946, when it merged with the *Lewisburg Journal*. Here is the printing office, sometime after 1909, with, from left to right, Edward and William McCall, William Hood, A. J. Zimmerman, Ambrose Askins, and editor Samuel B. Wolfe. (UCHS 89.5.15.4.1.)

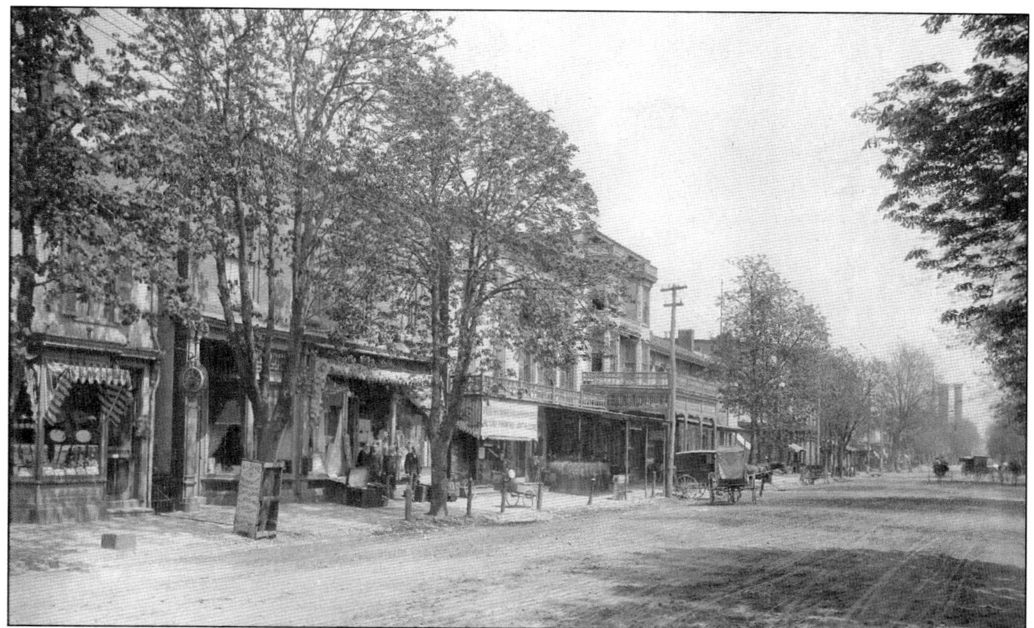

This undated scene shows the north side of the 300 block of Market Street. The advertising board on the sidewalk stands in front of eye specialist H. J. Nogel's shop. The group of men is in front of the Kline and Oldt Dry Goods store. On the right is a picture-framing shop (large awning to the right of a tree) and a shop dispensing ice cream (sign to the left of the utility pole). (UCHS 82.4.1.Aa.)

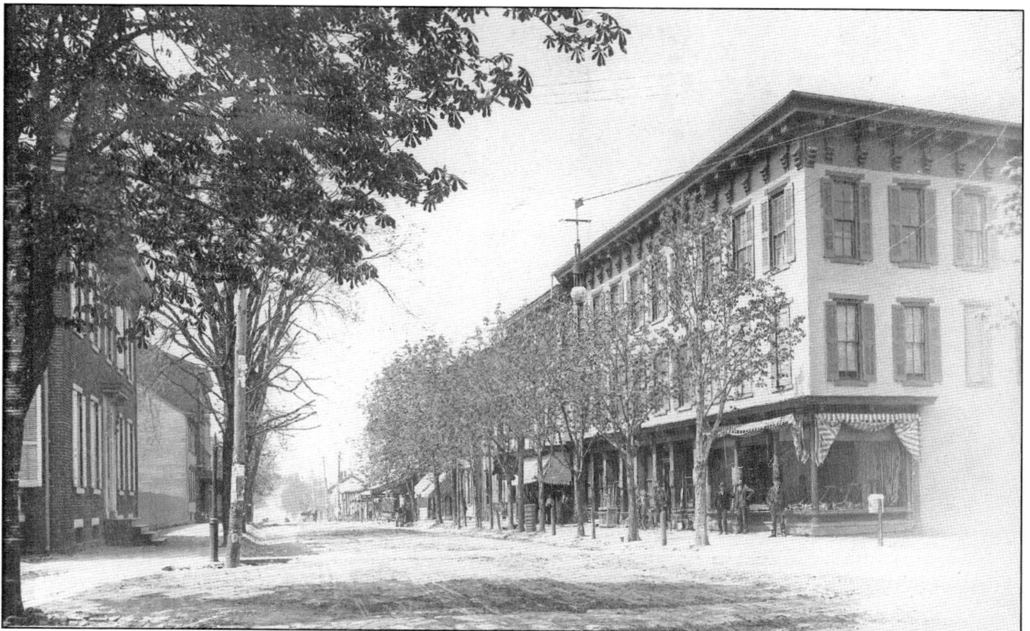

A companion image of the one above, this view looks west along Market Street from Fourth Street. The large structure that dominates this image is the C. Dreisbach Sons Hardware. The faint outline of the Chamberlin Building is discernible at the edge of the trees at the far end of this block. By around 1900, when this photograph was taken, the 500 block that straddled Bull Run was the western edge of the downtown business district. (UCHS 82.41.23.Ac.)

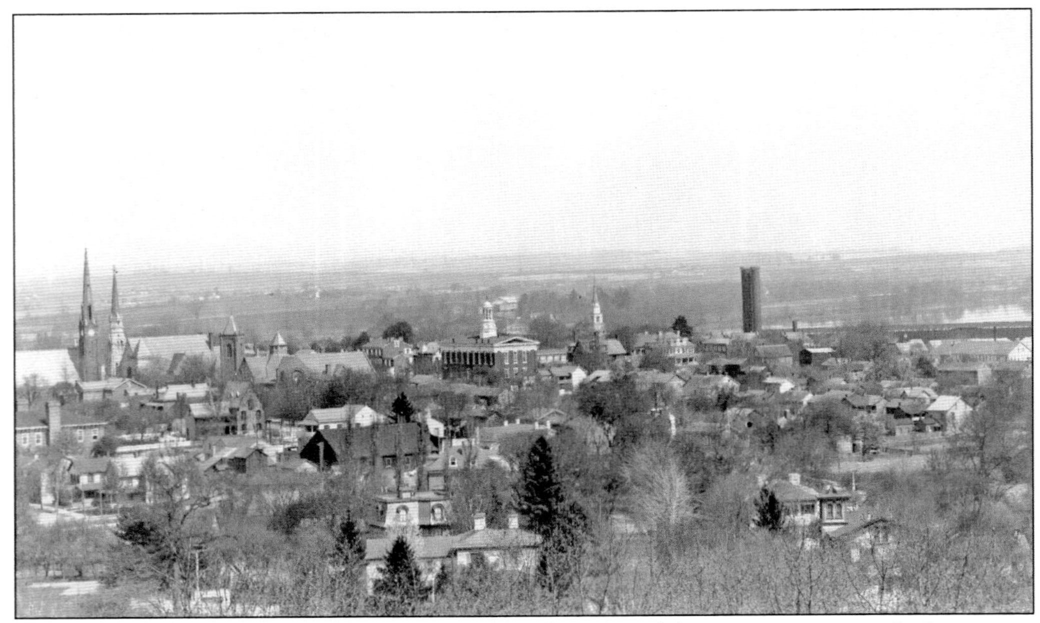

This pre-1906 view of Lewisburg presents an overall picture of the growing town at the beginning of the 20th century. The Union County Courthouse dominates the scene (center), with the Methodist and Lutheran churches on the left and the spire of the First Presbyterian Church to the right of the courthouse. The twin water towers of the Lewisburg Water Company loom just before the covered bridge on the right. (PHM.)

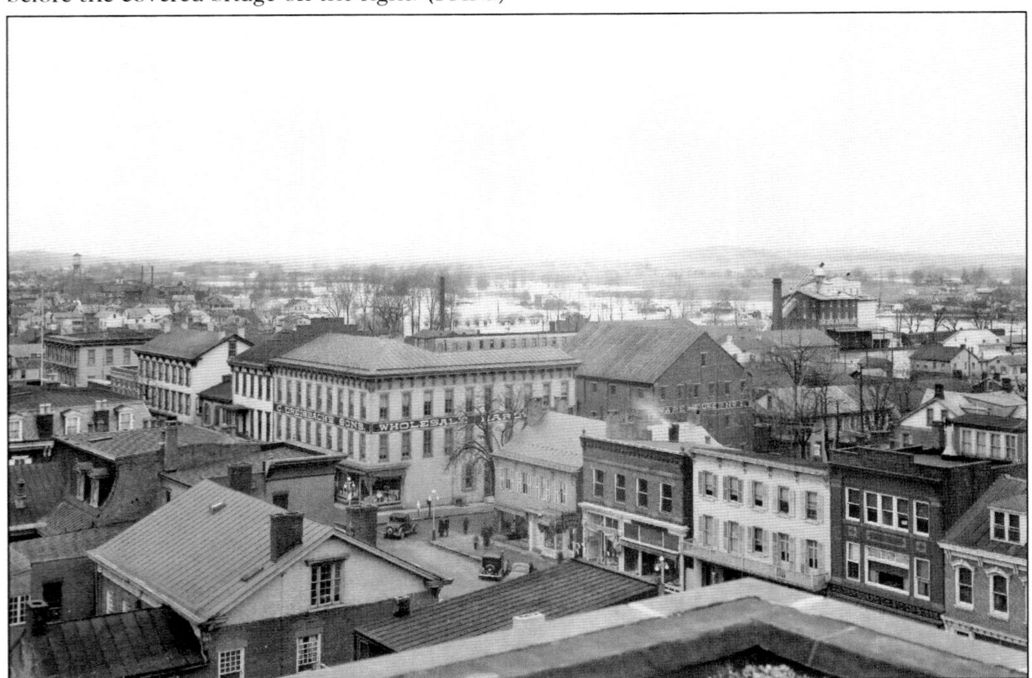

This 1936 view from the roof of the Federal Building shows high water from Buffalo Creek in the background at the height of the March flood. The C. Dreisbach Sons Hardware and warehouse are seen in the middle of this image. The water tower in the left distance marks the location of the Lewisburg Chair Company. (UCHS 89.15.19.1.)

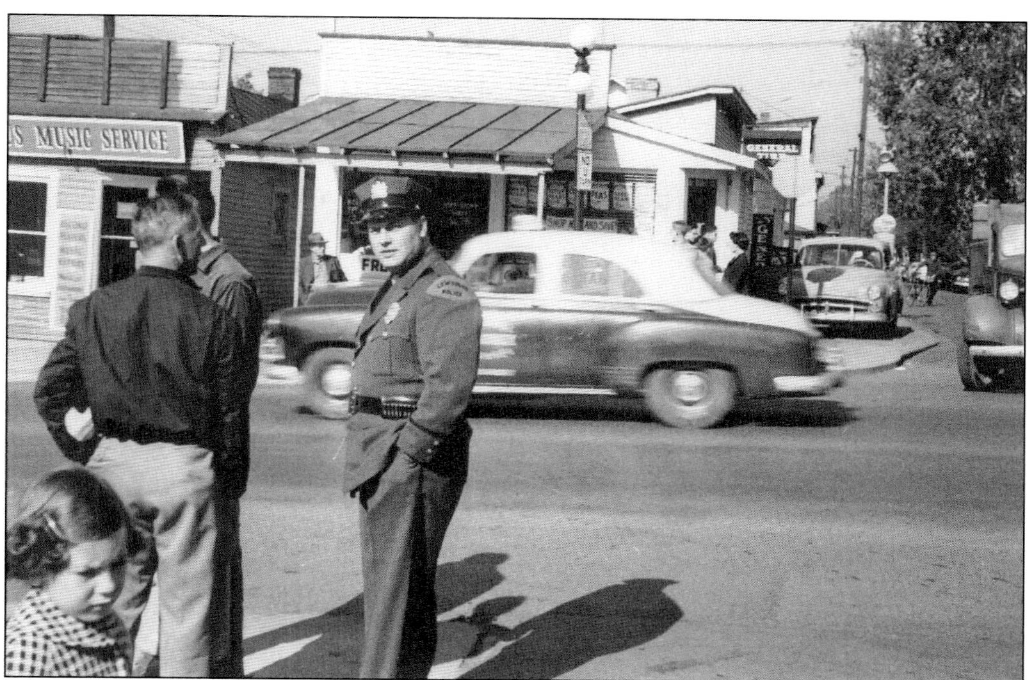

Lewisburg police officer Orvis Camel stands on the southern side of Market Street at Fifth Street in this undated photograph. Across the street is Flavio's Vegetable and Fruit Store, with an adjacent music store. Behind Flavio's on North Fifth Street is a small gas station. The corner is now a parking lot in front of a small office building. (Virginia Moore.)

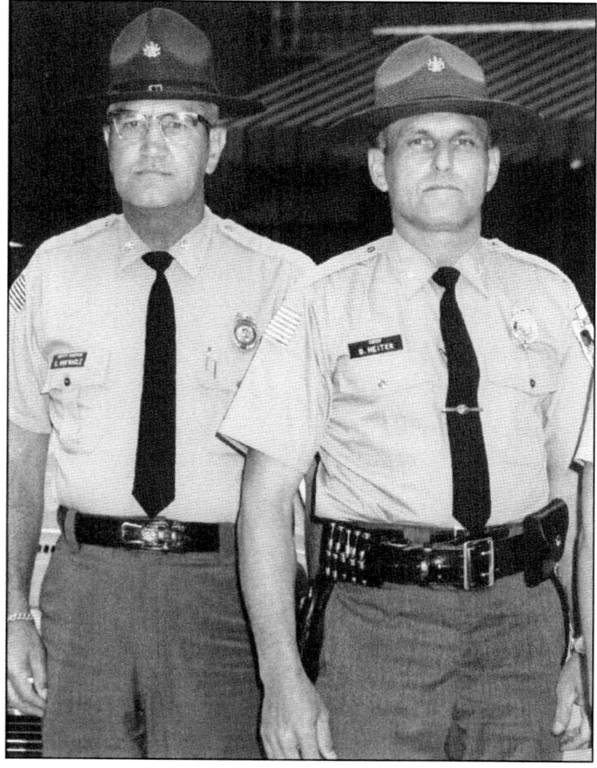

Gordon Hufnagle (left) was Lewisburg's chief of police from 1942 to 1970, when he was promoted to borough safety officer. He was succeeded as police chief by Donald Heiter (right), who filled the position until his death in 1996. Both were well loved in the community. Hufnagle Park and the Donald Heiter Community Center ensure that the names of both these men live on. (Paul Yost.)

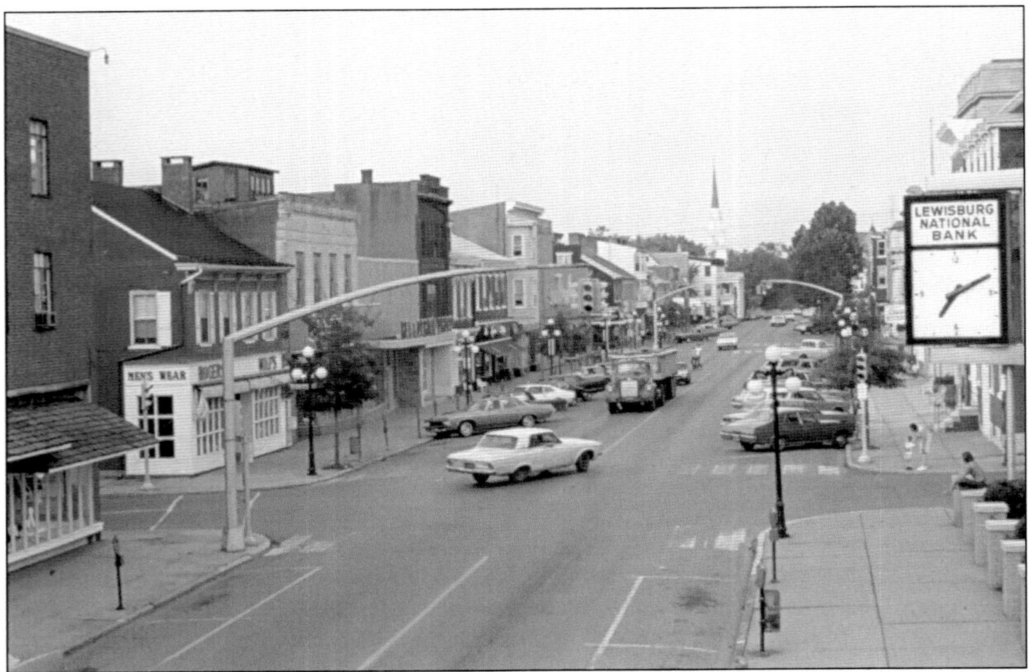

The intersection of Market and Fourth Streets is shown here in this 1960s-era image, looking east. The revolving clock of the Lewisburg National Bank was a local icon for decades before it was taken down in the 1990s after Northern Central Bank acquired the bank. Rea and Derick Drugs (in town since 1941, now CVS Pharmacy) and the J. J. Newberry dime store were among the staple businesses of a thriving downtown. (PHM.)

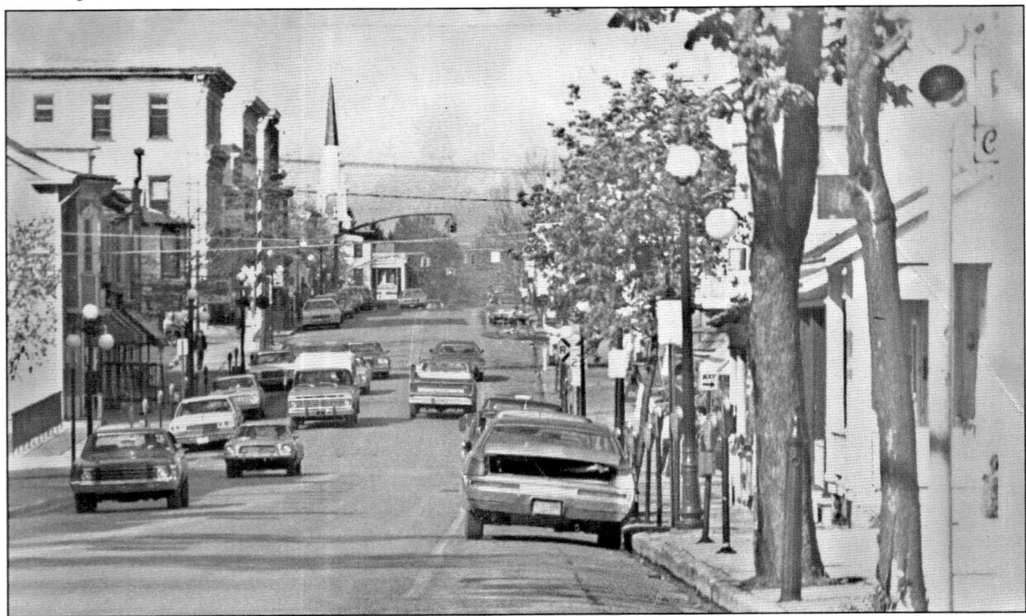

This image of the west end of the Lewisburg business district looks east on Market Street between Fifth and Sixth Streets. On the left is the Chamberlin Building, and in the distance is the spire of the First Presbyterian Church, with the columns of the Hotel Lewisburger in front. The dip in the road marks the location of Bull Run. (UCHS 89.5.24.19.)

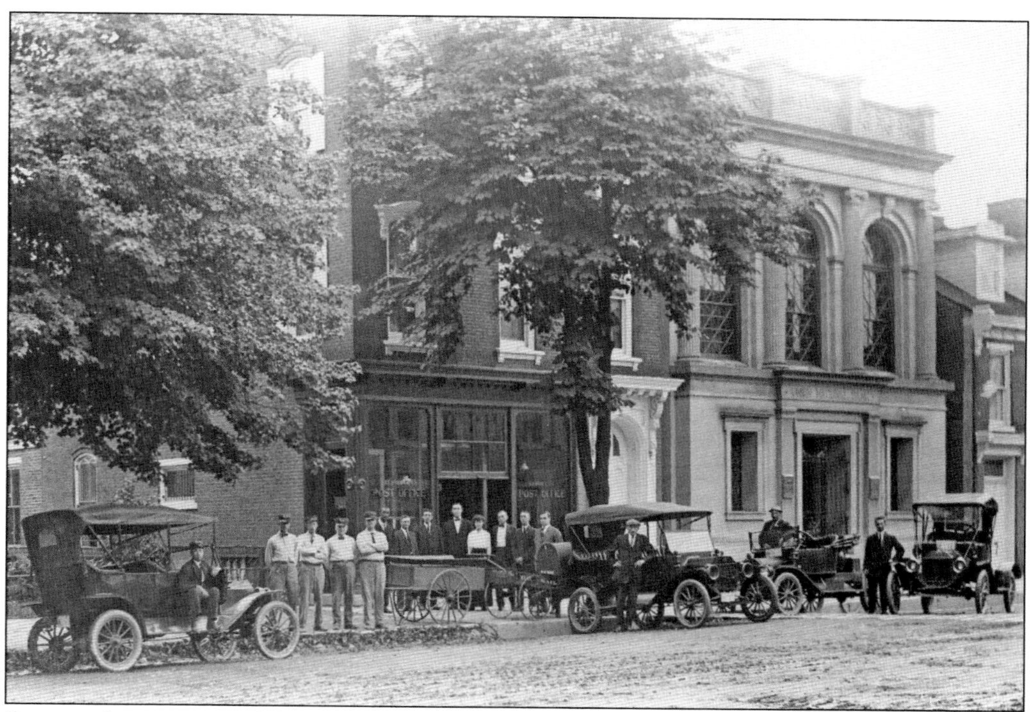

Prior to the opening of the Federal Building in 1933, the borough post office could be found at various locations. In 1913, the post office was located next to the Union National Bank on Market Street. In this image, postmaster Fred Kuntz wears a white shirt and stands to the right of clerk Bess Brown (the tallest man in the center behind the cart). The three men on the right are rural mail carriers with their vehicles. (UCHS 89.5.21.3.)

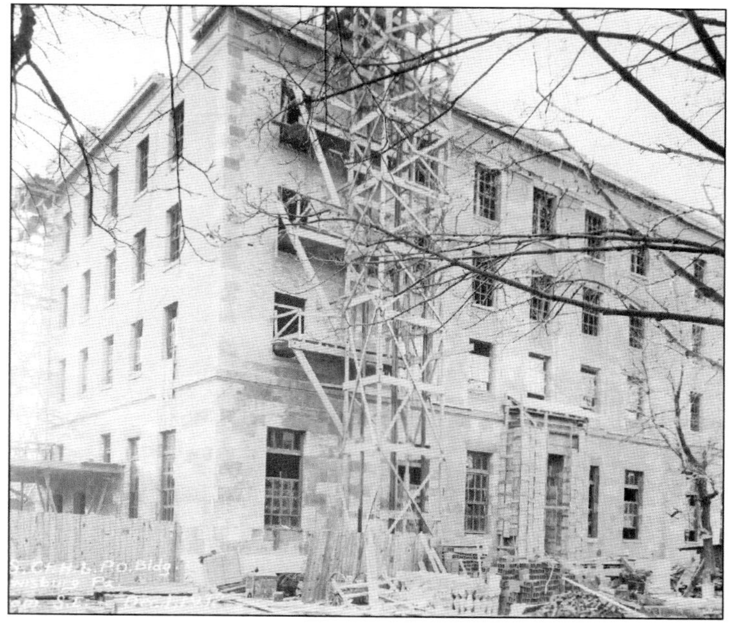

Taken on December 1, 1932, this photograph shows the construction progress of the new Federal Building, located on the southwest corner of Market and Third Streets. Dedicated in 1934, this structure housed the federal district court in its upper stories and the Lewisburg post office on the main floor. Although the post office remains in this building, the court was moved to Williamsport by 1987. (UCHS 2001.39.4.)

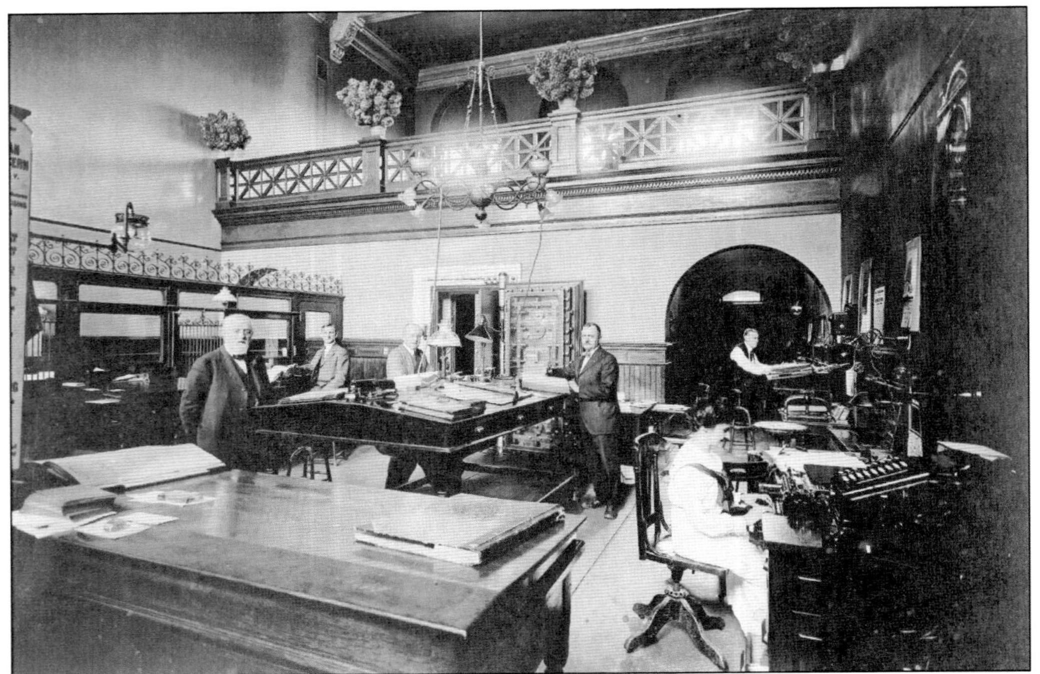

The interior of Union National Bank, now First National Bank, at 311 Market Street near South Third Street shows the use of both electric and gas lighting for illumination. In the photograph, taken around 1911–1912, the individuals are identified as, from left to right, J. K. Kramer, L. T. Butler, R. Hoffa, Mr. Forrest, Elva Baker, and C. Hoffa. (UCHS 1992.9.69.3.)

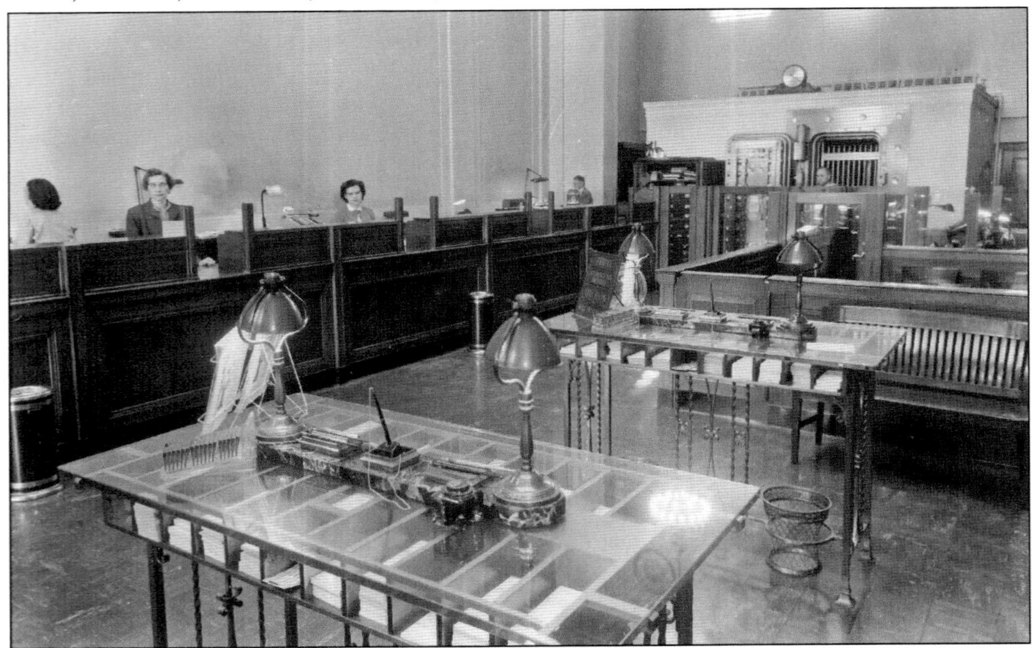

This more modern interior view of the lobby of the Union National Bank shows a sleeker, somewhat less personable environment. Here in 1957, behind protective high counters, the bank assures privacy and deters thieves. Individuals, identified only by last names, are, from left to right, Giunta, Eyer, Dougherty, Moyer, and Johnson. (UCHS 2006.45.11.)

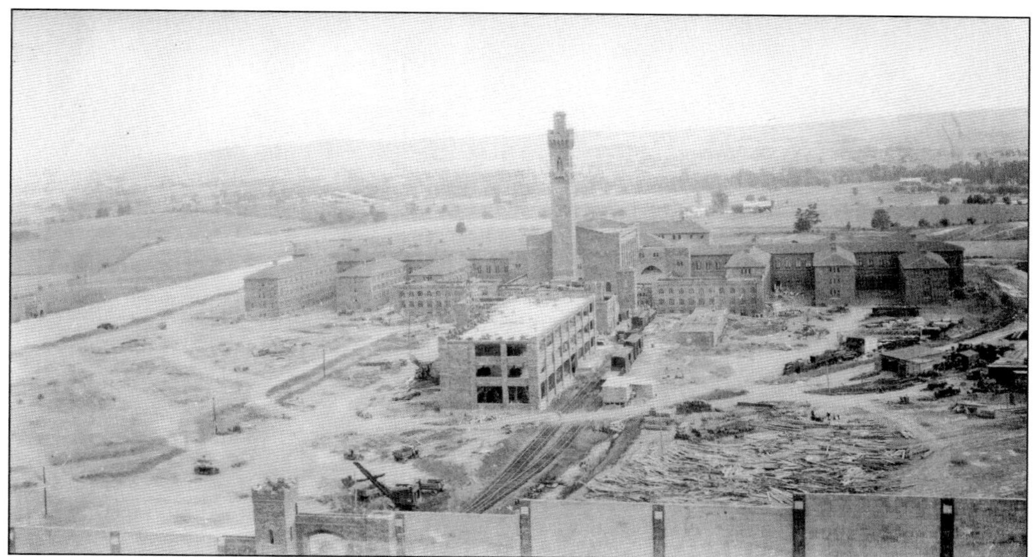

An aerial view shows the Northeastern Federal Penitentiary in Kelly Township under construction. Pres. Herbert Hoover signed the bill in 1930, authorizing the construction of a federal penitentiary in the northeast. The 1,000-acre site in Lewisburg consisted of 12 family farms that were sold to the government. Construction began in 1931. (Ronald Nornhold.)

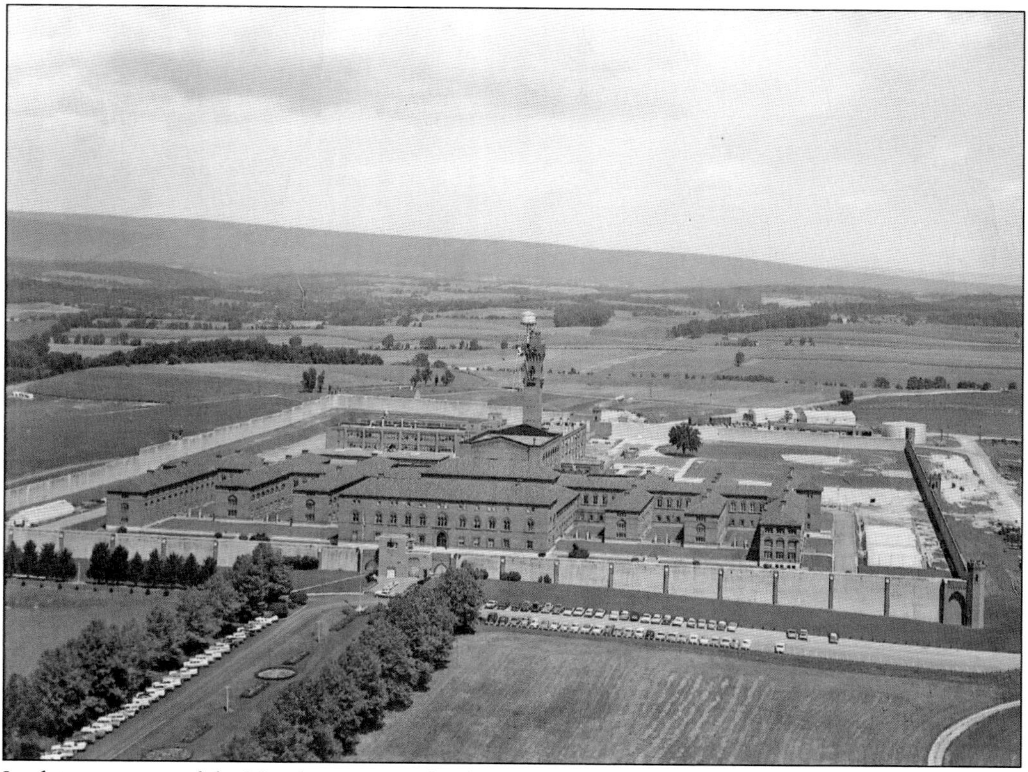

In this overview of the Northeastern Federal Penitentiary, the administration building is located directly behind the main entrance gate. A baseball diamond is visible in the upper right portion of the walled complex. The prison factory is located in the upper left corner. The smokestack, visible in the center, hovers over the prison theater. (National Archives.)

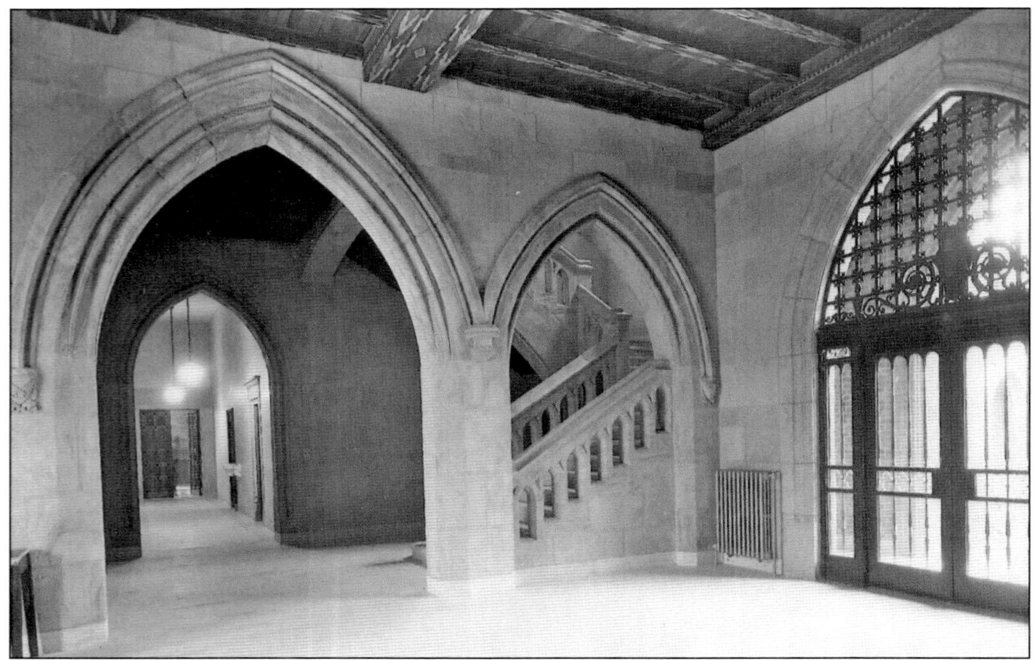

The entrance foyer of the administration building shows some of the Italian Renaissance–style features that characterize the penitentiary. Cast concrete was used to simulate the polychromed wooden ceiling, stone staircase, and arched doorways. The wrought iron gate at the right leads to the central courtyard. (National Archives.)

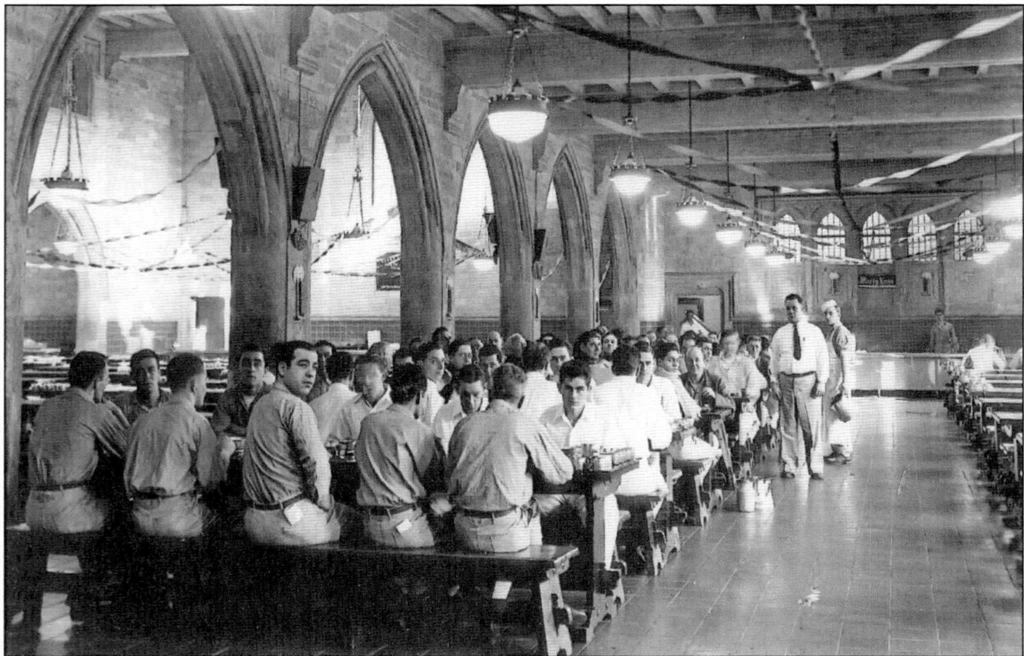

Inmates, shown here around 1950, eat in the prison's dining room. Alfred Hopkins, who was the architect for the whole prison complex, designed the tables and benches. When the construction was complete, pictures of the new penitentiary were never published for fear that the public would find the structure too plush. (National Archives.)

Three

Celebrating

Parades are, perhaps, the ultimate expression of community, and Lewisburg has had a lot of them. The town decorated itself and welcomed fraternal visitors from the region. Some exceptionally large parades celebrated the Odd Fellows. Annual homecoming and sports rally parades brought out the fans of the Lewisburg High School and Bucknell University teams. Other parades celebrated the nation's bicentennial in 1976 and Lewisburg's third century in 1985, holidays with children in Halloween costumes, Lewisburg's identity with a Victorian Christmas theme, Memorial Day, and the glorious return of World War I soldiers. Most recently, the Fourth of July parades have celebrated veterans of all wars and honored our national flag.

There were many other ways to celebrate. Clubs and leisure activities brought people together who shared similar interests. Drama clubs, civic clubs, the Opera House, sports teams, and school activities broke people out of their everyday work to times of special enjoyment. May Day events, especially those sponsored by the schools, are still remembered fondly. Hotels and motels attracted visitors on vacation. Restaurants, including the beloved Bechtel's with the cow on its roof, offered families a place to celebrate birthdays and anniversaries with a solid meal and many flavors of ice cream for dessert. Eventually the roads became good enough, and gasoline was still cheap enough to enjoy a ride in the country or to visit a local museum where memories are stored and reveal themselves to those who visit. Local photographers captured image after image of family members dressed in their finery. Even though they were pictured with stern faces, they were celebrating—a wedding, a birthday, a soldier's leaving, a young child's latest achievement, a new job, a garden, or a house. Photography itself is a celebration of a moment in time for the future.

Just as individuals have their own ways to celebrate and remember, the community has its ways. The celebration itself forges, strengthens, and maintains community in a way that binds us all to this place and to each other.

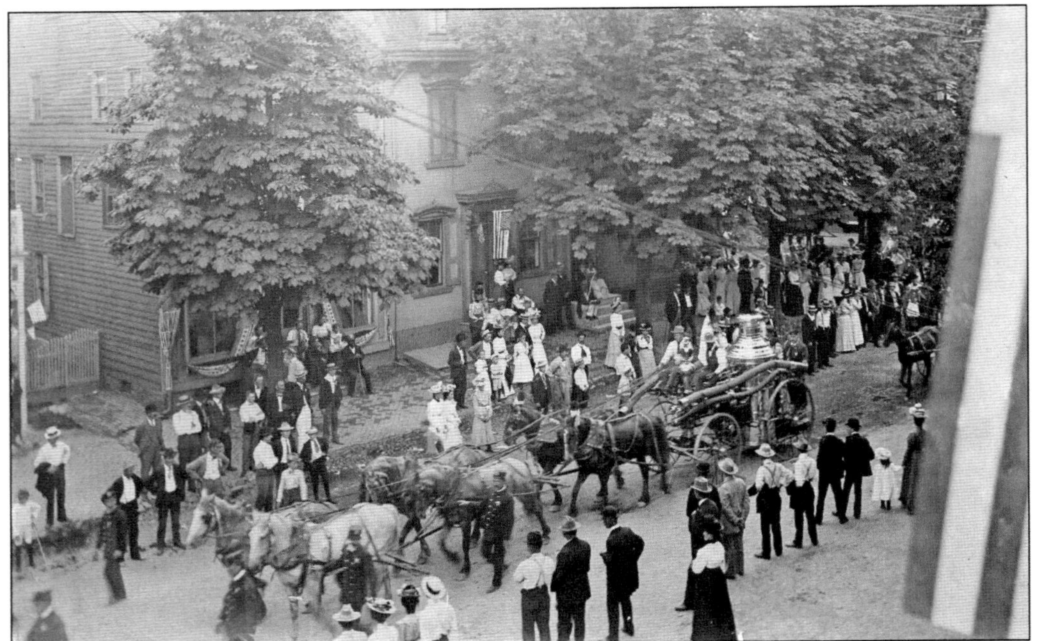

In this undated image, the original steamer purchased by William Cameron for the Lewisburg Fire Company parades through Lewisburg. Cameron paid $9,775 for the engine in 1874, together with carts and 2,500 feet of hose. This engine was in use until 1932, when it was retired and can be found today in the William Cameron Engine Company's museum. (PHM 1987.10.6.)

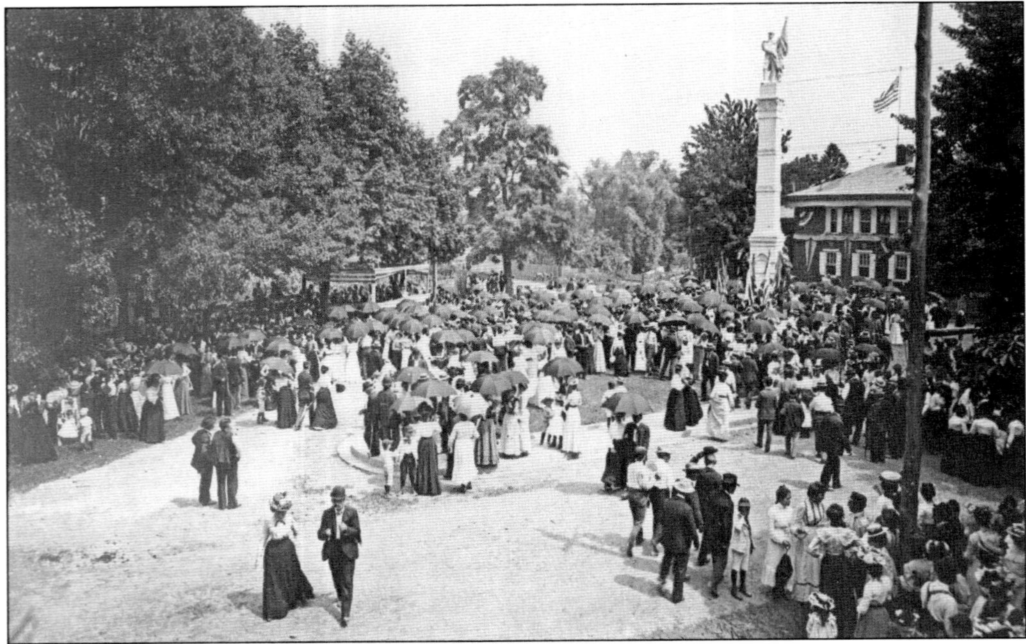

The erection of the Soldiers' Memorial Monument was celebrated in 1901. The monument commemorates Lewisburg's contribution to the Civil War, and similar ones grace focal points in other central Pennsylvania towns. It is a granite obelisk about 30 feet in height, topped by the figure of a Civil War soldier carved in granite. Copper figures of a soldier and a sailor stand on opposite sides of the monument's base. (UCHS 82.4.326Ba.)

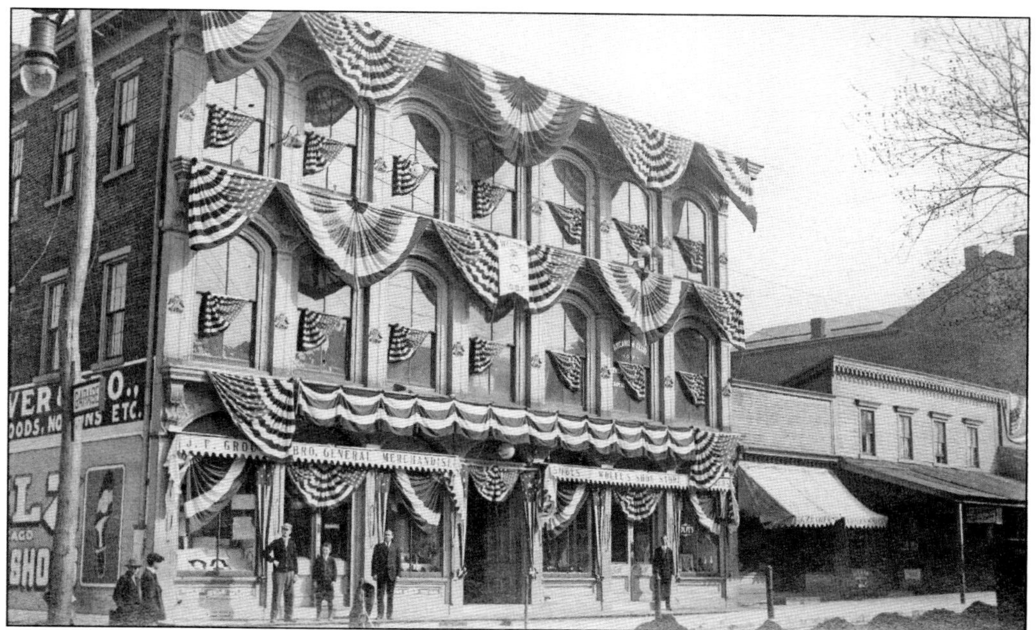

Architect William Palmer erected the Chamberlin Building at the intersection of Market and Fifth Streets in 1855. Also known as the "Iron Front Building," it is seen here decked out to celebrate an Odd Fellows convention in town. J. F. Groover's store occupied the left side of the building from 1904 to 1923, with Wolfe's Shoes on the right. In front of Groover's are three members of the Groover family—Obediah, Biehl, and J. Frank Groover. (Dorothy Reish.)

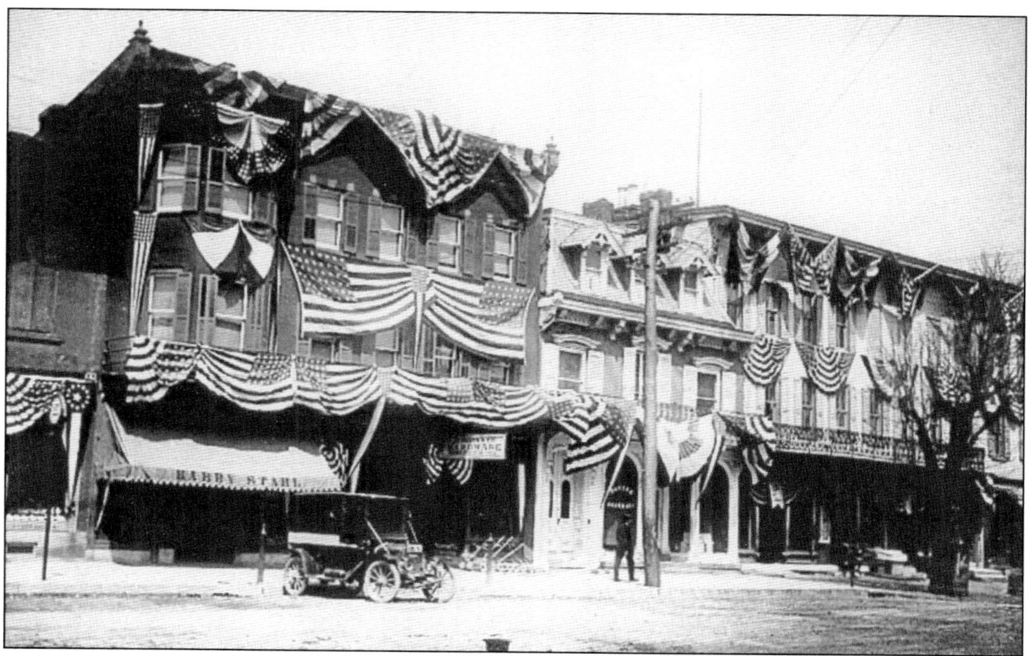

The north side of the 300 block of Market Street is decked out with flags in this undated image. Harry Stahl's grocery store is on the left, followed by a hardware store, pharmacy, dry goods emporium, and other stores. Lewisburg has always had a vibrant downtown, offering local residents the staples they need to maintain their households. (PHM.)

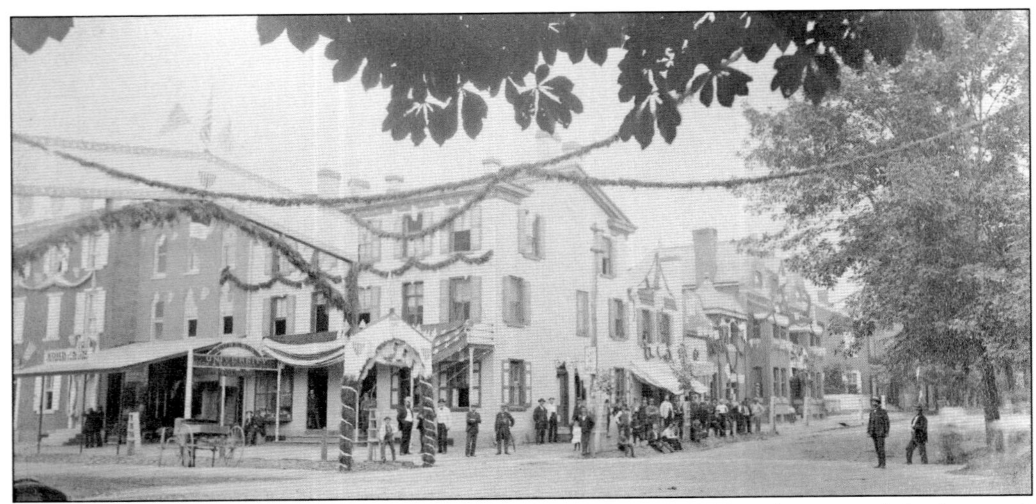

This was the southeast corner of Third and Market Streets in 1885 at the time of the fireman's convention. The parade route was festooned with arches, as was the custom of that time period. The large house on the corner no longer stands; it was demolished to make way for the Lewisburg Trust and Safe Deposit Company. (UCHS 85.221.)

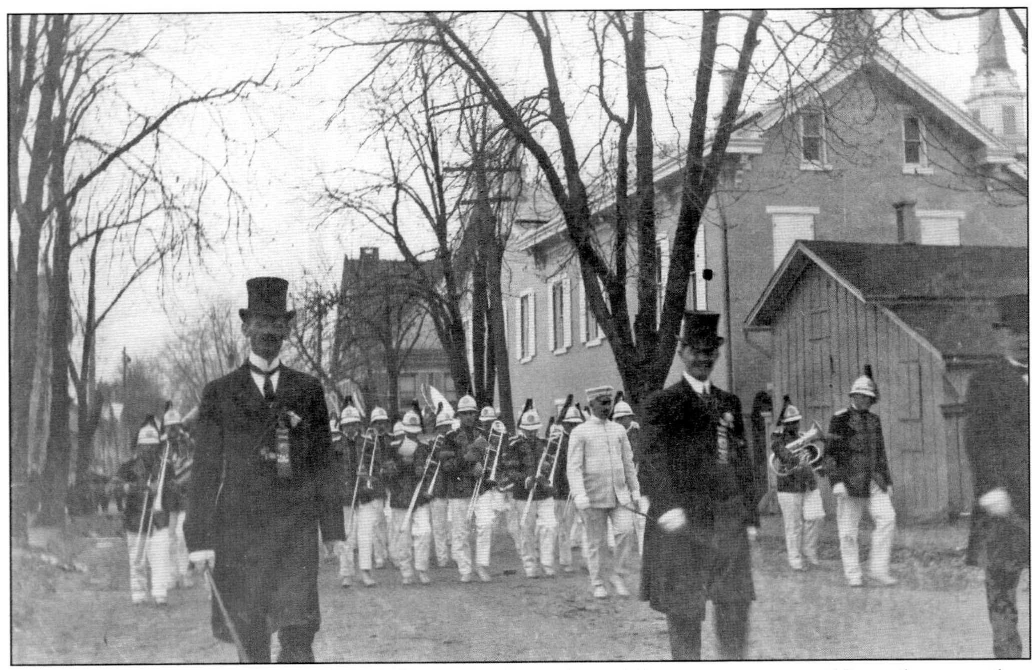

Parades have always been a big hit in downtown Lewisburg. This scene, captured by a photographer on April 24, 1912, shows the Berwick Cornet Band marching on North Front Street before swinging onto Market Street as a unit in the Odd Fellows parade that year. Newspapers indicated that perhaps 10,000 people watched this parade. (UCHS 95.1.1.)

Benjamin Focht (1863–1937) was a Republican politician, serving in the state legislature (1893–1897, 1901–1905) and in the national House of Representatives (1907–1913, 1915–1923, 1933–1937). He also established the *Saturday News* in 1882. Here he stands with son Brown in front of his newspaper office in 1918. He spared no expense to celebrate the end of World War I. (UCHS 89.5.1.12C.)

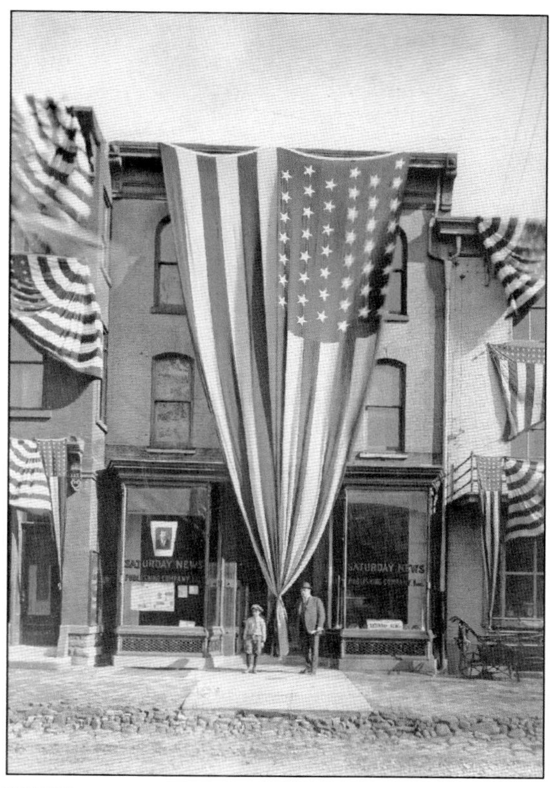

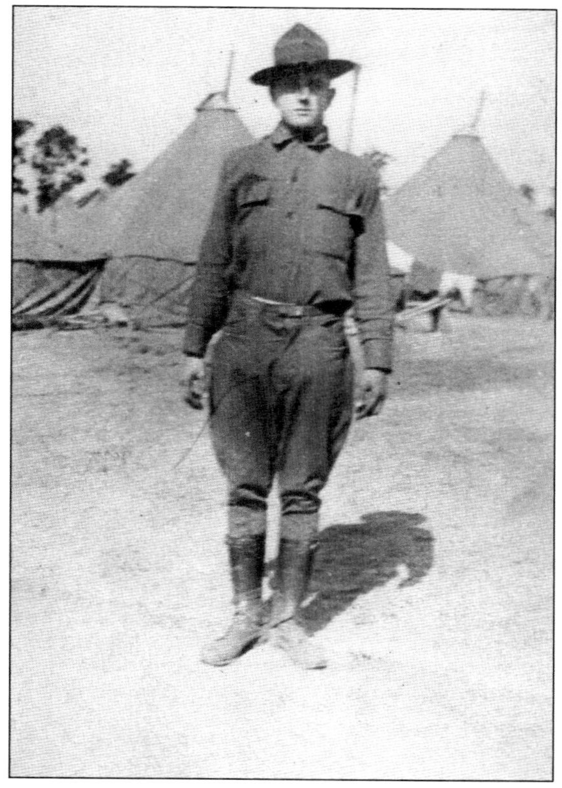

Bright Kratzer was born on a farm in East Buffalo Township. He enlisted in the army in 1917 and was assigned to a trench mortar battery. On September 26, 1918, a shell set off a munitions dump; Kratzer was one of six Lewisburg boys killed. His remains were brought back to Lewisburg in 1921 and buried in the cemetery. (June Harmon.)

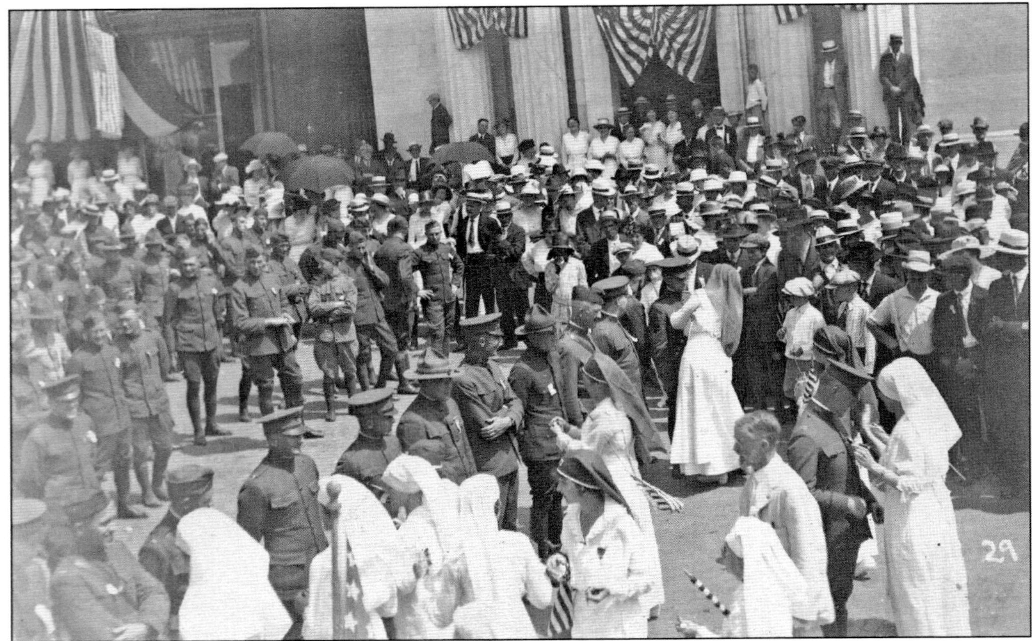

The 1919 World War I Homecoming Parade was reported to one of the best seen in the county for years. It was estimated that between 5,000 and 6,000 people were in the town. About 300 soldiers marched through the streets. Here the marching units are seen greeting one another in a real photo postcard produced by photographer Nelson Caulkins. (UCHS 2001.27.3.)

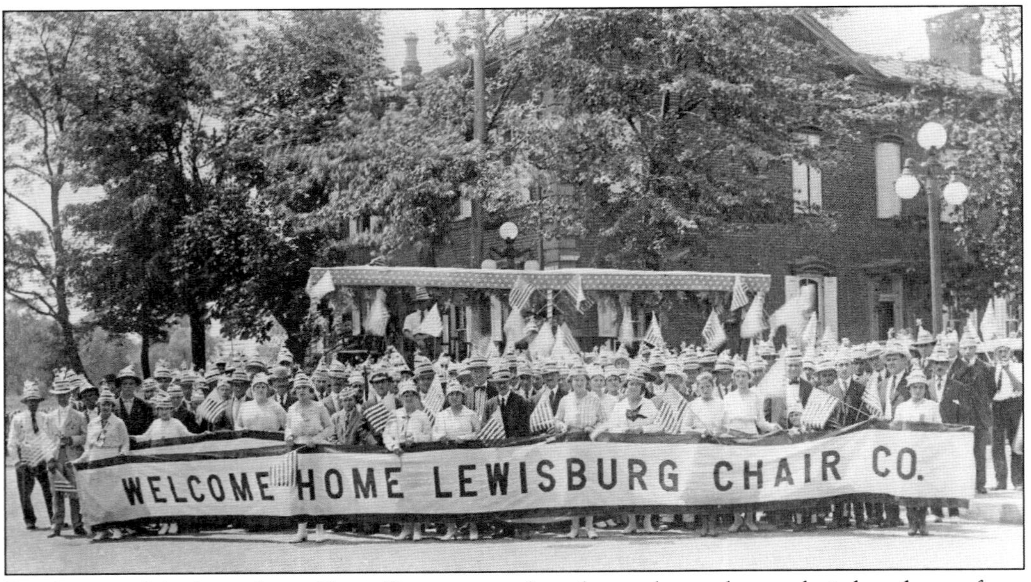

Employees of the Lewisburg Chair Company gathered to welcome home their loved ones from World War I. This company had its origins with the 19th-century chair maker David Ginter; in 1961, the Lewisburg Chair Company became Pennsylvania House, a major employer in Lewisburg until its demise in 2004. (UCHS 89.5.14.20.)

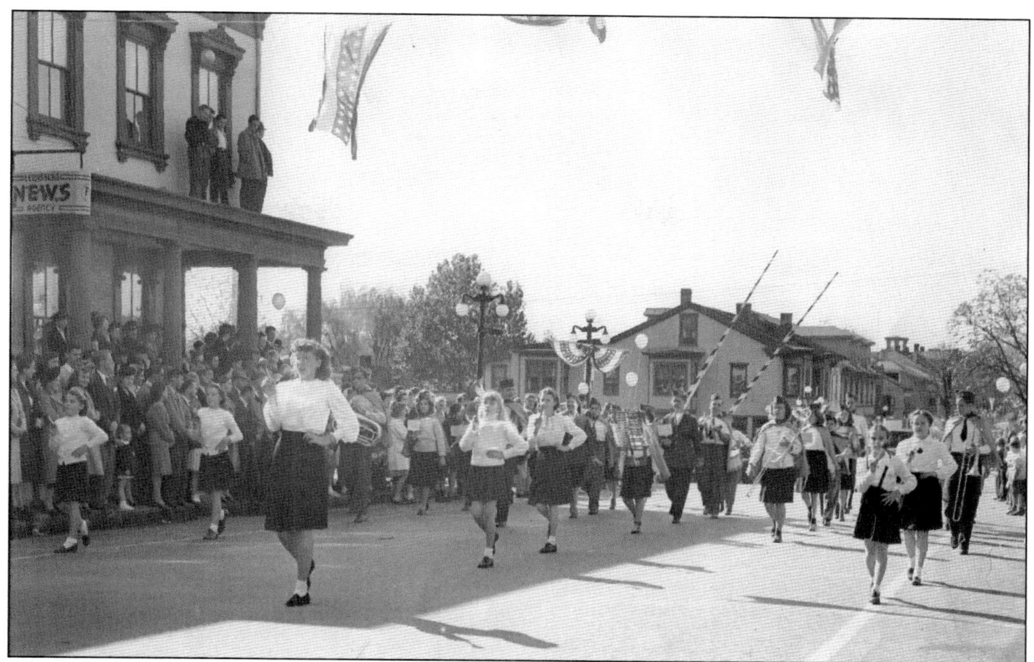

The Lewisburg High School marching band is pictured here, sometime in the late 1940s, marching east on Market Street as part of a parade. The high school adopted green and white as its colors sometime before World War II and has maintained those colors ever since. At some point, the high school's mascot became a green dragon. (UCHS 2006.46.23.)

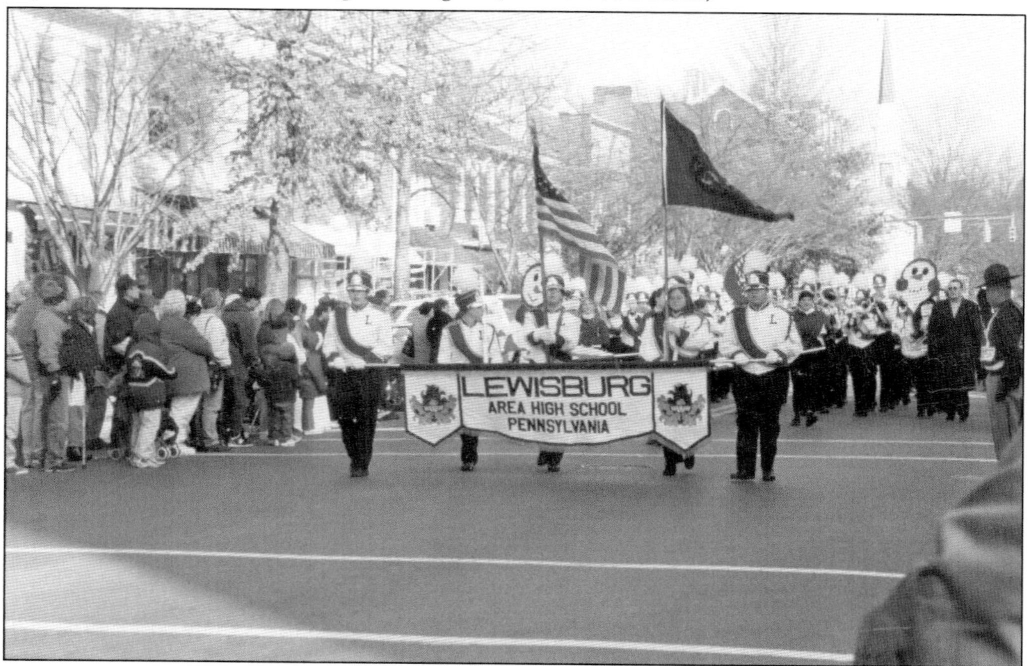

Lewisburg began a Victorian-themed holiday parade in the 1990s. Bands, costumed Victorian marchers, floats, Civil War reenactors, and an Abraham Lincoln impersonator have been part of this parade ever since. This scene shows the Lewisburg High School band marching in the December 2, 2000, parade. Band director Kenneth Campbell marches with them. (Ruth McCord.)

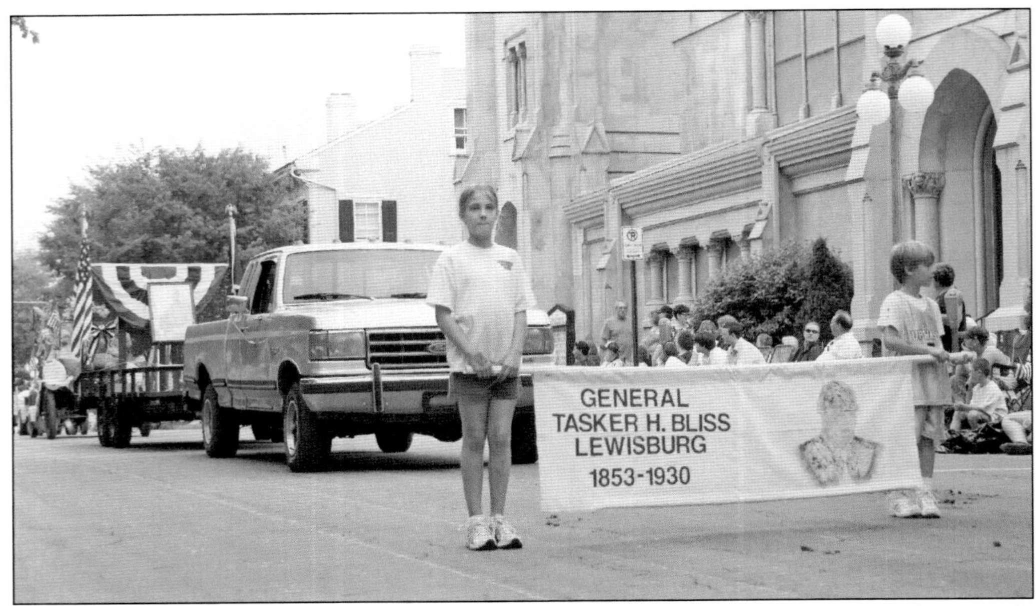

This Fourth of July parade entry remembered Gen. Tasker H. Bliss, perhaps Lewisburg's only native-born general. Bliss (1853–1930) graduated from West Point in 1875, and thereafter had a long, distinguished career as an army officer, culminating in his role as chief of staff in 1917–1918 at the onset of American entry into World War I. His report from Europe led to a rapid American deployment to France in 1918. (Tiffini Scott.)

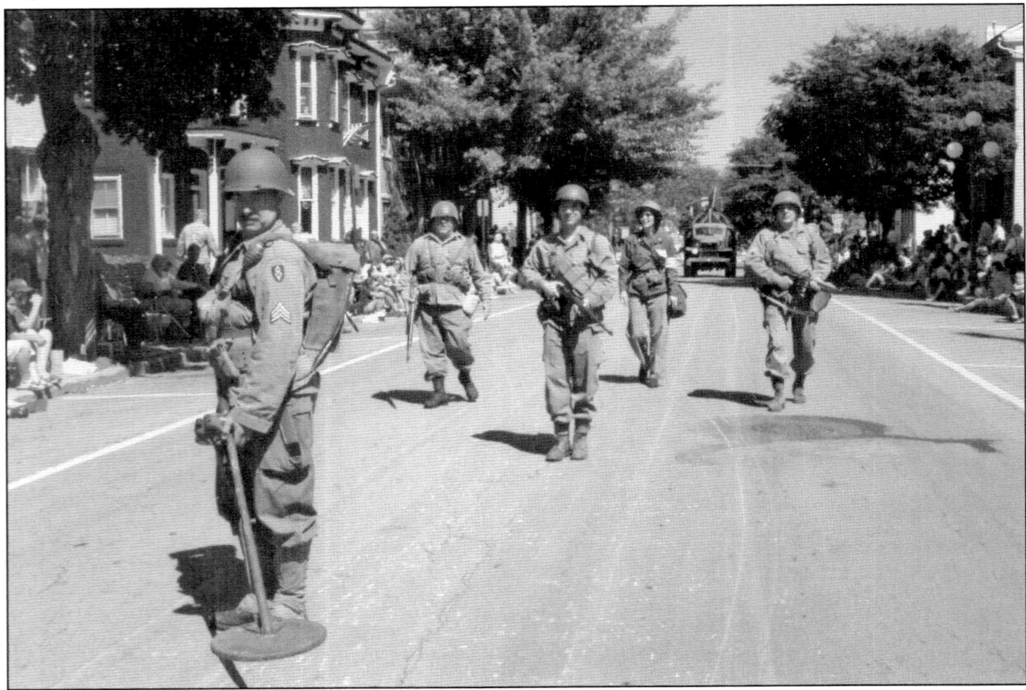

Ever since attorney Graham Showalter rejuvenated the Lewisburg Fourth of July parade in 1995, it has been centered on honoring American men and women in uniform. Every parade features a series of reenactors portraying all periods of American military history. Here is a group of World War II reenactors. (Tiffini Scott.)

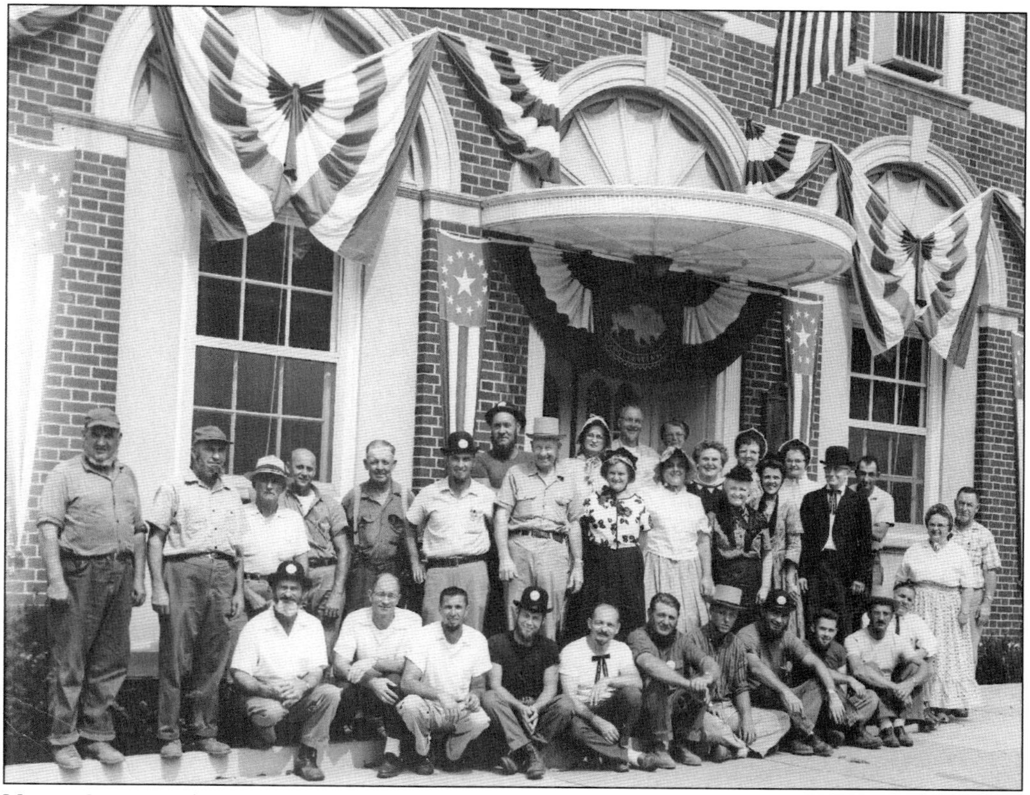

Union County celebrated its sesquicentennial in 1963 in a variety of ways. A huge extravaganza took place at the Bucknell University Memorial Stadium, and many small publications appeared relating to county history. Here, posed in front of the Buffalo Valley Telephone Company building on South Second Street, are the company's employees, decked out in faux fashion of the year. George Ruhl, company president, stands in his dark suit near the right. (Nada Gray.)

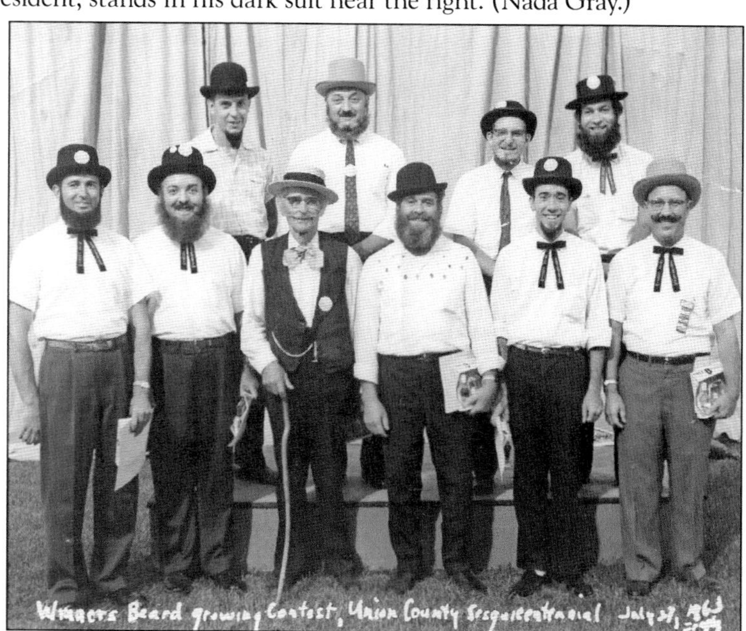

One of the events that took place during Union County's 1963 sesquicentennial celebration was a beard-growing contest. These were the winners of this contest, which was judged on July 27 during the weeklong celebration. These "brothers of the brush" sport a range of beard styles, from goatees to bushy beards to a handlebar moustache. (UCHS 84.4.4.13.Da.)

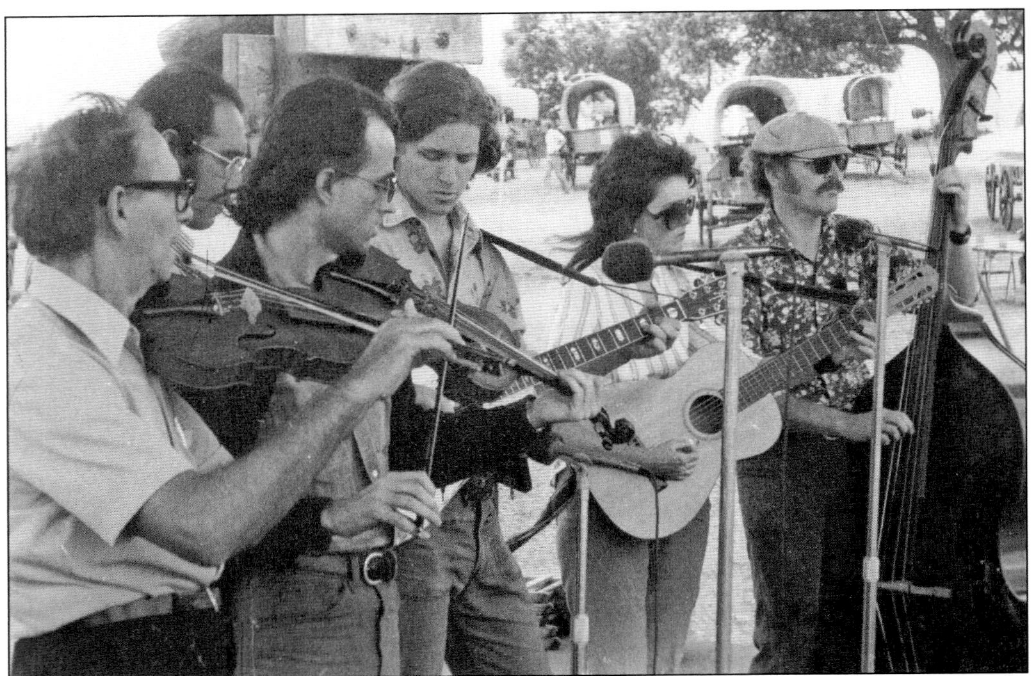

The United States celebrated its bicentennial in 1976, and Lewisburg was not left out. Union County Day at Valley Forge was August 1, 1976. The musical group, which added to the festivities, included, from left to right, area fiddlers Harry D'Addario and Robert Taylor, Michael Moynihan (guitar), David Andrew Pearson (guitar), Janice Pearson (guitar), and David Pearson (bass). (UCHS 89.5.14.26K.)

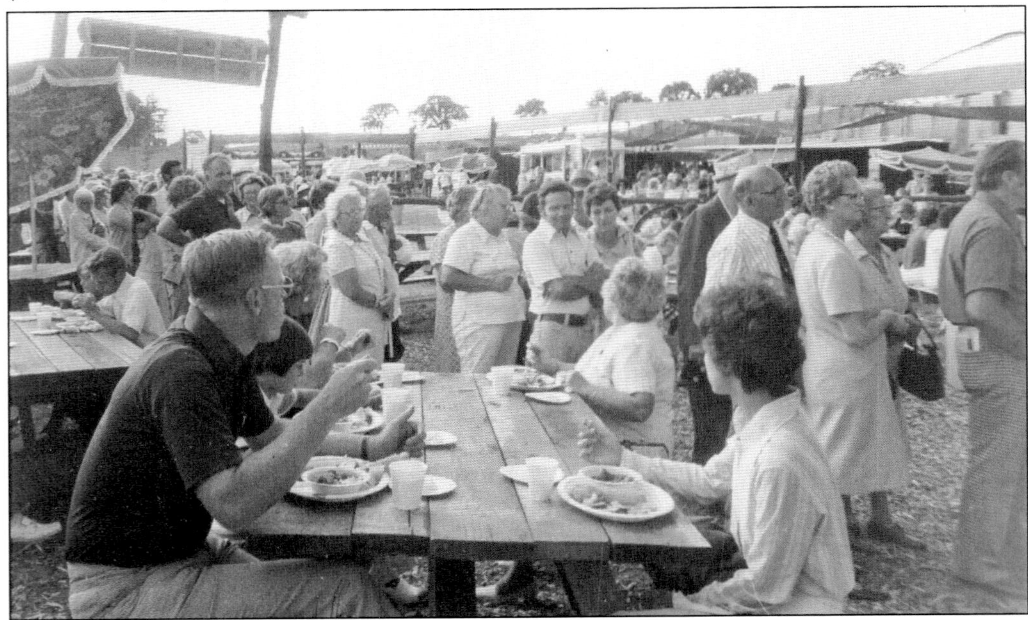

Union County Day at Valley Forge entailed food and fun. Union County residents arrived by bus and stood in line for popular foods. The bicentennial, with its covered wagons on display, showcased various aspects of life through traditional craft demonstrations. Sherman Doebler served as master of ceremonies for the Union County presentation. (UCHS 89.5.14.26V.)

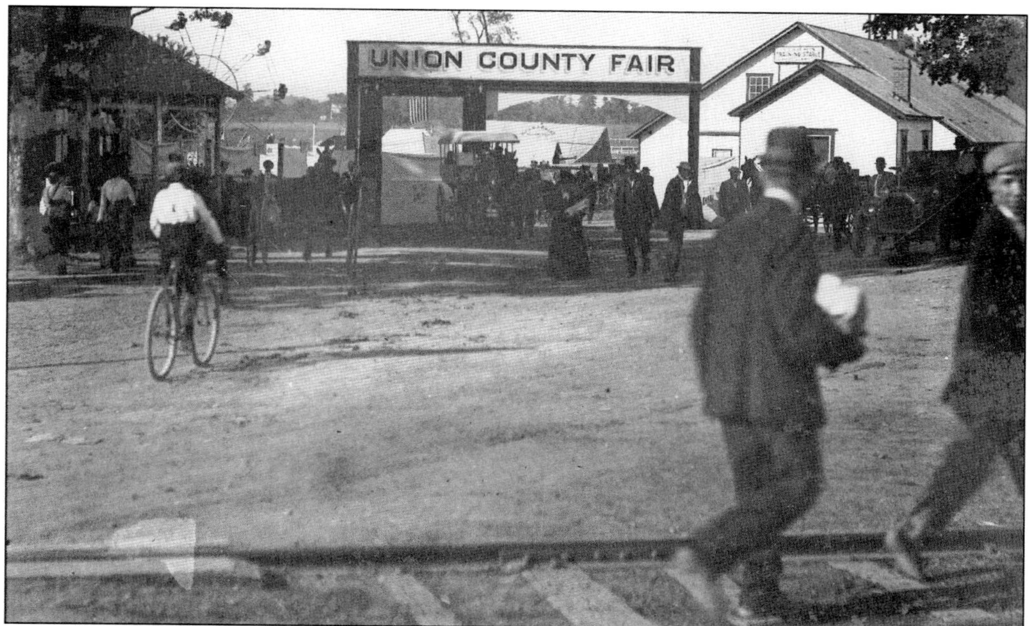

Once located at Brookpark Farm on ground now occupied by the Lewisburg Farmers Market in East Buffalo Township, the Union County Fair began in 1857 on 10 acres purchased by the Union County Agricultural Society. The grounds included a grandstand from which spectators could watch horseracing. The grandstand was demolished in 1937, and the fair moved to the western end of the county. (UCHS 97.3.1.)

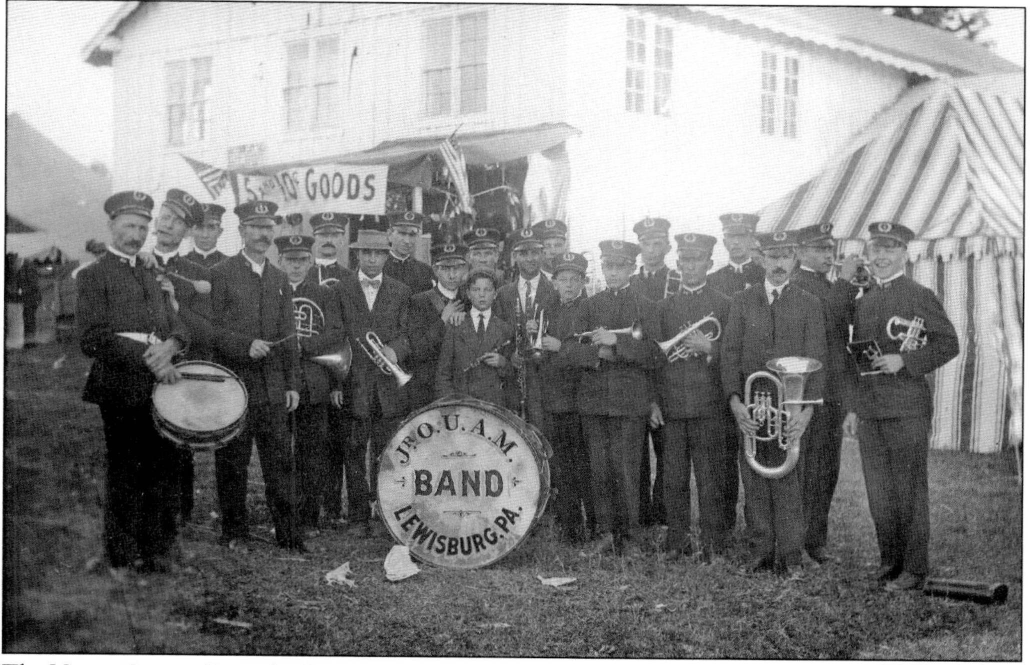

The Union County Fair, which was held in Brook Park, had its 19th-century roots in New Berlin and then by Grove's Mill in Buffalo Township. In the early 20th century, it featured many bands. The Junior Order of United American Mechanics Band (Jr. O.U.A.M.), like many other local small-town bands, dressed in uniforms and consisted mainly of percussion and brass. (UCHS 92.9.92.1.)

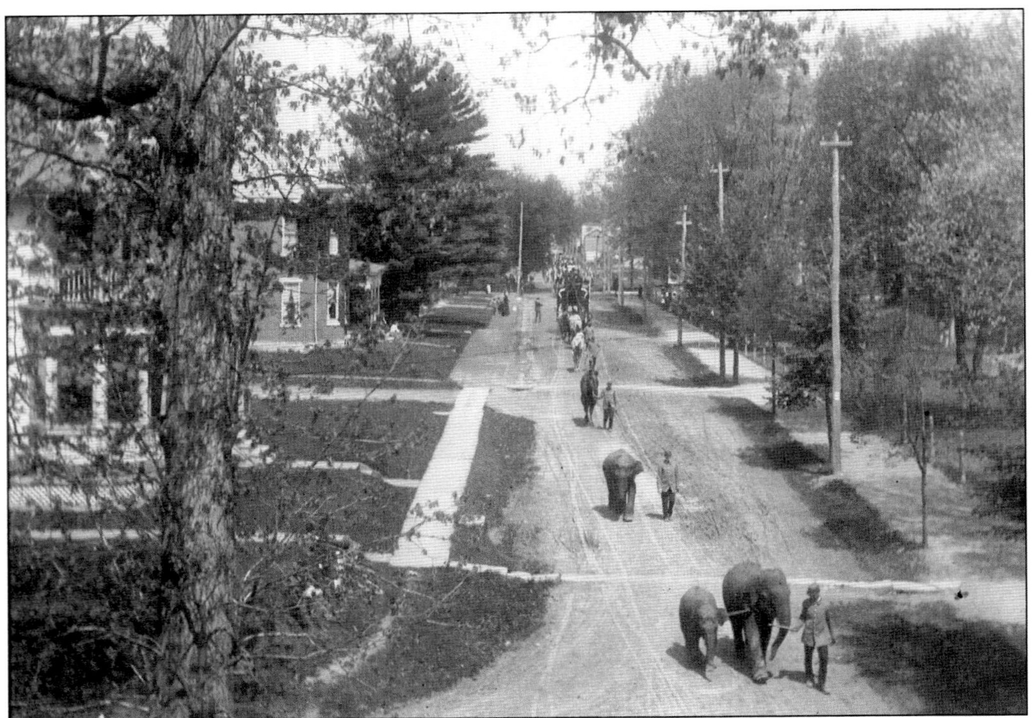

Circuses were at one time an extremely popular event in towns all across America. Lewisburg was certainly no exception. A glance through old newspapers will reveal that numerous circuses visited throughout the years. This scene was certainly not a rare one in the early 20th century. Here trainers lead a group of elephants along South Sixth Street. Circus wagons can be seen in line behind the pachyderms. (UCHS 89.5.14.23.)

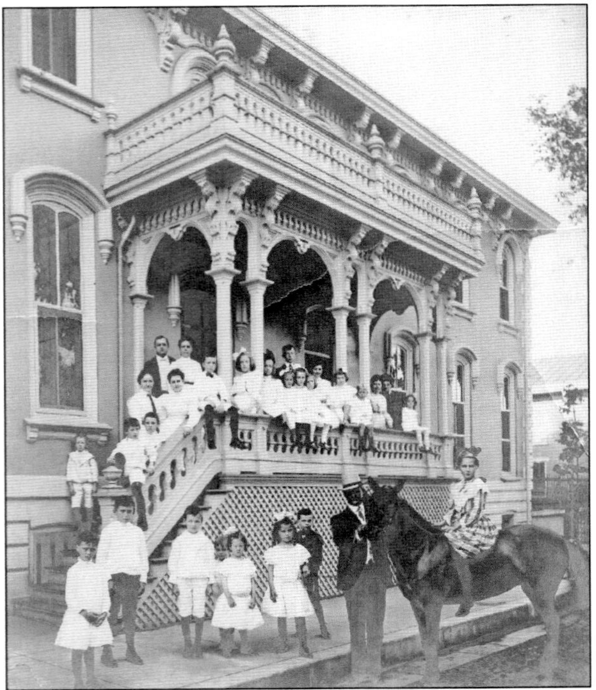

Benjamin Focht throws a birthday party for his daughter and invites several of her friends. The three-story Italianate house at 60 South Second Street was constructed by L. B. Christ in 1860. It became a home for Benjamin Focht, who served for 10 years as a representative in the U.S. Congress and was founder and editor of the Lewisburg *Saturday News*. Since the 1950s, the building has been divided into apartments. (UCHS 89.5.7.115.)

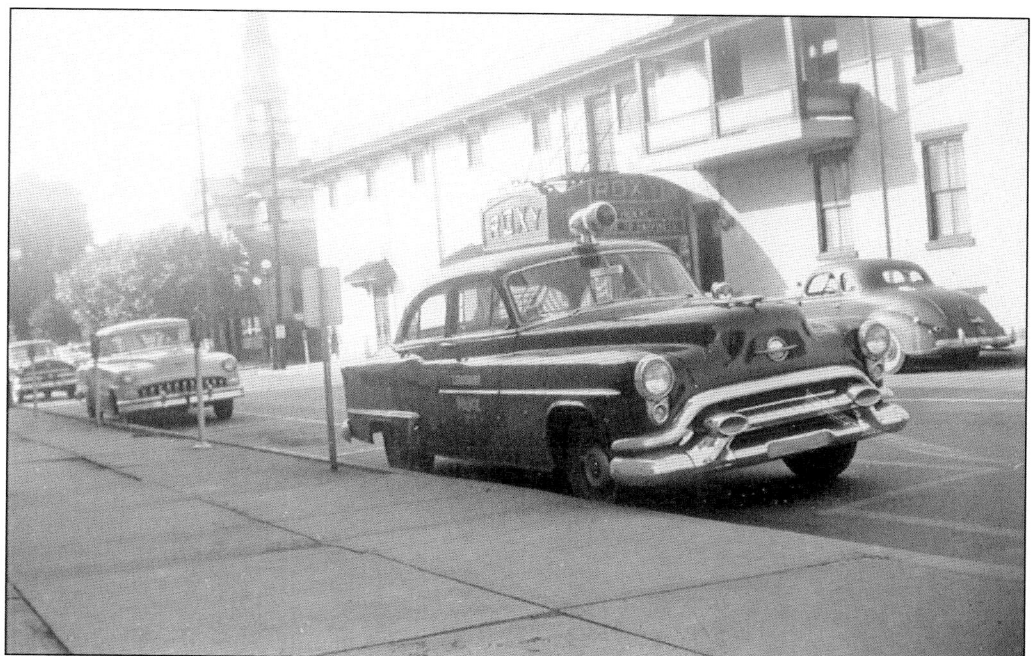

Lewisburg's first moving picture theater opened early in the 20th century on North Third Street. Its original name was the Orpheum; in 1931, it changed owners and became the Roxy. The theater closed in 1960 and was demolished to make way for a parking lot. This 1940s view of the Roxy shows a Lewisburg Police Department cruiser parked across North Third Street. (Virginia Moore.)

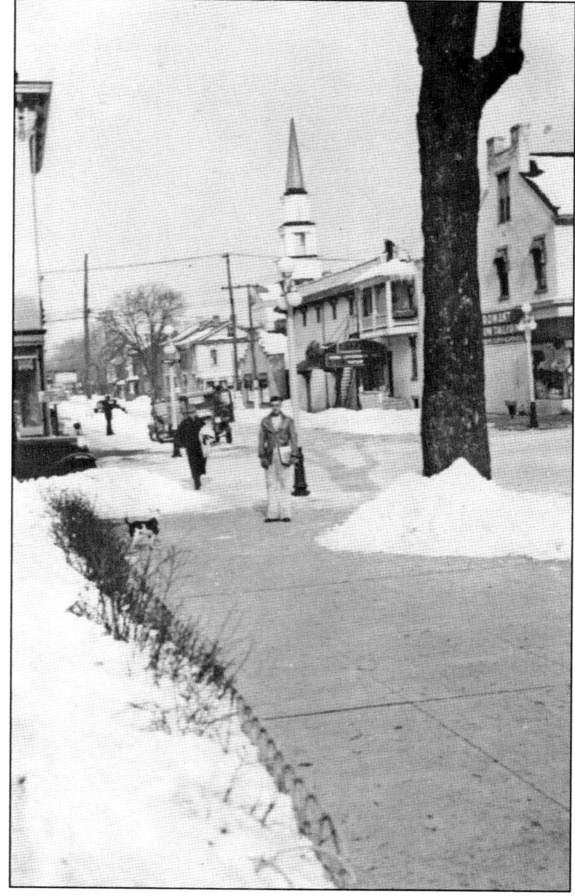

A photographer stood on the sidewalk adjacent to the Federal Building and snapped this image with snow on the ground early in 1936, looking across Market Street and up North Third Street. To the left of the tree stands the Roxy Theater and beyond that is the spire of the Christian Church. Both buildings were demolished in the early 1960s. (UCHS 89.5.15.7.)

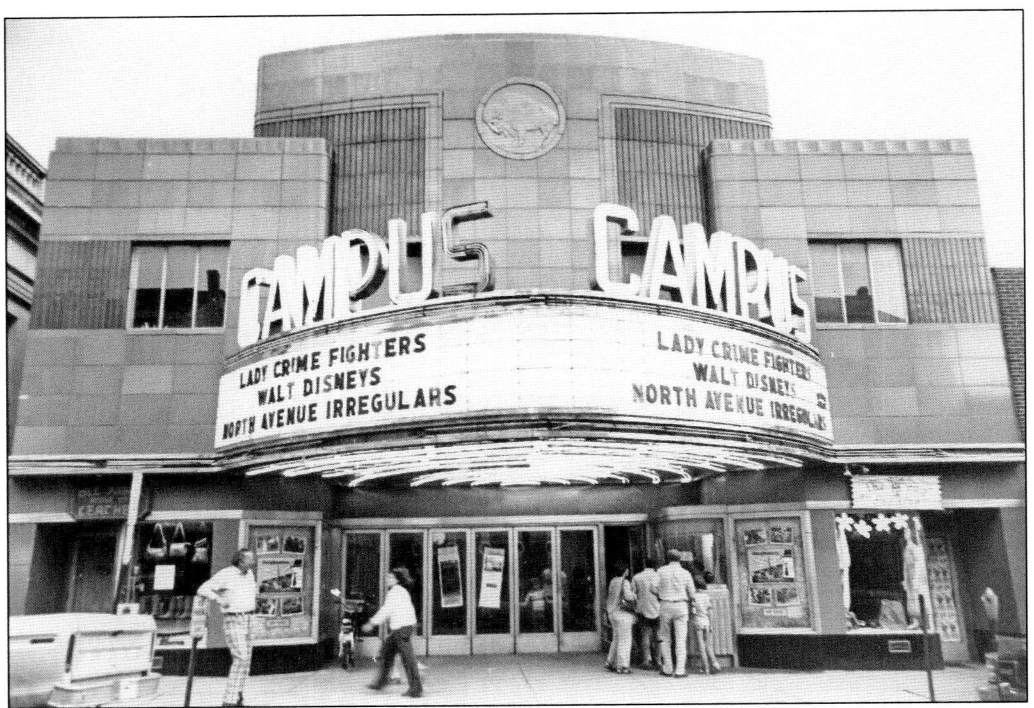

The Campus Theatre, designed by Philadelphia architect David Supowitz, was constructed in 1940 in the art deco style. The photograph shows former owner Harold Stiefel in his characteristic pose, leaning on the parking meter where he would greet passersby. A major renovation in 2004 refurbished the facade and marquee. (UCHS 89.5.15.16.)

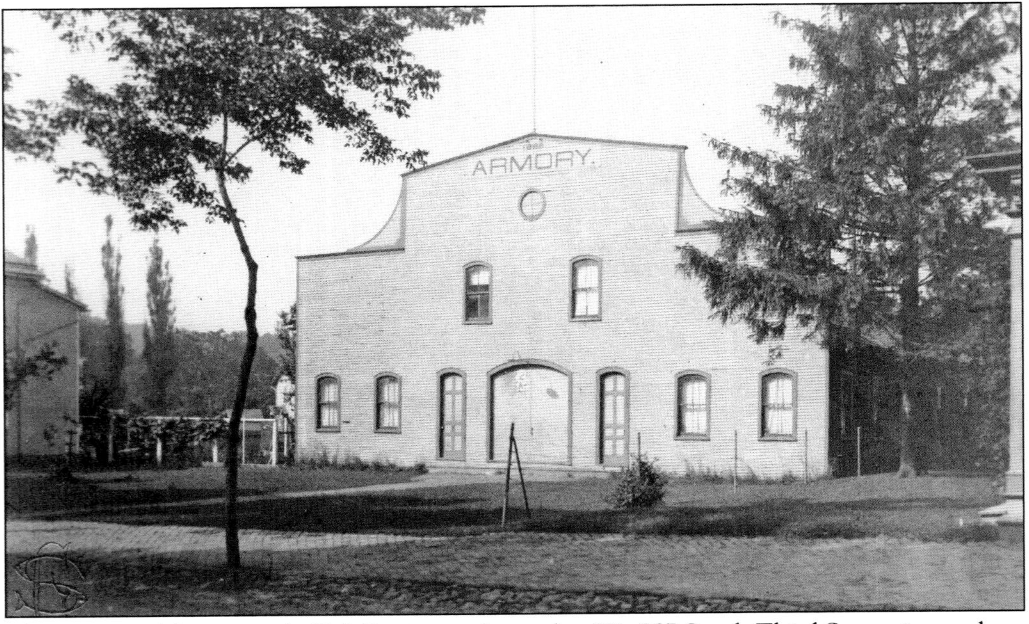

The armory of Company A, 12th Regiment, located at 221–237 South Third Street, is seen here around 1905. It was the site for dancing classes, dinners, and balls. The town's Assembly Balls were held with formally gowned and dressed couples in the days of high social protocol. In 1938, a new National Guard armory was constructed on Route 15. (UCHS 87.7.10.)

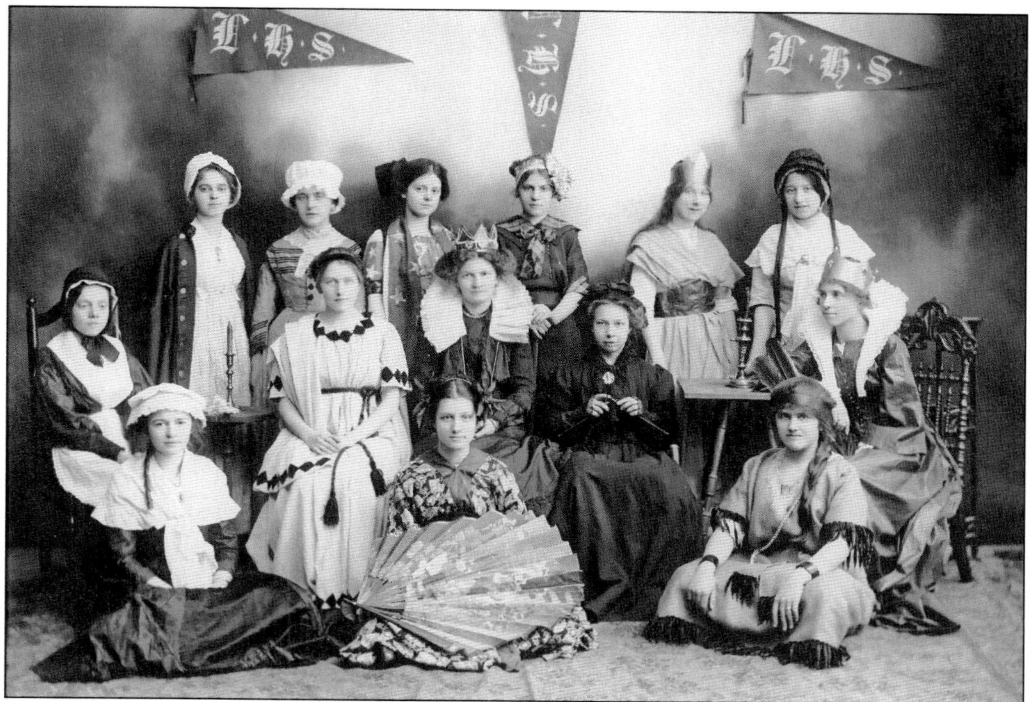

Plays have always been popular in Lewisburg High School. They were an extracurricular activity that involved substantial teamwork, creativity in designing sets and costumes, and plenty of practice and effort to ensure that each play was successful. This early-20th-century image shows the cast of one such play, the play's name is not etched on the reverse of this undated image. (UCHS 88.27.4.)

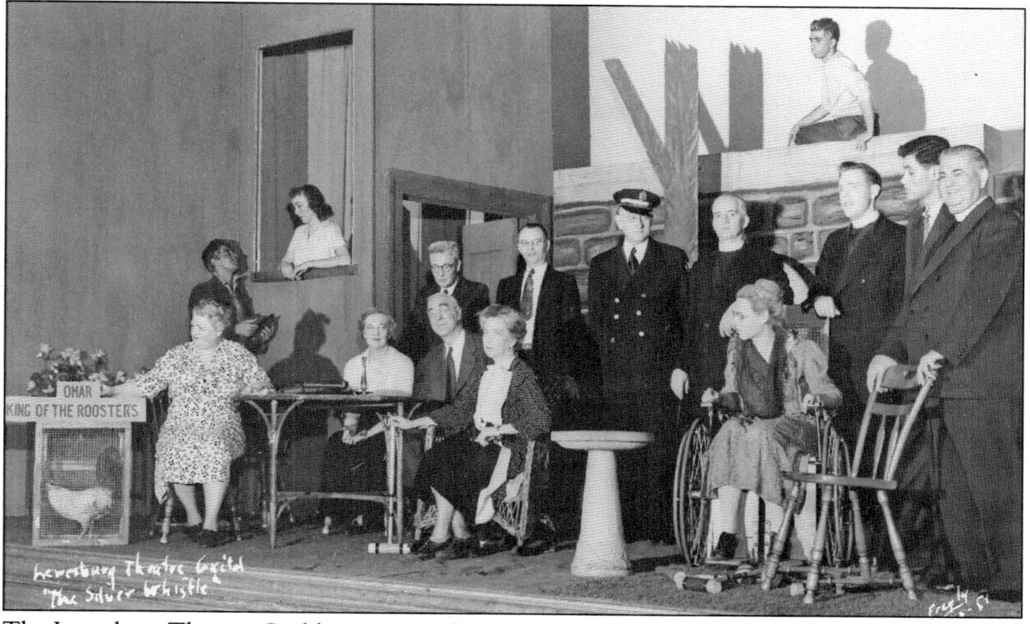

The Lewisburg Theatre Guild was active throughout much of the 20th century. Here is the cast of Robert McEnroe's comedy entitled *The Silver Whistle*, a story about a group of unhappy senior citizens who have their lives shaken up by a newcomer. This play debuted on Broadway in 1948 and ran for 219 shows. Lewisburg saw it in early 1951. (UCHS 87.17.24.)

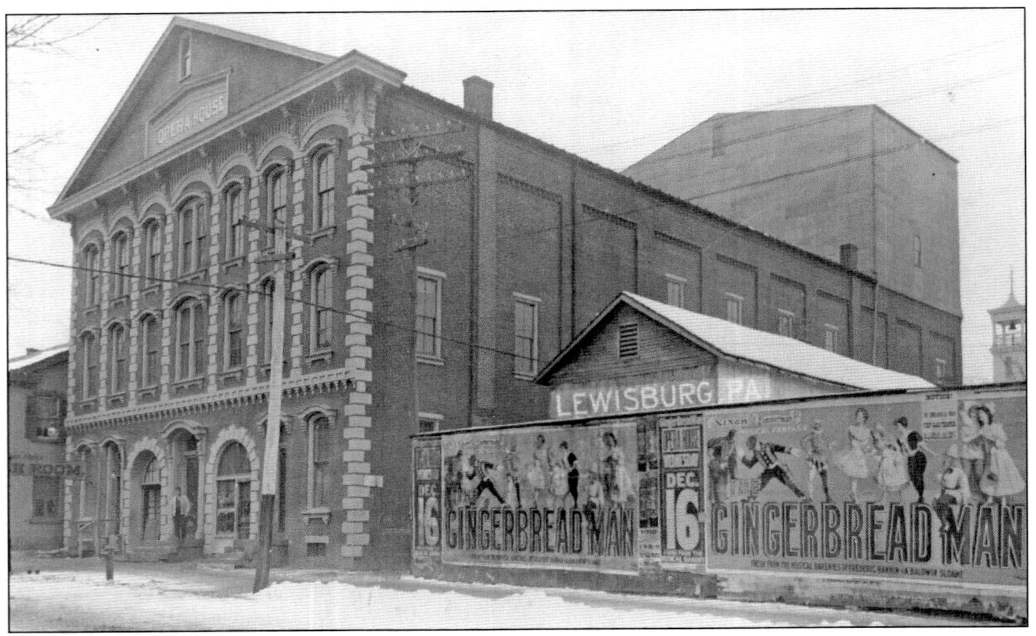

Lewisburg, like so many other towns, once had an elegant opera house. The town's new Music Hall was dedicated in 1879 by Massachusetts senator Charles Sumner. The structure, which could hold an audience of 1,000, was located on South Third Street. In 1893, the hall was extensively renovated and its name changed to the more grandiose Opera House. The building was completely destroyed by fire on December 27, 1908. (UCHS 98.15.2.)

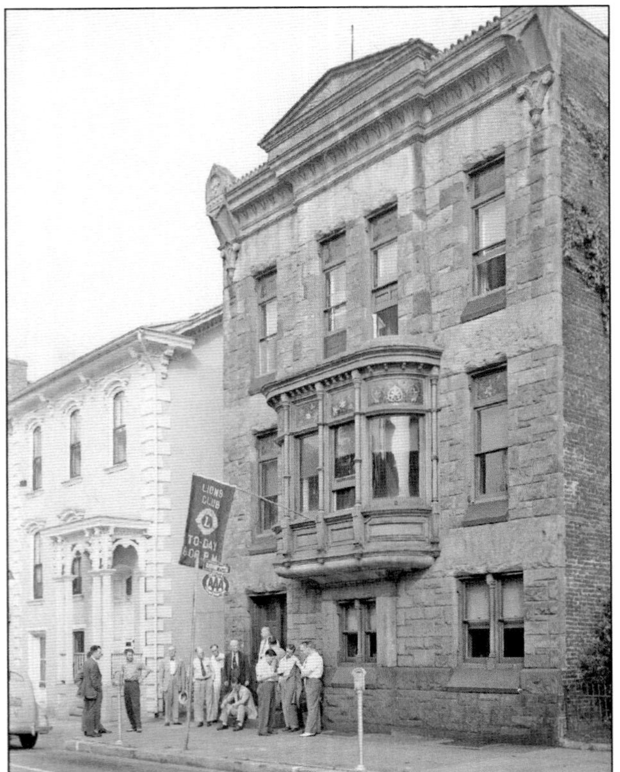

The Lewisburg Club building, pictured here in 1945, was originally a simple brick structure erected between 1800 and 1814. Joseph Nesbit and his wife, Rebecca, converted it into a fashionable brownstone mansion and sold it in 1911 to the Lewisburg Club for its activities. The building became the home for the service clubs (Kiwanis, Lions, and Rotary) and community activities. (UCHS 2006.42.)

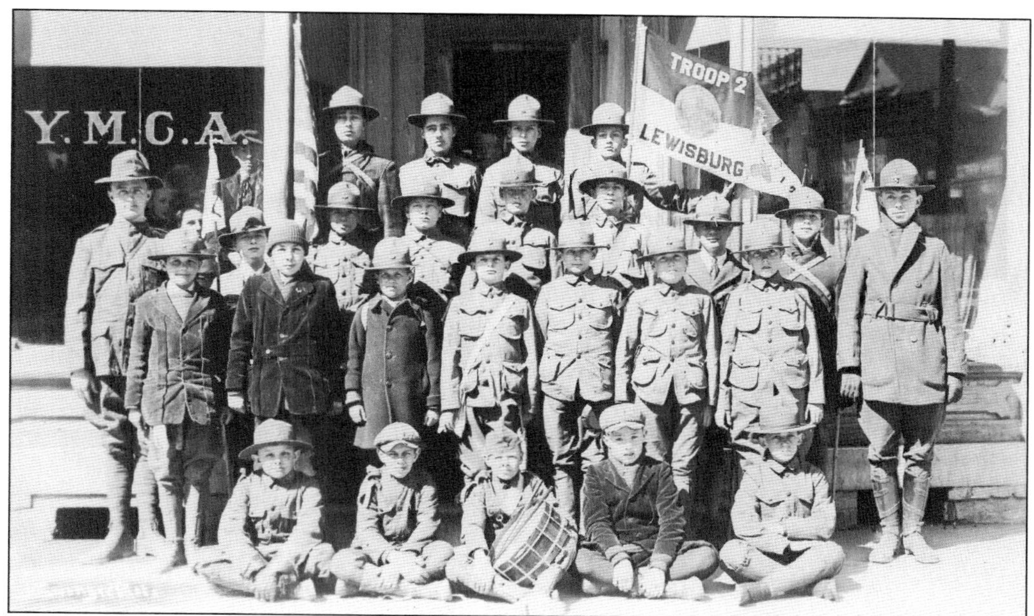

Lewisburg has been home to numerous Boy Scout troops since the movement began after 1900. Here, Troop 2 stands in front of Lewisburg's YMCA in this undated image. The ages of the boys vary from youngsters to teenagers. The troop has a drummer, its own guidon, and neat uniforms. (UCHS 84.60.3.)

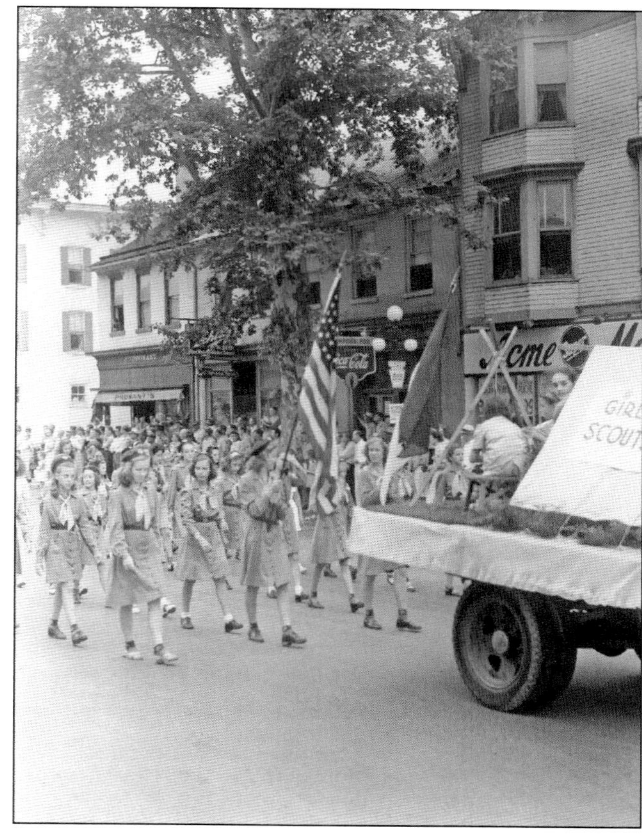

A local Girl Scout troop marches in one of Lewisburg's many parades. The girls are moving east in the 200 block of Market Street. Prowant's Men's Wear is on the end of the block, with Acme Markets, a local food store, just behind the truck. The side of the J. J. Newberry building is on the left of this photograph. (UCHS 82.4.1.26AK.)

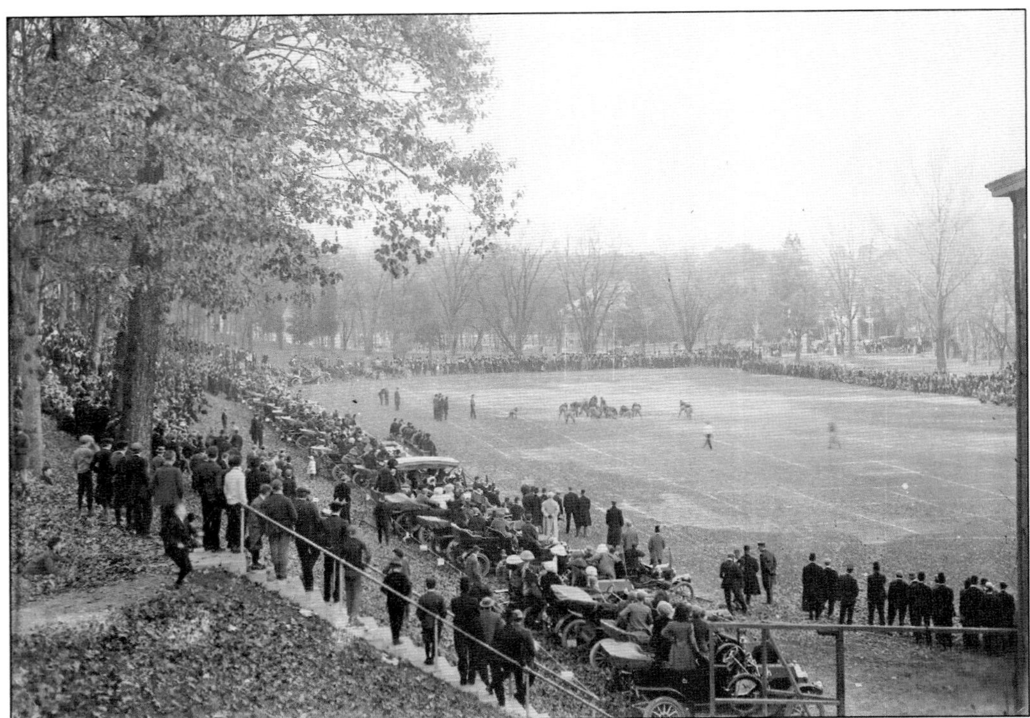

Football is played around 1906 on Loomis Field, Bucknell's first athletic field. By the 1920s, alumni were pressuring the Bucknell trustees to provide better athletic facilities. According to Bucknell historian J. Orin Oliphant, of all the building projects carried out by the university during the 1920s, the most expensive by far was that of the stadium, which was completed in 1924. Loomis Field now contains the Gateway dormitory complex. (UCHS 89.5.3.27.)

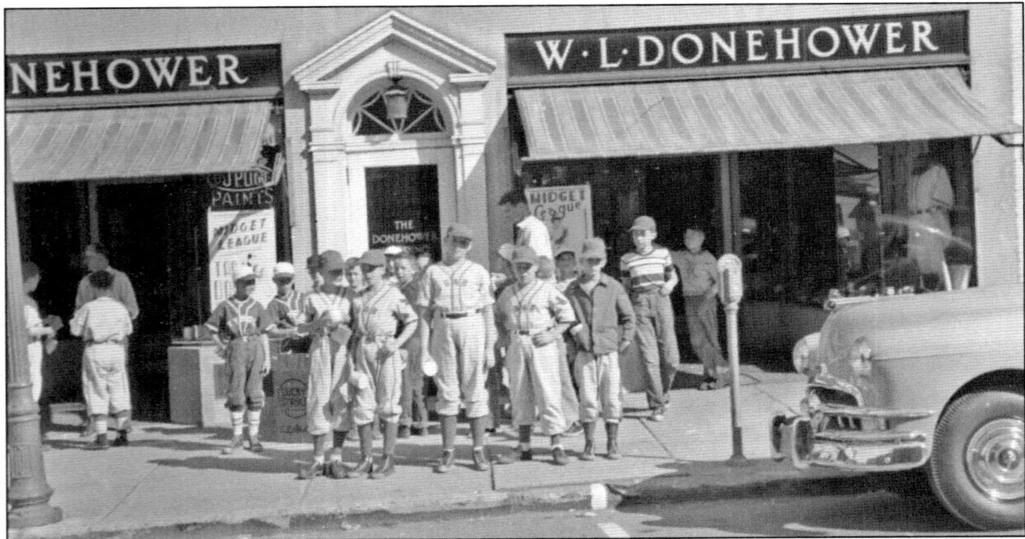

The Donehower business opened in Lewisburg in 1877, selling sporting goods and wallpaper, among other items. Its Market Street location opened in 1936 and remained until 2009. The Donehower family was always generous to local sports teams, annually supporting youth baseball, as seen in this 1950s snapshot of a "midget league" (youth league) team standing outside the store. (UCHS 96.19.12.)

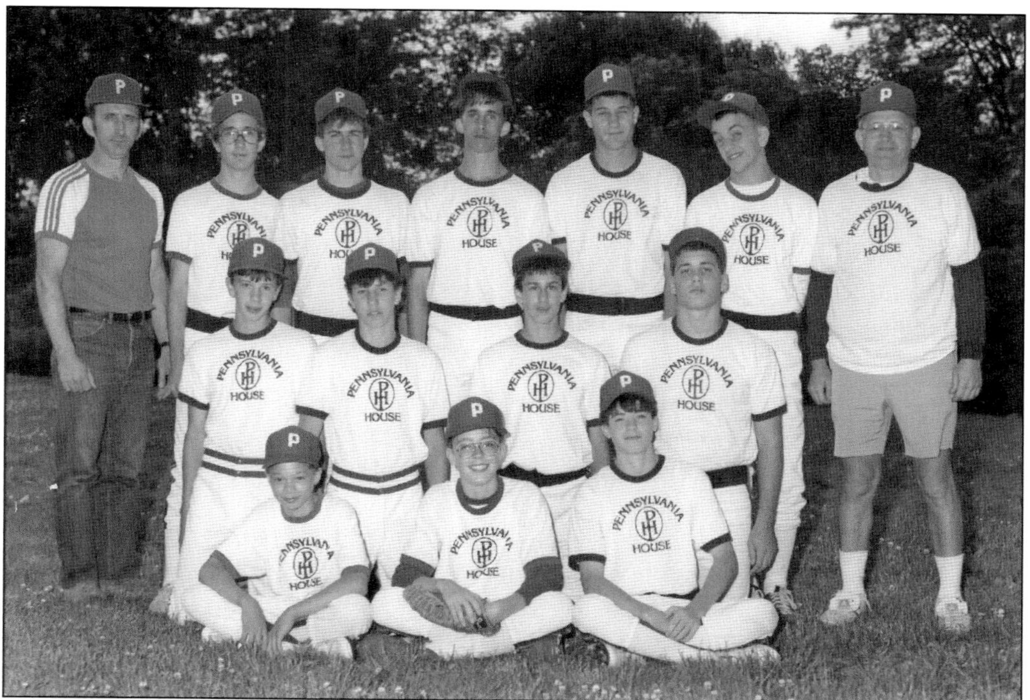

The softball team sponsored by Pennsylvania House could thank Daniel F. Green that they have a place to play. Green, president of the Lewisburg Trust and Safe Deposit Company, was active in philanthropy. He donated land for a playground and softball field, which was named in his honor in 1955. This complex is located on North Seventh Street and is still a center of sports activity. (UCHS 2004.54.44.)

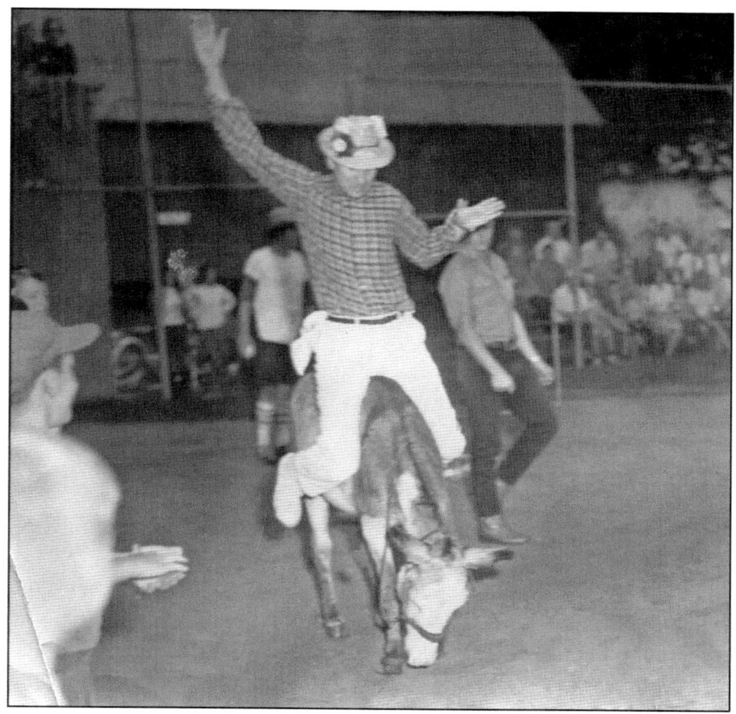

Sports involving donkeys have been a source both for fund-raising and amusement. Lewisburg civic organizations have provided this source of fun for decades. This September 1965 image shows a donkey baseball game sponsored by the Lewisburg Jaycees at Daniel Green Field. David Mensch, a Lewisburg real estate business owner, is trying to stay on a donkey. (David Mensch.)

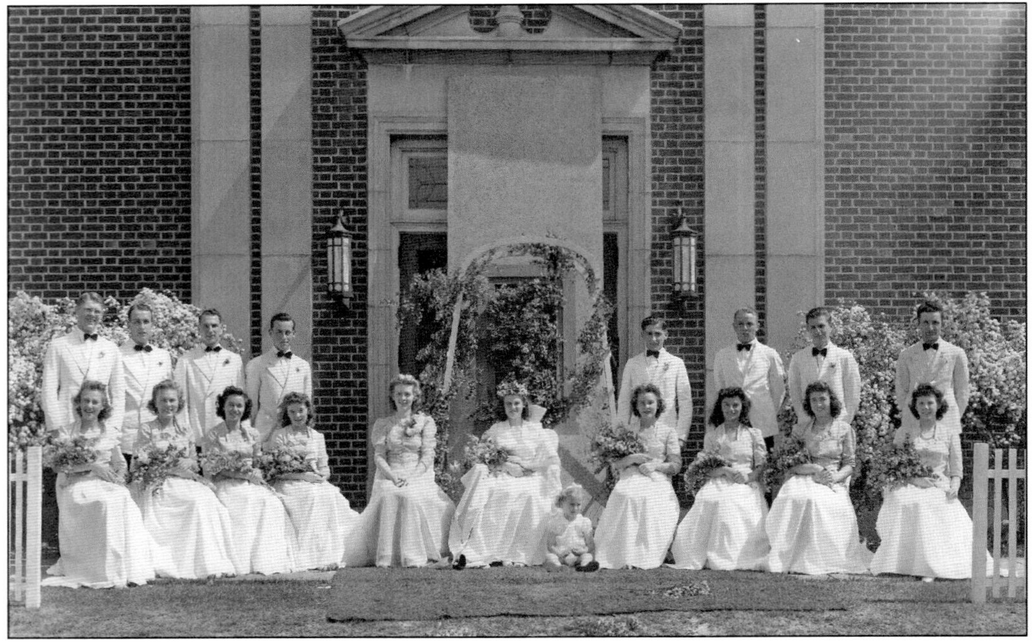

May Day was once celebrated at high schools and colleges on or close to May 1. A queen was selected from the junior class by students, here crowned by a wreath of flowers and formally posing with her court in front of Lewisburg High School. The young men standing behind the women were chosen by the teachers. (UCHS 82.4.2.25Ca.)

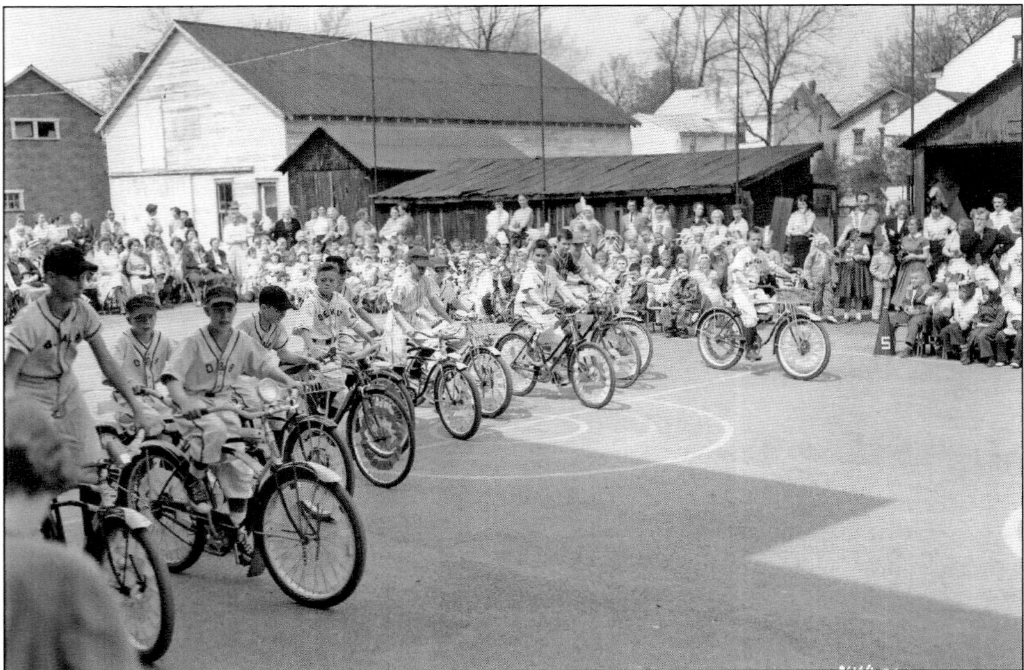

The younger grades also celebrated May Day with school-sponsored festive activities. On May 3, 1956, these students from North Ward Elementary School on North Second Street dressed in their team uniforms and showed off their decorated bicycles, which they then rode around the building in a parade. (UCHS 89.5.3.70L.)

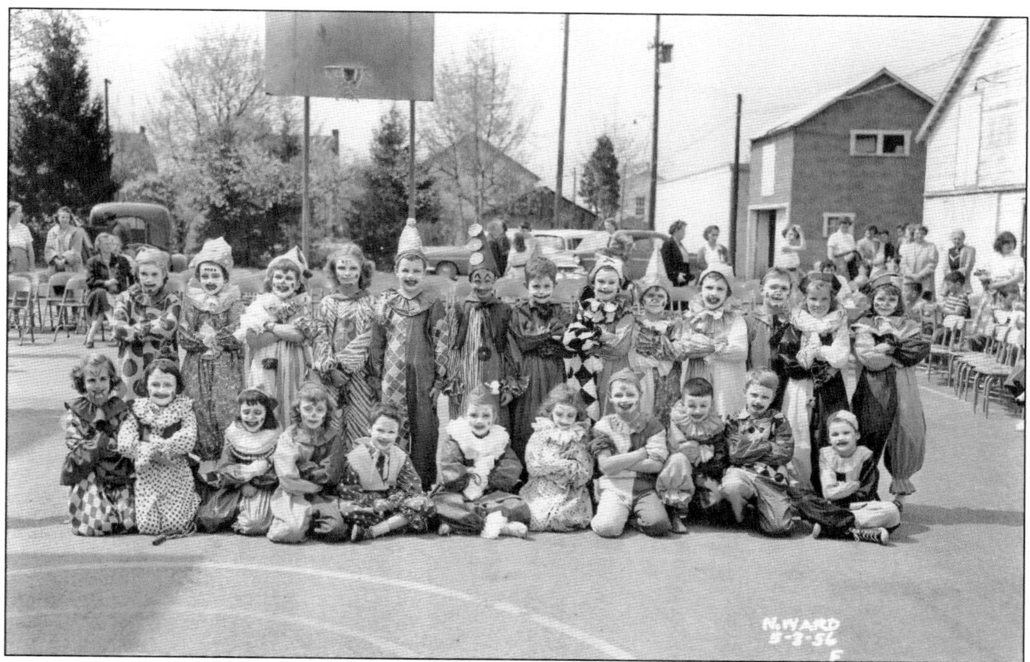

The "Clown Group" was part of the North Ward School May Day festivities in 1956. On some May Days, the North Ward students were taken to the high school to participate in the themed festive events there. By the 1960s, school-sponsored May Day activities no longer took place. (UCHS 89.5.3.70n.)

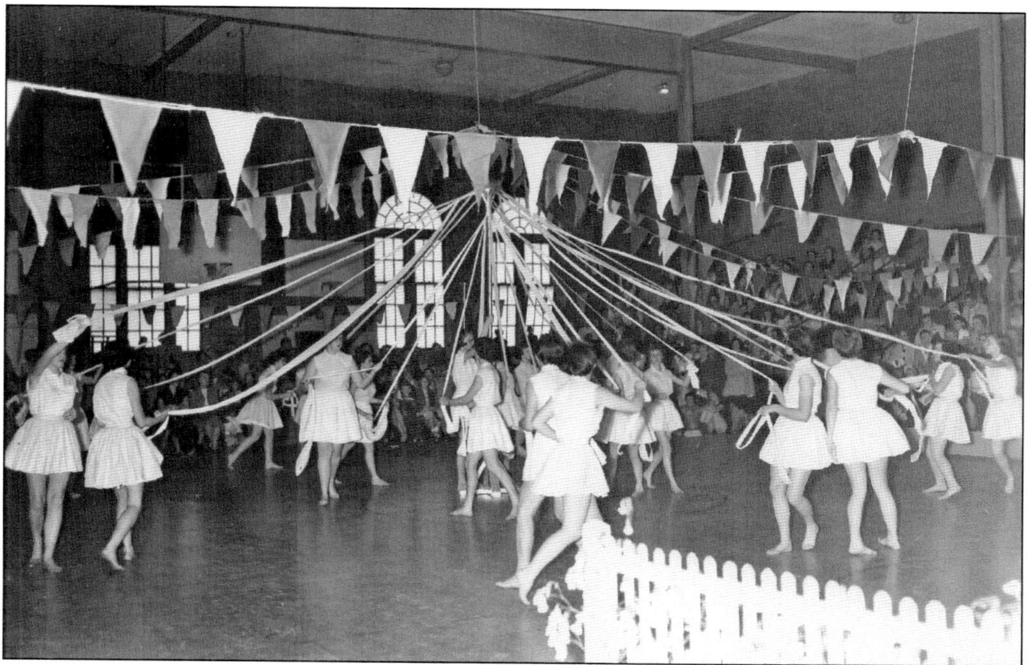

The tradition of the maypole dance was part of the Lewisburg High School May Day celebration. The girls, here barefooted, danced in an elaborate fashion while holding ribbon streamers attached to a pole. The maypole dance pictured here occurred on May 12, 1954. May Day events also included skits and performances. Each year the festival had a different theme. (UCHS 89.5.3.221.)

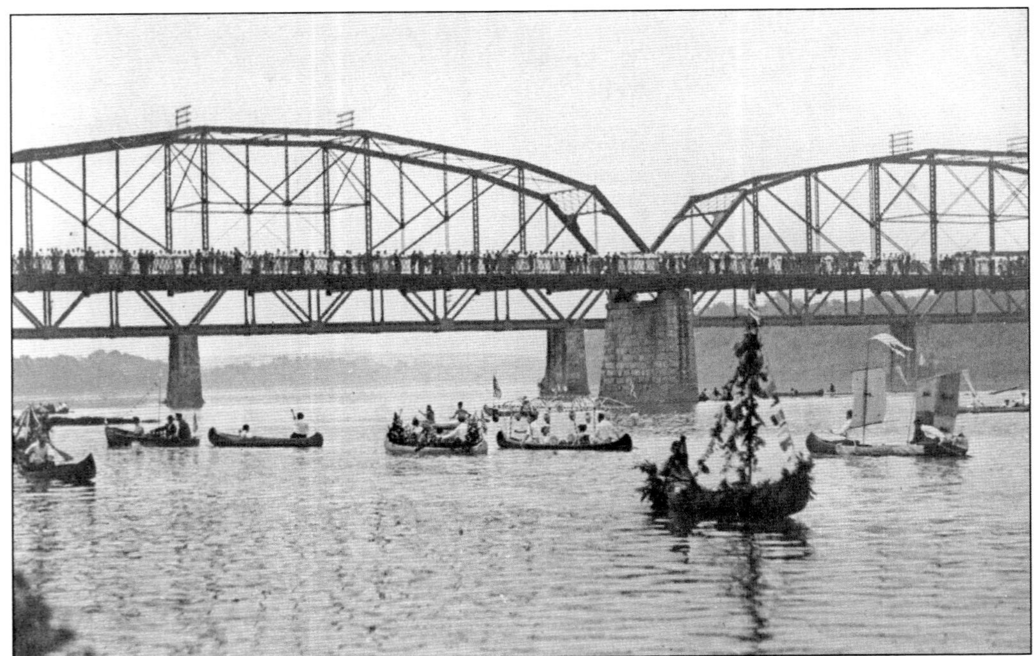

An early 1900s canoe regatta was held on the Susquehanna River near the Lewisburg free bridge, pictured here crowded with spectators. The free bridge (non-toll bridge) was constructed beginning in 1906 and dedicated in 1908. In 1912, the steel railroad bridge, which can be seen behind the free bridge, was built on the piers of the 1865 wooden toll bridge. (UCHS.)

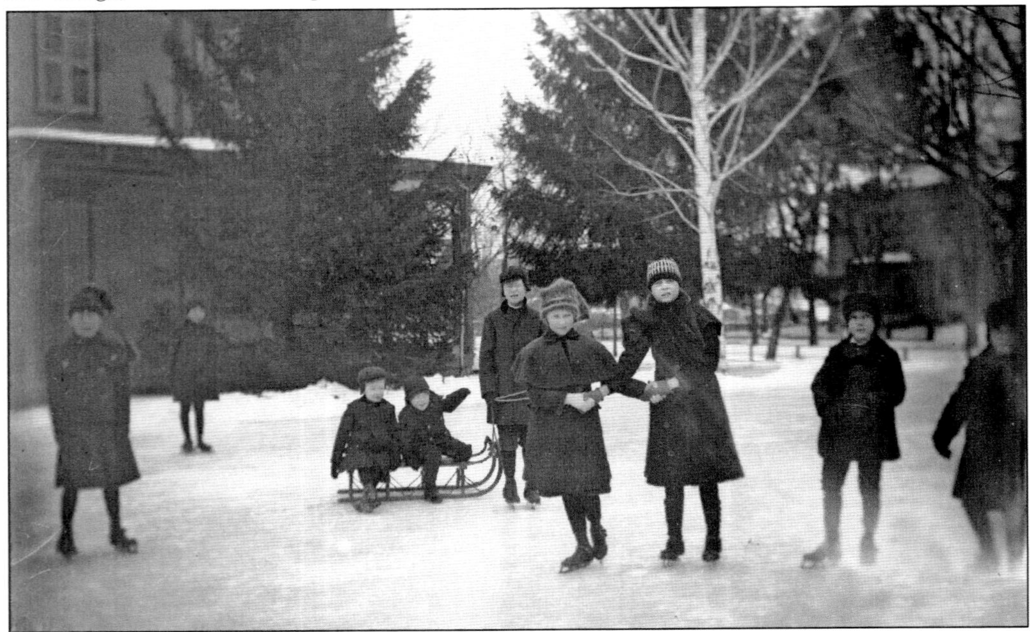

Winter leisure activities have not changed much over the decades. This early-20th-century image shows a group of children sledding and skating on ice somewhere in Lewisburg. The Lewisburg area had several small streams and ponds that easily froze during most winters, allowing local residents to have seasonal fun. In decades past, even the Susquehanna River froze over and was used for skating. (PHM 1987.03.107.)

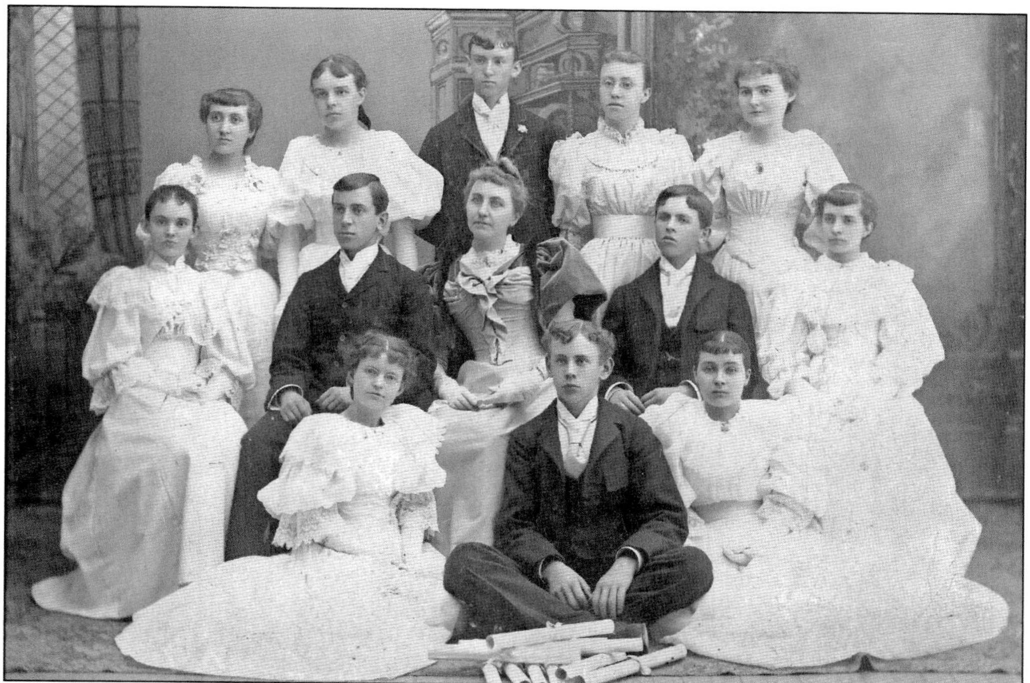

Graduating from high school was a festive occasion, meant to be remembered and commemorated well into the future. This formal photograph, taken by Lewisburg photographer Tilman Pross, shows the Lewisburg High School class of 1894 of nine women and four men. The high school at that time was held at the West Ward School on North Eighth Street, presently called the Colonial Apartments. (UCHS 95.15.18.)

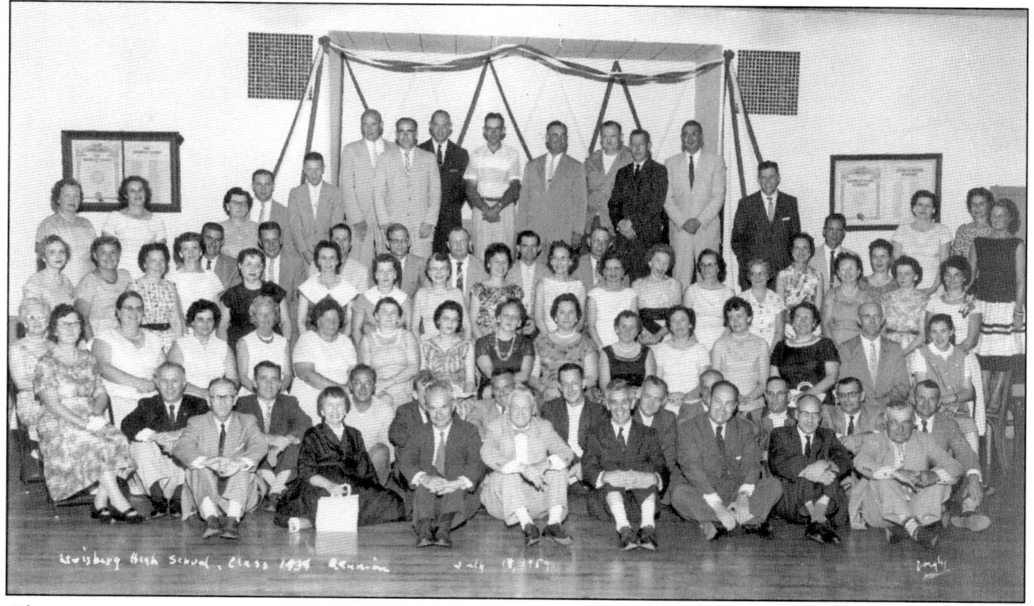

Class reunions commemorate a time of youth and its passage. This photograph, more informal than the one above, shows the 25th reunion of the class of 1934, taken in 1959. This group would have spent a delightful evening recounting memories of 25 years ago and celebrating their coming together again. (Alan Richard.)

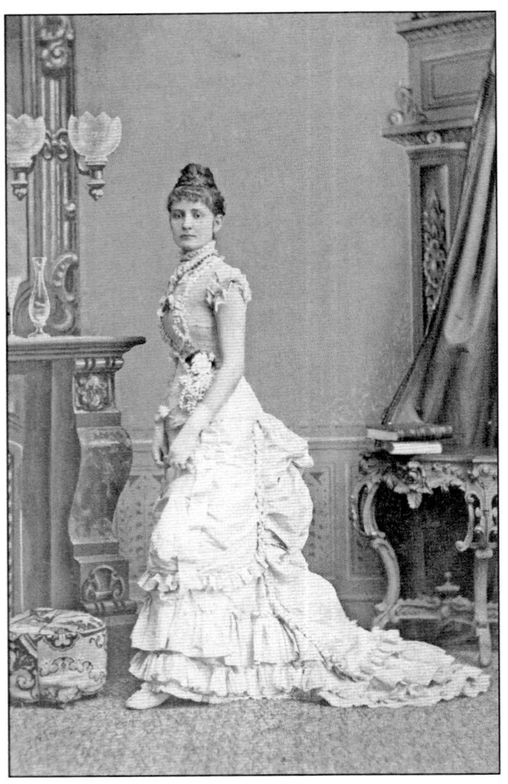

Jennie Frick married Lewisburg attorney George Barron Miller; this image is her formal wedding portrait. Frick's gown, posture, and studio background harken to the days of such formal photographs in an age of slowly evolving technology. Lewisburg has been home to several good photographers over the past 150 years including William M. Ginter (1869–1910), J. Wesley Cornelius (1880s), Fred Lindig (1886–1910), Donald Ross (1925–1980), and John Gardner (1980 until the present). (PHM 1998.01.33.)

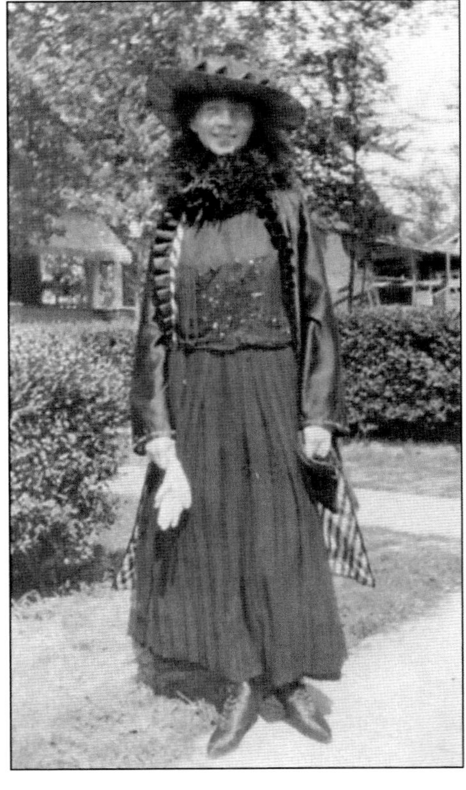

Pictured here was one of Lewisburg's "town characters." Edith Hedges Kelly Fetherston (1885–1972) was a descendant of one of the early pioneering families in the area. After graduating from Bucknell in 1905, Kelly had a brief career as a teacher before her marriage to John Fetherston. The couple retired to Lewisburg in 1936 and were the founders of the Packwood House Museum. Edith was well known for her lavish costumes. (PHM.)

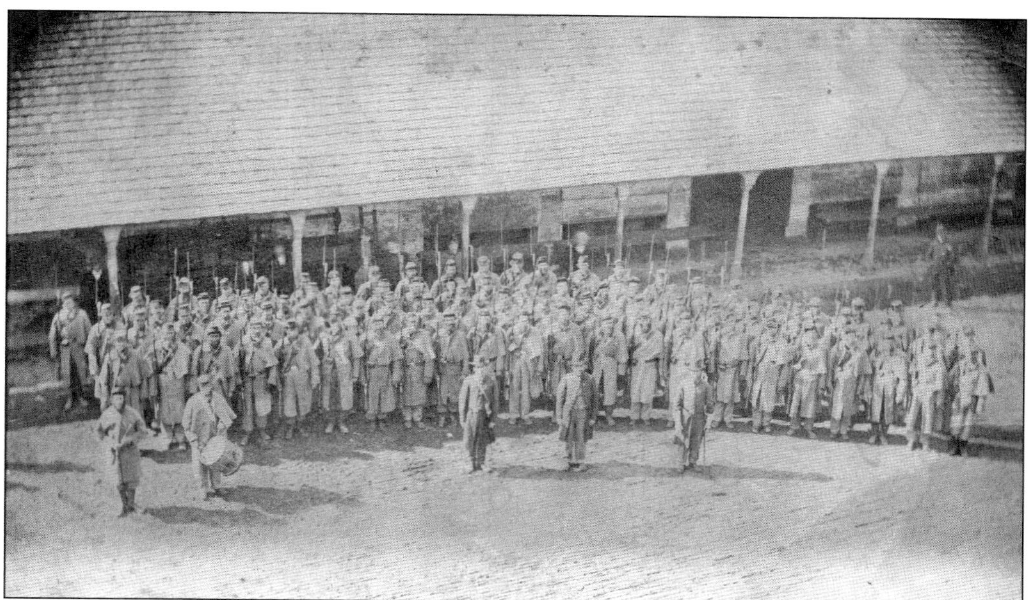

Here is Company I of the 192nd Pennsylvania Volunteer Infantry in formation in Market Square in Harrisburg. Capt. J. Wilson Hess and his two lieutenants stand in front, with the fifer and drummer on the left. This company was organized in the Lewisburg area in March 1865 and spent some time in the Shenandoah Valley, but saw no fighting. By this time, the Union army was well supplied, as evidenced in this previously unpublished image. (PHM 1988.01.)

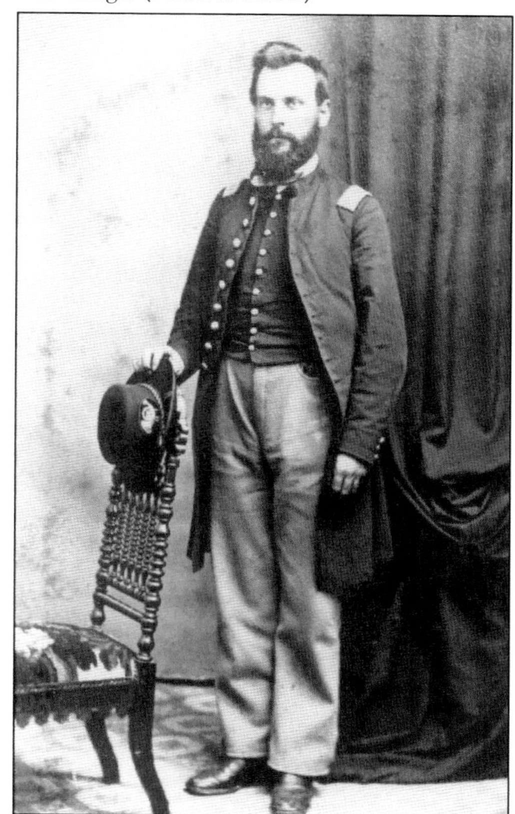

Lewisburg resident Henry F. Mangus enlisted in Company E, 53rd Pennsylvania Volunteer Infantry in 1861 and survived the war, despite being wounded at Fredericksburg (left foot) and Gettysburg (right leg) and spending time in five Confederate prison camps after being taken prisoner in June 1864. Mangus began as a sergeant and ended the war as captain of his company. (Ronn Palm Museum, Gettysburg.)

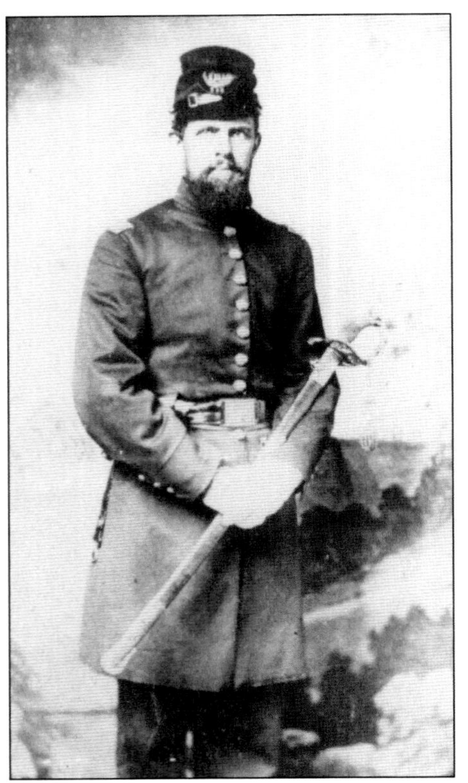

James Merrill Linn was a Lewisburg attorney who enlisted for three months of service in April 1861. He then came home and raised Company H, 51st Pennsylvania Volunteer Infantry, and became its captain. Linn saw battle in North Carolina, Virginia, Mississippi, and Tennessee before resigning in April 1864 because of poor eyesight caused by hard service. Linn's brother John was the author of *Annals of Buffalo Valley*. (Ronn Palm Museum, Gettysburg.)

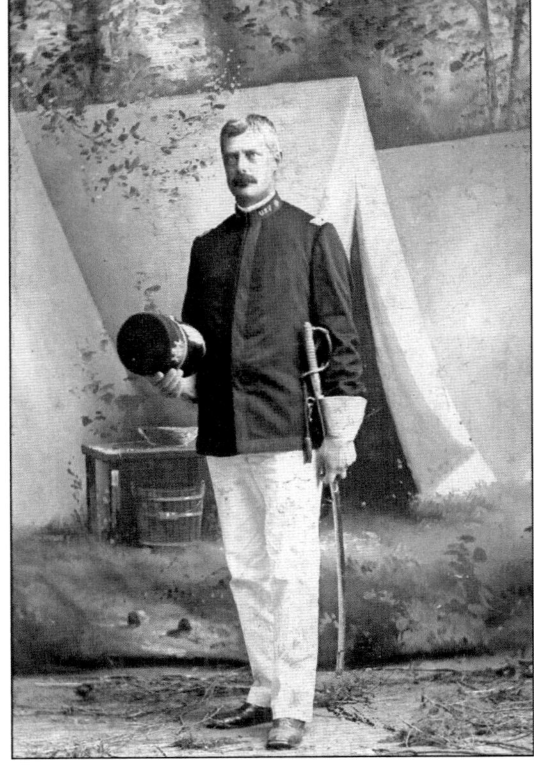

Dr. Martin Luther Focht poses in his army uniform while serving with the 12th Pennsylvania regiment during the Spanish-American War. Focht (1856–1928) was a Bucknell graduate. He studied medicine and became a physician in 1881. He practiced medicine in Lewisburg for 47 years. Politician and newspaper owner Benjamin K. Focht was Martin's brother. (PHM 1989.09.04b.)

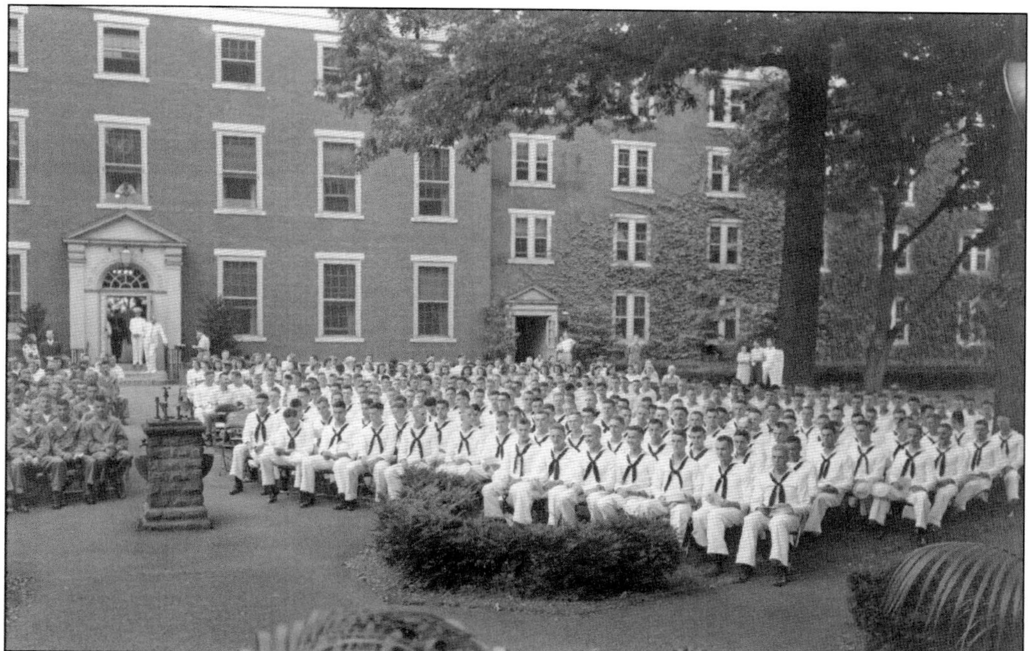

Members of the naval and marine units of the V-12 program at Bucknell University are seen here graduating in 1943. The V-12 college program was called an "Accelerated College Program for the Duration of the National Emergency." In 1943–1944, Bucknell had the largest enrollment in its history up until that time and the largest income. (Bucknell University.)

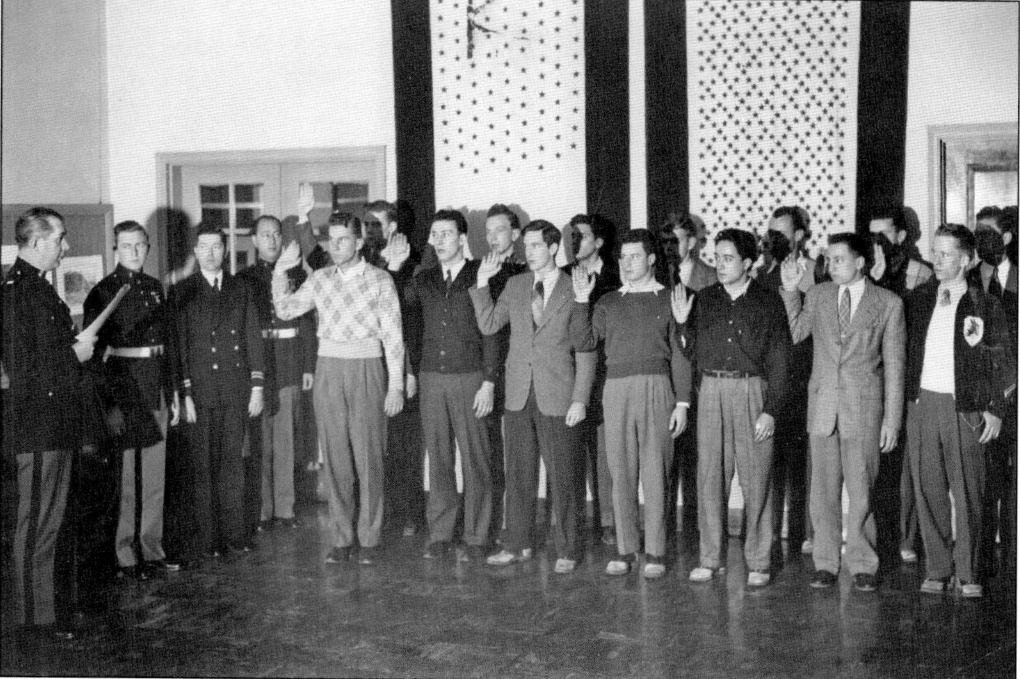

A U.S. Marine Reserve Unit is seen being sworn in at Bucknell University. By June 1945, the number of Bucknell men and women undergraduates who entered the armed forces totaled 3,000. By the end of the war, 43 Bucknell men had lost their lives in the struggle. (Bucknell University.)

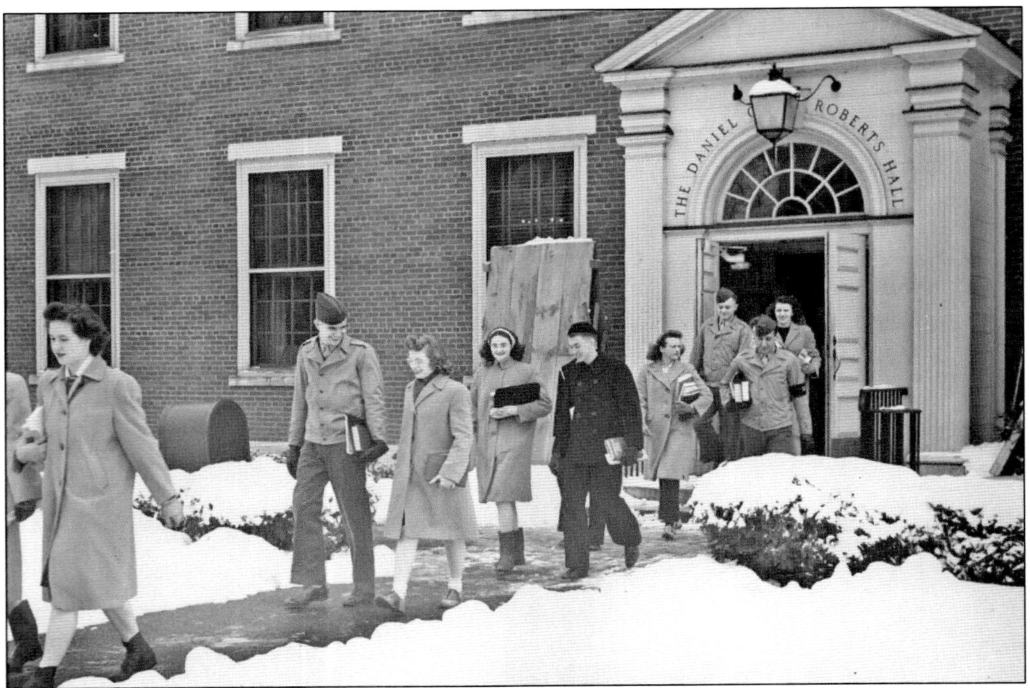

Uniformed students studied alongside regular university students during the war years. Those in the accelerated continuous program attended 48 weeks of college courses per year. The additional sessions placed a significant burden on the faculty because of increased enrollments. There also were fewer faculty members since a number had left to join in the war effort. (Bucknell University.)

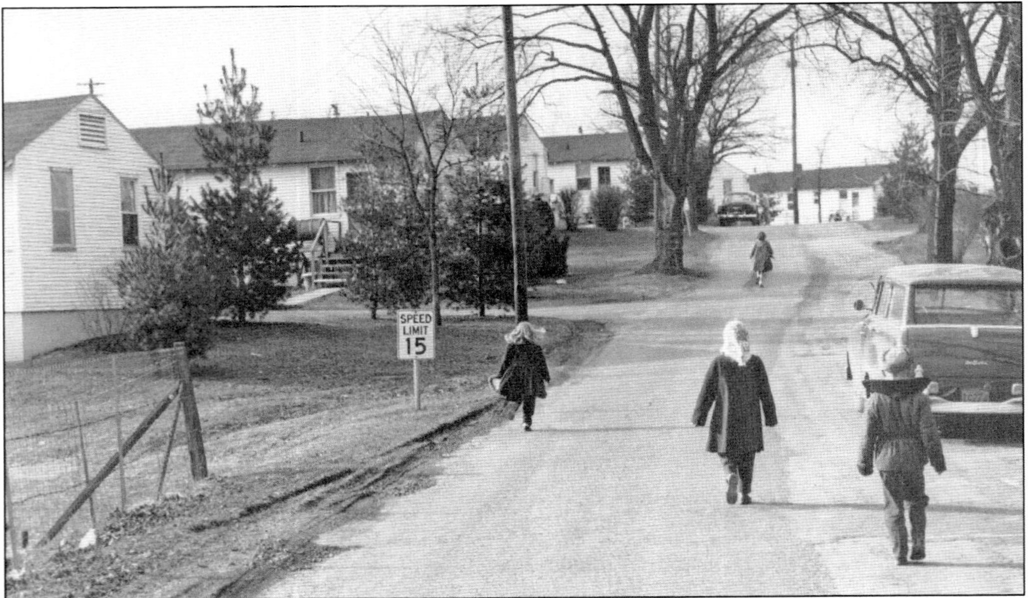

Veterans flooded into colleges and universities in the postwar years. Bucknell Village was Bucknell University's response to the need for adequate housing for veterans who were married. Bucknell Village included 16 reconverted barrack-like structures on the west side of Route 15. Today's modular student housing units sit on the footprint of those Bucknell Village buildings. (Bucknell University.)

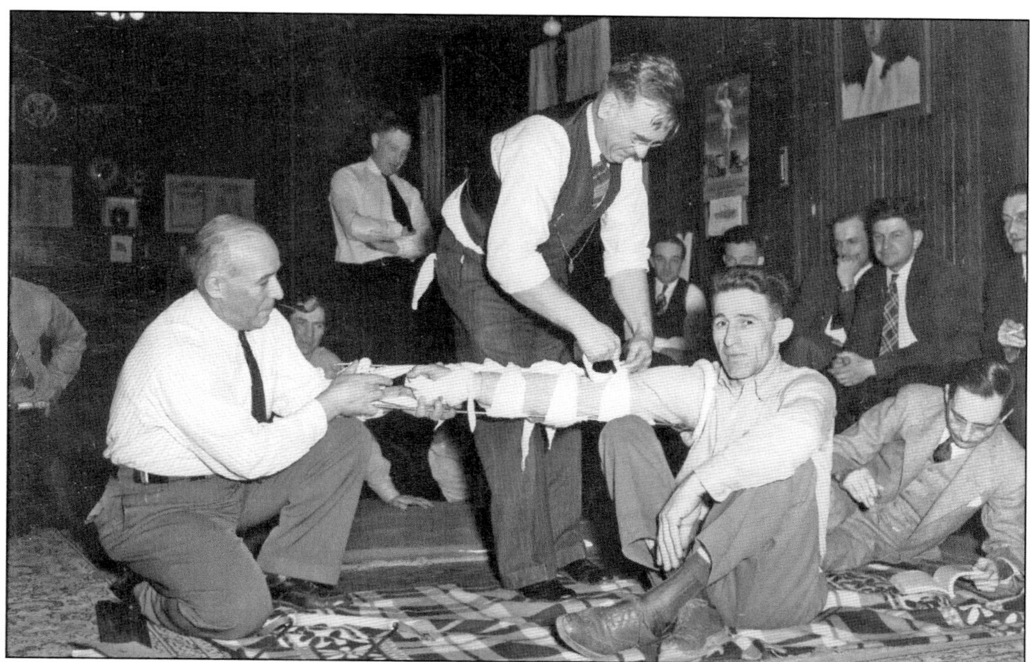

During the war years, Bucknell University offered civilian defense courses. J. Orin Oliphant is seen here in 1942 instructing local air raid wardens. These courses were an effort to prepare noncombatants in case of military attack. The borough was divided into sectors, each of which had a designated warden. The warden's main purpose was to patrol the streets during blackout and to ensure that no light was visible. (Bucknell University.)

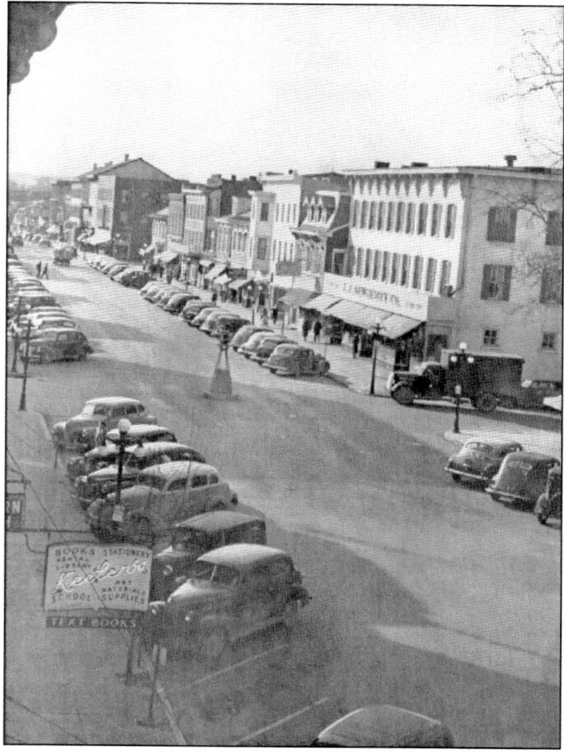

This undated scene, likely from 1945, looks west on Market Street. The traffic light stands in the middle of the Third Street intersection. Lewisburg's famous tri-globed street lights can be seen, as are dozens of parked cars on a busy day after gas rationing must have been lifted. J. J. Newberry Company's large building is on the right with the equally large C. Dreisbach Sons Hardware building at the Fourth Street intersection. (Owen Mahon.)

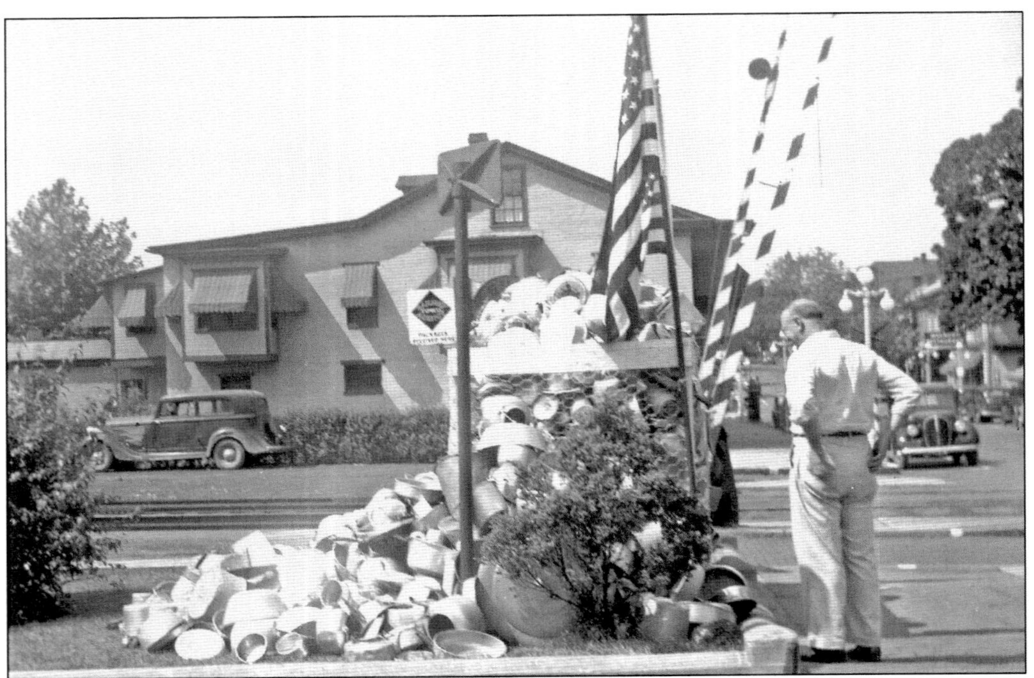

Area residents donated household items of aluminum toward the war effort. This photograph, taken in the early 1940s, shows a substantial pile of pots, pans, lids, and plates on the corner of Fifth and Market Streets. The metal was to go toward making airplanes. (UCHS 2006.5.02.)

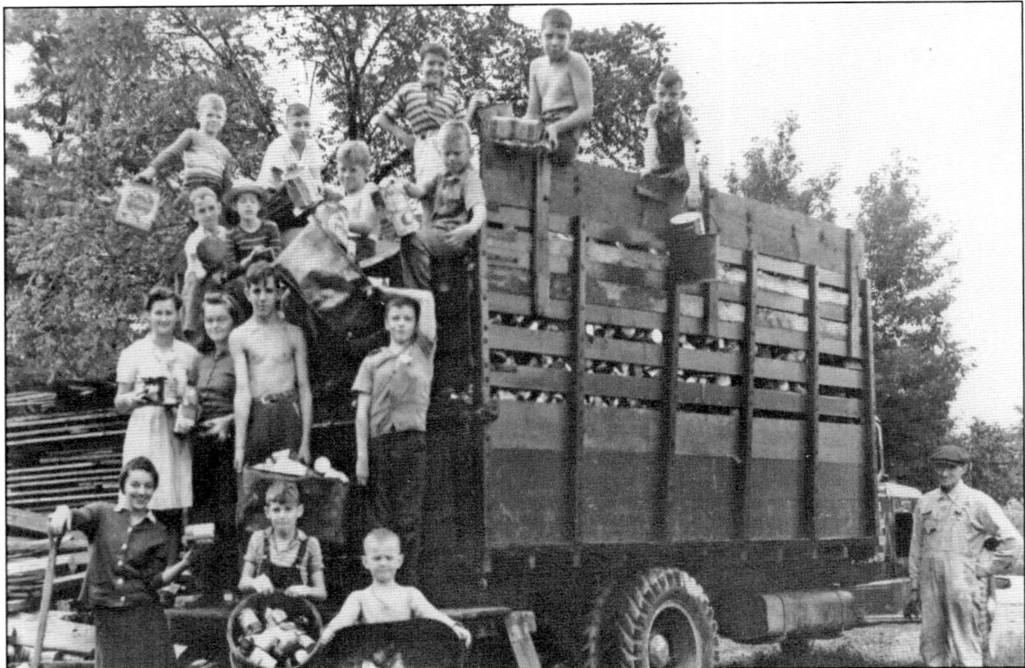

All Americans contributed in one way or another during World War II. Here a group of children help gather scrap metal for the war effort. Toothpaste tubes, food cans, old gas cans, and other assorted cans can all be seen in this previously unpublished image of a scrap drive in the Lewisburg area. (Michael McWilliams.)

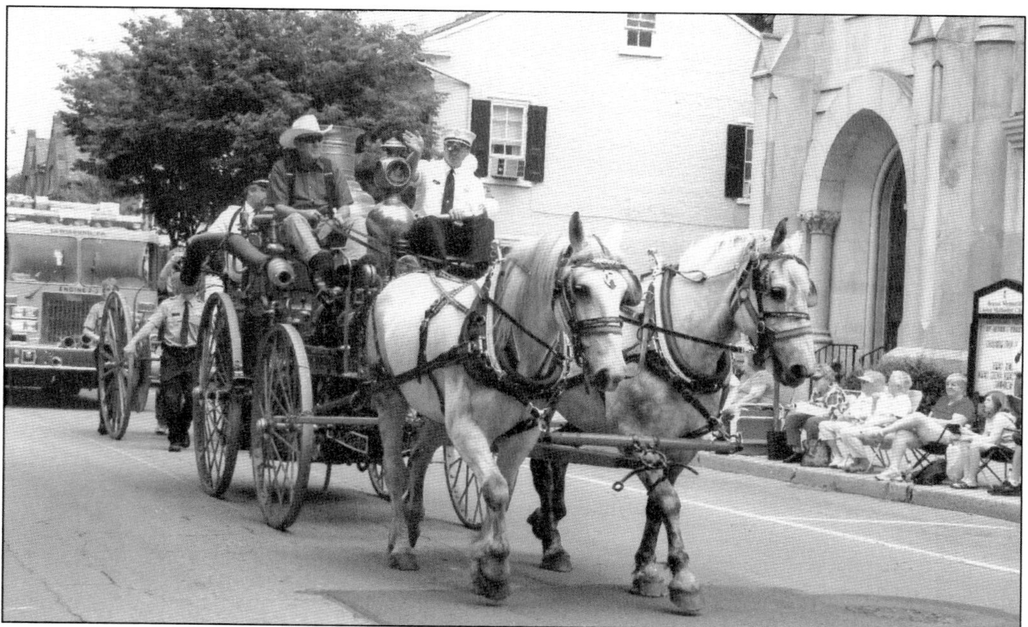

The original Silsby Steamer purchased by William Cameron in 1874 for the Lewisburg Fire Company was retired in 1932. It is on display in the company museum on Buffalo Road, and, on occasion, can be seen in a parade through Lewisburg. The steamer here passes the Beaver Memorial Methodist Church on South Third Street during a Fourth of July parade. This is the same steamer pictured on pages 33 and 90. (Tiffini Scott.)

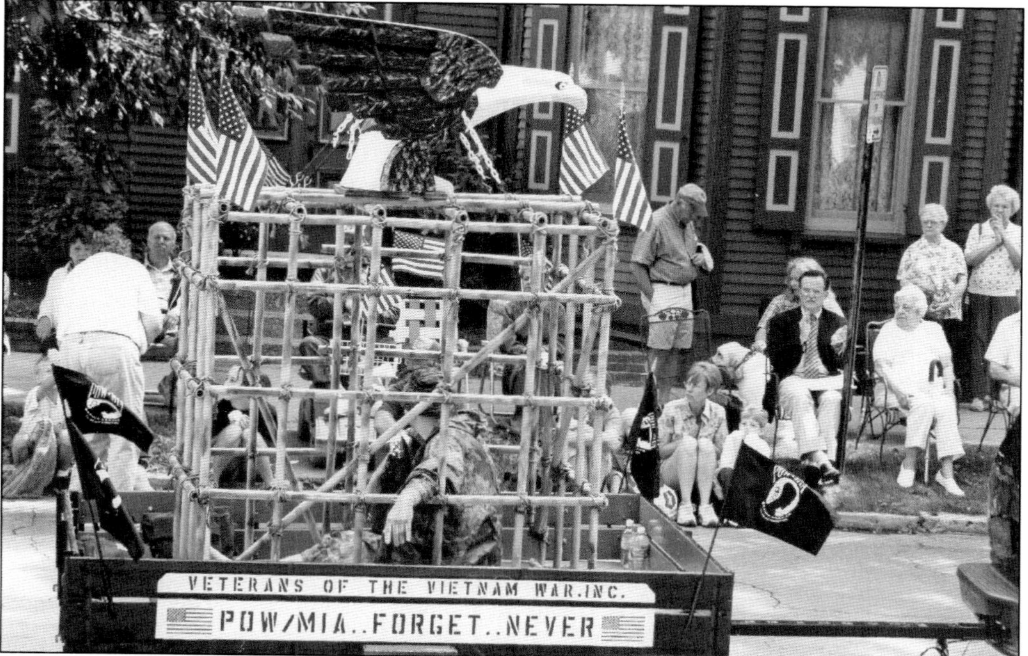

The veterans of the Vietnam War constructed this float as part of Lewisburg's Fourth of July parade in 2008. The men who had been captured still vividly recalled their horrible captivity, at times stuck inside a cage such as this one they built from memory. Good weather for such parades always draws huge crowds from throughout the area. (Tiffini Scott.)

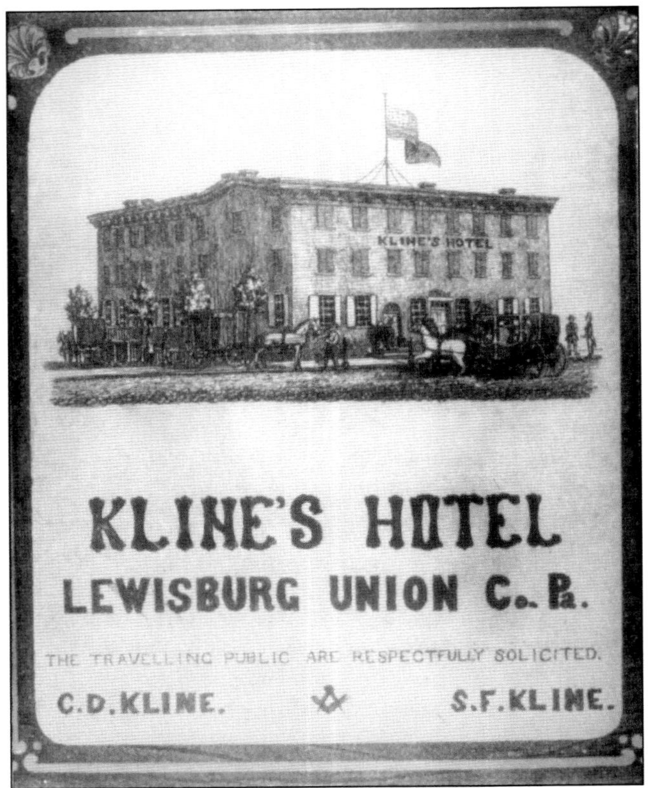

Kline's Hotel opened at 136 Market Street in 1834 as a two-story structure. Prof. Stephen Taylor, the first acting president of the new University at Lewisburg, lived here from 1846 to 1851; the formal dinner after the first university commencement in 1851 was held in the hotel dining room. (PHM.)

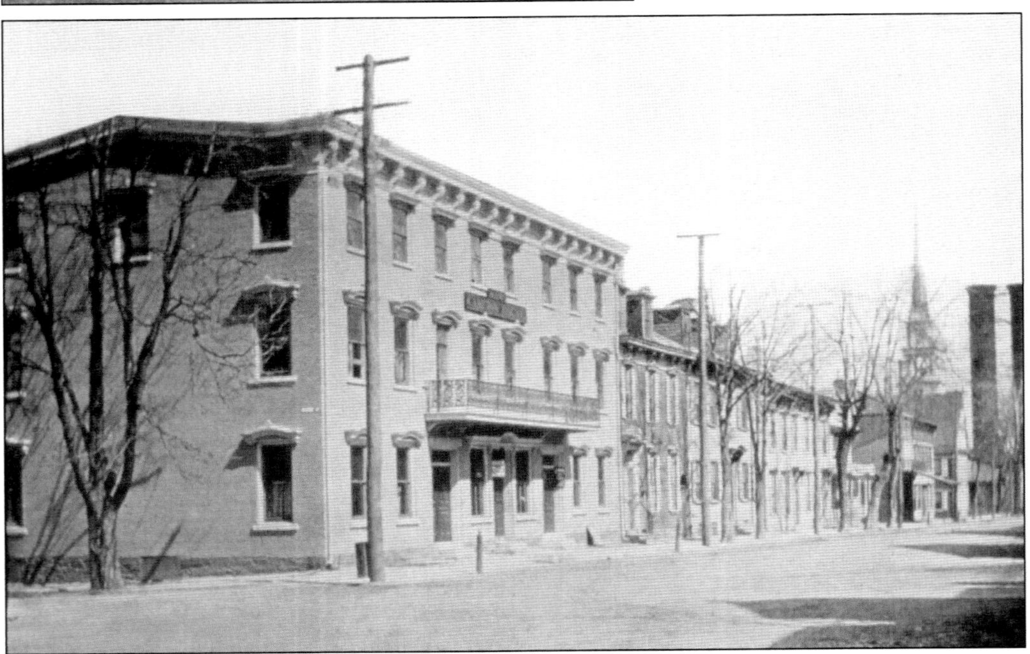

William Cameron purchased the old Kline Hotel (then in business as the Reviere House) in 1874 and turned its management over to his daughter Jane Cameron Harrison, who presided over occasional renovations as she delegated the daily operations to a series of competent managers. The Cameron House, shown in this postcard, retained its name until 1934. (PHM.)

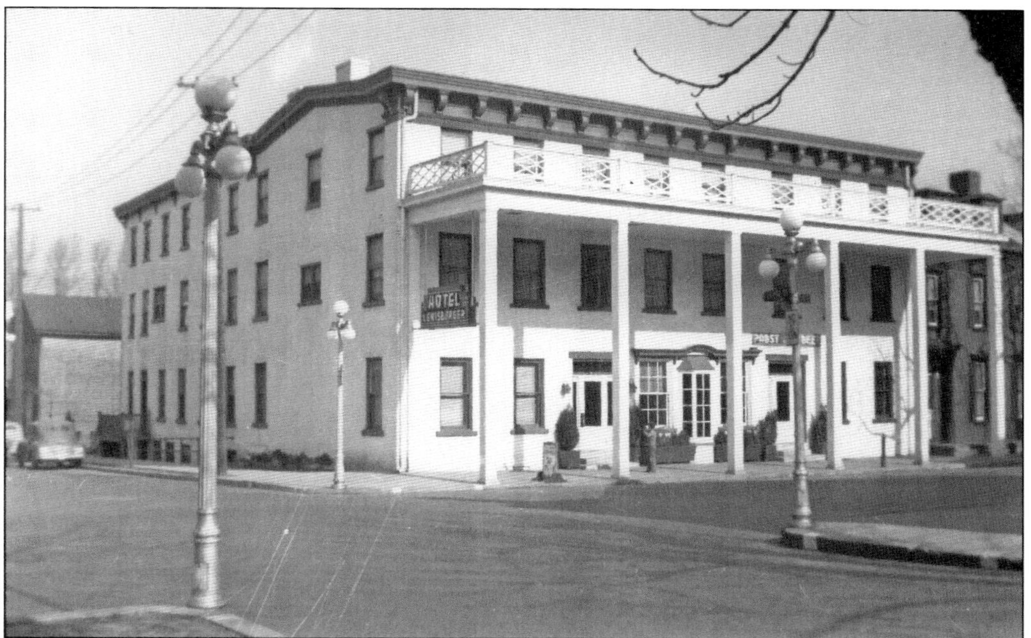

W. W. Watkins purchased the Cameron House in 1934, renovated it, and changed its name to the Hotel Lewisburger. He added the Mount Vernon porticos in 1938. Today they remain an easily recognizable feature of downtown Lewisburg. The hotel closed in 1993, was purchased by Norman Buck, and reopened in 1997 as the Lewisburg Hotel. (UCHS 83.45.1.)

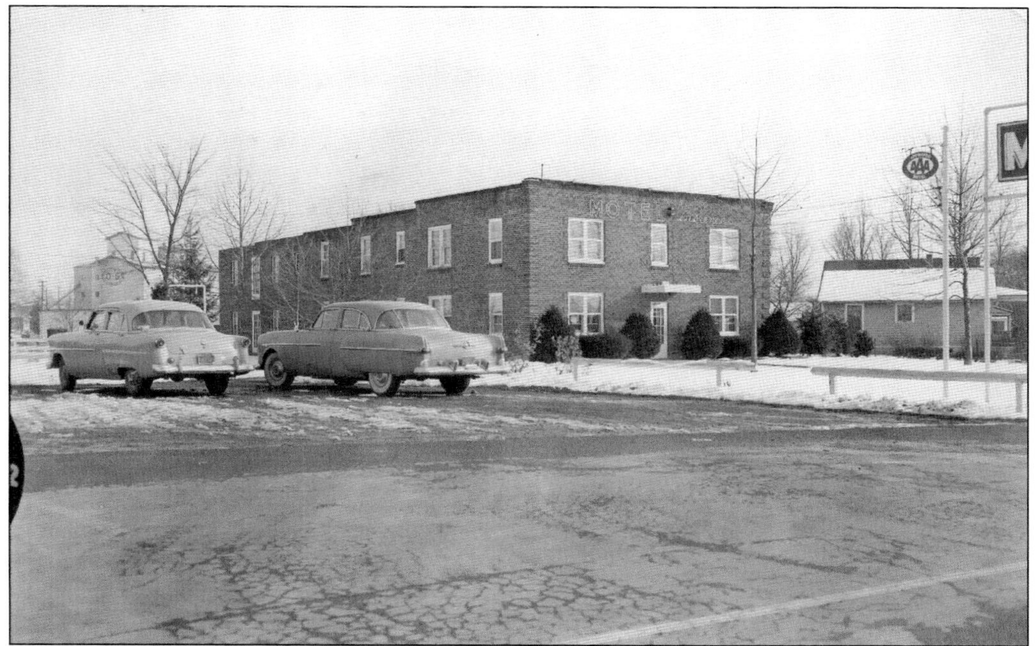

The Larry Hunt Motel, seen here, was typical of the sprawl that spread along Route 15 as automobile travel increased after World War II. Cheap motels catered to drivers looking for places to stay as they traveled through the area. The stamp of approval by the American Automobile Association meant that the Hunt Motel had an edge over other local inns that were not in the AAA guide. (UCHS 82.4.C524Cj.)

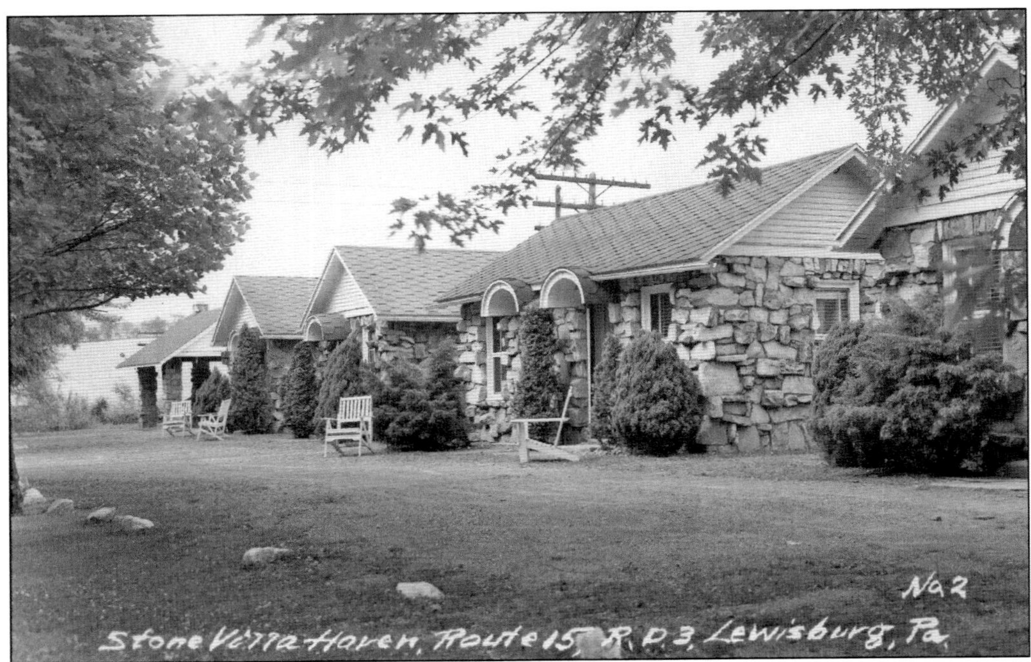

Located north of Lewisburg along Route 15, the Stone Villa Haven Motel was one of the fancier hostelries constructed for the comfort of travelers. The motel consisted of a number of separate cottages faced with stone, thus giving the motel its name. The motel went out of business and was razed when Route 15 was widened to four lanes. (UCHS 90.40.12.)

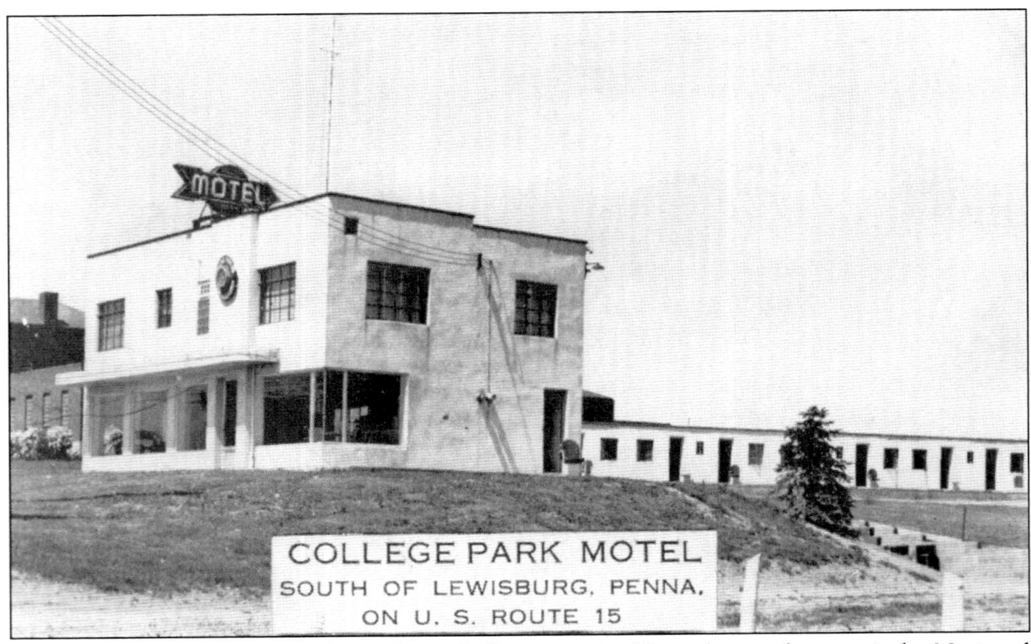

The College Park Motel was located on a hill just south of Lewisburg, adjacent to the National Guard Armory. The motel's advertising card commented, "We are located on top of a plateau, overlooking many valleys, and seldom without a breeze. Our Dutch generosity and atmosphere will add to your pleasant stay with us." (UCHS 92.9.92.67.)

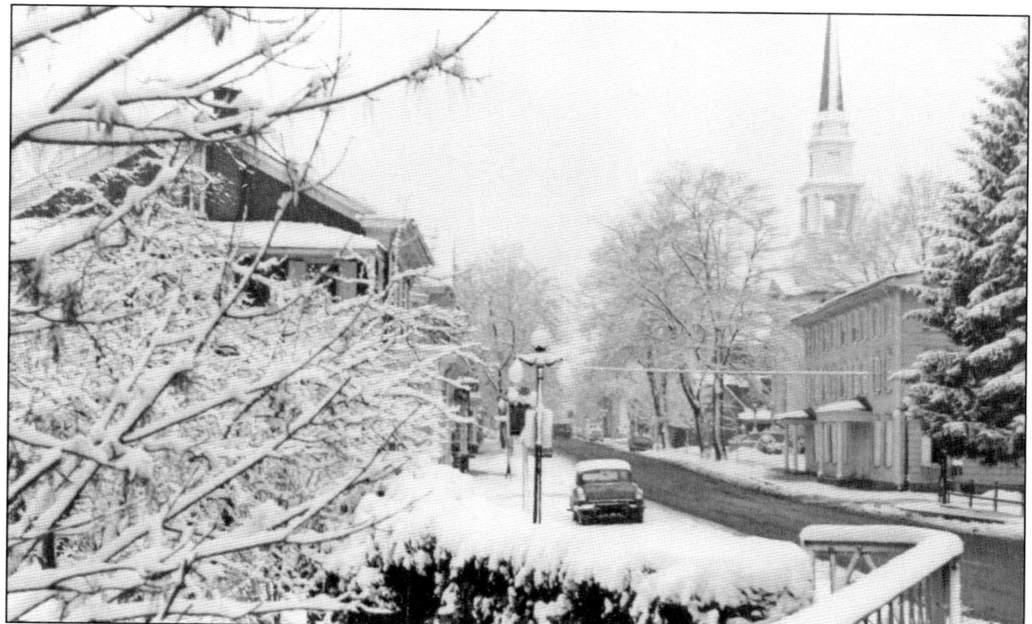

This snowy scene looks west from the Market Street Bridge. The structure to the right was erected in the 1790s as a two-story log tavern and then was enlarged to become the American House Hotel in the 1830s. When the hotel closed, the building was converted into apartments and then was reunited in the late 1930s by John and Edith Fetherston. After Edith's death in 1972, her home became the Packwood House Museum. (PHM.)

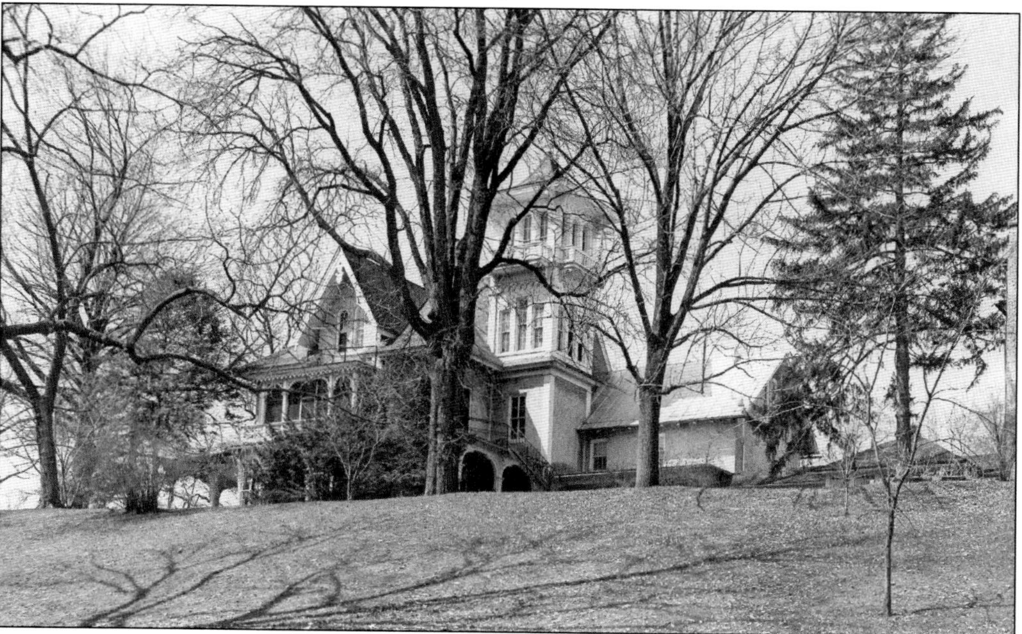

Noted architect Samuel Sloan built this magnificent Victorian home for Eli Slifer (1818–1888) in 1860. Slifer had come to Lewisburg years earlier and was both a politician and successful businessman. As secretary of the commonwealth during the Civil War, Slifer aided Gov. Andrew Curtin in maintaining the state's war effort. The Evangelical Association bought the mansion in 1915, and it was part of a retirement home until 1976, when it opened as a museum. (PHM.)

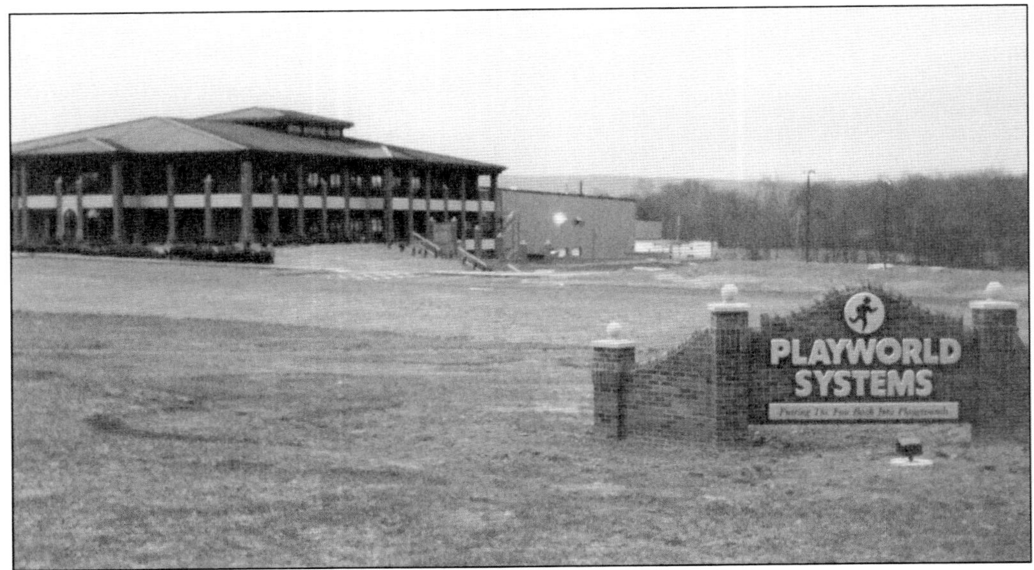

Playworld Systems, a third-generation, family-owned business, produces recreational equipment for all ages. It serves parks, schools, and public playgrounds with an emphasis on school-age children. Kidsburg in Lewisburg's Hufnagle Park is a local example; many other parks nationwide purchase Playworld products. (Playworld Systems.)

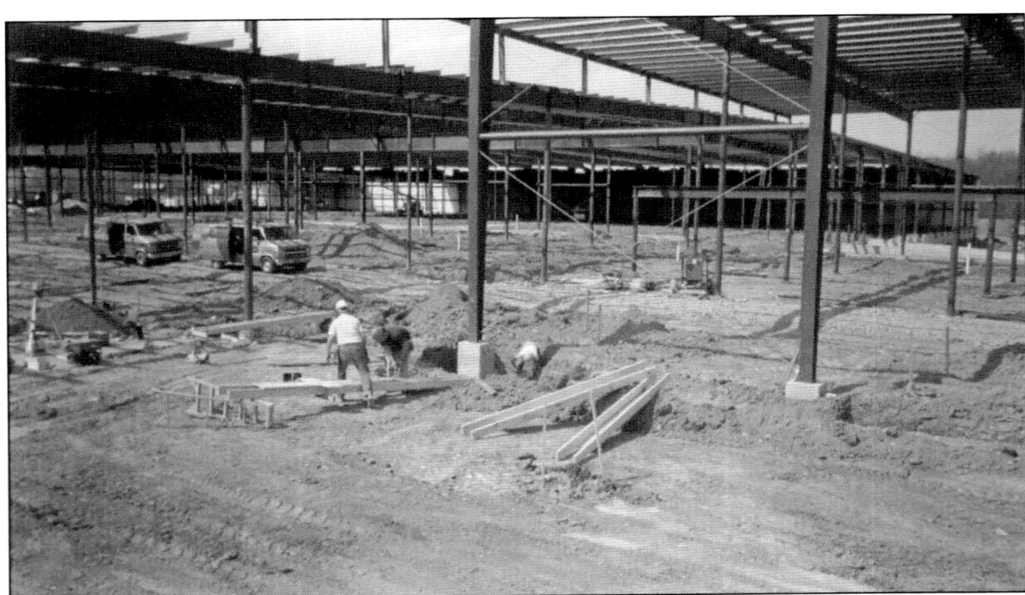

Playworld Systems moved its corporate headquarters to Lewisburg in January 1999. The construction of the headquarters building began in 1998 and is located at the intersection of Fairground Road and Buffalo Road (Route 192). Playworld Systems represents a type of industry likely to be attracted to Lewisburg in the future. (Playword Systems.)

Lewisburg in the 21st Century

Lewisburg, for the foreseeable future, will continue to exhibit the same charming qualities that have drawn residents and visitors for centuries. While change is inevitable, it stands to remain a quaint and vibrant small town due to its location, historic fabric, strong economy, proximity to exceptional natural resources, and the determination of its residents.

Unlike many central Pennsylvania communities, where population decline has become the norm in recent decades, the Lewisburg area is poised to experience a significant increase in populace. This will bring with it greater diversity of age, income, race, and ethnicity. These residents, some of whom will be retirees, university alumni, singles, and young families looking to escape the faster pace of metropolitan areas to raise a family, will bring entrepreneurial energy and fresh ideas, making Lewisburg a center of innovation in the county and region. Lewisburg will build on its current and past prosperity with creativity, knowledge, and technology as the new economic capital. Health care, education, professional services, small businesses, and hospitality and tourism will be the foundation for employment, as manufacturing will have faded except for a few highly skilled applications.

The town proper has spread well beyond the borough. As a result, new growth and development attributed to the expanding population will occur in the adjacent townships of East Buffalo and Kelly. The abundant agriculture and open-space land that abuts Lewisburg's doorstep is as much a key to the community's sense of place as the town itself. Therefore, how this surrounding landscape is transformed and conserved over the ensuing years will have a tremendous influence on the continued maturation and success of Lewisburg. The future vision is to create denser, mixed-use neighborhoods that mimic the scale and characteristics of the traditional town pattern originally laid out by Ludwig Derr—where walkability, livability, and efficiency are emphasized over the suburban sprawl that has become commonplace in modern times. Part of Lewisburg's allure is the ability to be in the historic downtown one minute and the next minute be peering across fertile farm fields or sitting along the idyllic Susquehanna River enjoying a moment of relaxation.

—Shawn R. McLaughlin
Union County Planning Director

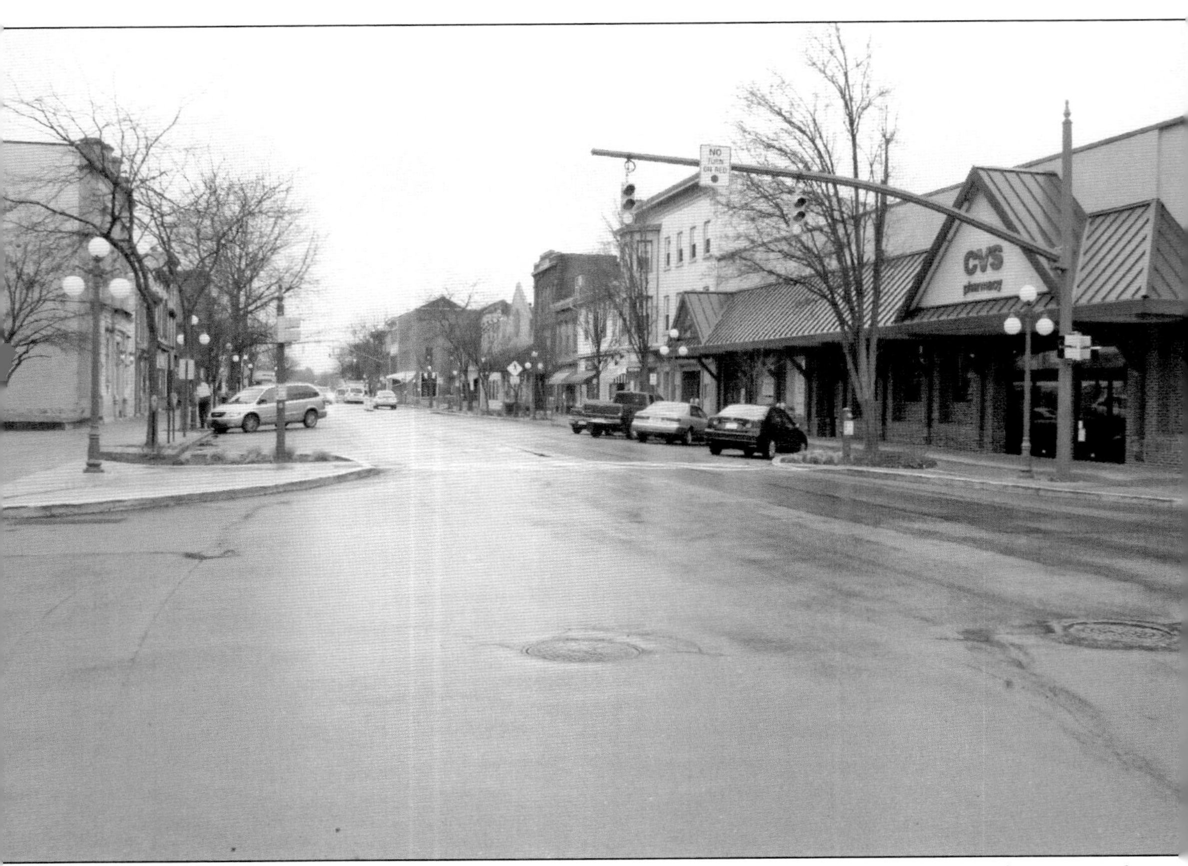

This March 2010 image was taken from the same location as the snow scene on the cover of this book. Notice the changes that have occurred during the past 80 years. The old Newberry building on the right burned and has been replaced, as has the Driesbach building in the center background. Businesses still fill this 300 block of Market Street. (Tiffini Scott.)

BIBLIOGRAPHY

Blake, Jody, and Jeannette Lasansky. *Rural Delivery: Real Photo Postcards from Central Pennsylvania, 1905–1935*. Lewisburg, PA: Union County Historical Society, 1996.

Goover, Claire. *As It Used To Be*. Winfield, PA: Claire Groover, 1976.

Historic Preservation Plan of Union County, Pennsylvania. Part I: An Inventory of Historic Sites and Landmarks. Prepared by the Institute of Regional Affairs at Bucknell University for the Union County Planning Commission, 1976.

Kalp, Lois. *Silhouettes: The Historic, Memorable, and Notable Women of Union County Pennsylvania 1785–1985*. N.p., 1985.

———. *A Town on the Susquehanna, 1769–1975*. Lewisburg, PA: Lois Kalp, 1980.

Lewisburg Journal. Various issues, 1908–1924.

Linn, John Blair. *Annals of Buffalo Valley, Pennsylvania, 1755–1855*. Harrisburg: Lane S. Hart, 1877.

Mauser, I. H. *Centennial History of Lewisburg*. Lewisburg, PA: I. H. Mauser,1856; annotated and reissued as a special issue of *Heritage*, volumes 9–10 (1984–1986,) by the Union County Historical Society.

Merkel, Jim. "Cameron Name Won't Be Forgotten." *Union County Journal*, November 5, 1981.

Oliphant, J. Orin. *The Rise of Bucknell University*. New York: Appleton-Century-Crofts, 1965.

Reed, Doris H. *Delta Place*, 1769–1976. N.p., 1976.

———. *Delta Place II: A Sequel to Delta Place*, N.p., 1991.

Saint John's United Church of Christ, 150th Anniversary, 1824–1974. N.p., 1974.

Snyder, Charles M. *Union County Pennsylvania: A Celebration of History*. Lewisburg, PA: Union County Historical Society, 2000.

Theiss, Lewis Edwin. *Centennial History of Bucknell University, 1846–1946*. Williamsport, PA: Grit Publishing Company Press, 1946.

Consistent with our mission to preserve history on a local level, this book was printed in South Carolina on American-made paper and manufactured entirely in the United States. Products carrying the accredited Forest Stewardship Council (FSC) label are printed on 100 percent FSC-certified paper.

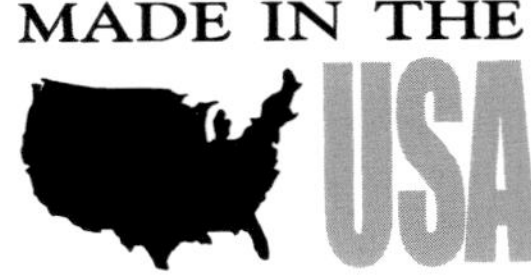